The JOY Of ACCOUNTING

A GAME-CHANGING APPROACH THAT MAKES ACCOUNTING EASY

PETER FRAMPTON & MARK ROBILLIARD

The Joy of Accounting: A Game-Changing Approach That Makes Accounting Easy

An imprint of
Wealthvox Press
Craig MacGillivray, CEO
64 New Cavendish Street, London, W1G 8TB United Kingdom

First U.S. edition September 2020

For the following opportunities, email easy@wealthvox.com
• Bulk orders and educational school and university supplies
• Remote or on-site accounting and finance workshops (see notice at end of book)
• The authors are available to speak at your live event on the subject of
effectiveness in personal and business finance, and financial leadership.

The contents of this book and the system upon which it is based draw on the
work of numerous Color Accounting Learning System™ educators and partners
around the world. The book is dedicated to this great family of business advocates
who passionately believe "there's a better way."

Authors: Peter Frampton and Mark Robilliard
Producer: Catherine Bronstein
Content Advisors: Dave Kolitz, Toby York, Adam Wilkinson
Illustration: Drew Foerster
Editing: Red to Black Editing
Layout: Jetlaunch
Publication Consultant: Stephanie Chandler

ISBN Hardcover: 978-1-7353129-1-0
ISBN Paperback: 978-1-7353129-2-7
ISBN ebook: 978-1-7353129-3-4

Rugged Green R134 G152 B116
Bold Orange R244 G124 B39
Royal Purple R94 G86 B165

CONTENTS

FOREWORD

Accounting has a reputation it does not deserve. You've heard the stereotypical old tropes about accountants being boring, conservative and pedantic. Even among its academics, accounting is commonly viewed as little more than a functional skill – the poor cousin of "finance".

Its image, however, is a result of its extraordinary success. Accounting is ubiquitous and so deeply embedded in our lives that we've lost sight of it. It's become the water that fish will never discover. It's everywhere in your life, enabling almost everything you do, from catching a bus to building or renting your house to supporting your preferred charity to shopping and saving.

Arguably, the three most important social technologies in the history of human civilisation are literacy, numeracy, and accounting. Most surprisingly, accounting might predate the other two.[1] Recent academic research suggests that accounting did not arise from the increasing complexity of economies, but has been present in all but the most rudimentary societies for about 10,000 years.

Double-entry bookkeeping, which is accounting perfected, is a comparatively new innovation, dating back to the 13th century, possibly earlier, and is the subject of the best-known book about accounting, Luca Pacioli's *Summa de arithmetica, geometria, proportioni et proportionalita,* (Summary of arithmetic, geometry, proportions and proportionality), first published in 1494. Pacioli's bookkeeping method uses the left and right side of a book, or ledger, to set out the double entries. This is an effective recording mechanism, but it is not an effective learning method.

Today, not much has changed, either in terms of record keeping or accounting education—I was told "debit the window—credit the door", because the window was on the left of the classroom and the door was on the right. To the teacher, however, the opposite was true, so it wasn't a satisfactory learning aid, it did nothing to explain why each entry was on a particular side, and completely useless if you found yourself in a place where the windows were on the other side of the room.

This book is different. The accounting concepts are entirely orthodox, but the methods used to teach them are novel. Peter Frampton and Mark Robilliard provide some deceptively simple twists, including using different colours instead of two sides of a ledger; and showing the complete accounting framework in a unique and memorable form—what they call the "Color Accounting BaSIS Framework". These may sound like trivial innovations, but the effects on learners are dramatic. I have been using their method in classrooms and workshops for some years and the speed of learning and depth of understanding of participants never fail to amaze me.

---

1. Professor Denise Schmandt-Besserat—a leading authority on prehistoric clay objects—has written extensively about record-keeping for commodities, claiming that this kind of accounting was the precondition and impetus to the invention of writing as well as abstract counting.

The essence of accounting today is no different to the system that Pacioli described, but it is not its historical longevity that makes reading this book a worthwhile investment—accounting, and specifically double-entry bookkeeping, will never become obsolete, even when the robots take over. It is hard to see how it can be improved and, astonishingly, it is a universal technology used by individuals, communities and organisations throughout the world, regardless of their size, location, area of operation or complexity. There's only one system to learn, and once learned you can carry it with you for the rest of your life.

Don't worry—this book will not turn you into an accountant, but it will make you accounting literate: you will feel confident to ask the right questions when using financial information. Whether you are in politics, in business, in work or just everyday life, understanding accounting gives you a voice. Not being accounting literate is like not understanding grammar. You'll get by, but you may well be limited and miss out on wonderful opportunities to be the best person you can be.

Toby York
Middlesex University, London, UK

"Where were you when I was getting my MBA? This changes everything."

 "[The approach] has the advantage of showing how accounting works visually. We all tend to see problems and relationships more easily visually, so the approach takes advantage of how we learn most effectively. As such, I believe that it is of value to anyone who is interested in understanding how accounting works (from high school students to undergrads to MBAs to business executives)."

—**Paul Healy, James R. Williston Professor of Business Administration, Harvard Business School**

"This is a seminal accounting book that is changing the way that my colleagues and I teach accounting. Students are responding with strong 'a-ha moments' and lightbulbs of clarity going off."

—**Sean Crevier, Accounting & Finance Teacher, Illinois, USA.**

BDO "The system is a fantastic, fun, one-of-a-kind approach that demystifies accounting, making it so easily understood for our clients. With hundreds of attendees having gone through the course in New Zealand, on average they have rated a 90 percent increase in their knowledge, which is amazing! The graphical framework allows clients to immediately visualize the impact of a transaction on the profitability and equity of their business—this promotes more informed and sound decision-making."

—**Justin Martin, Partner, BDO New Zealand, together with ServiceIQ**

 "The way The Joy of Accounting explains accounting is a revolution in financial education. It helps our CPAs communicate clearly and makes accounting accessible to anyone."

—**Tom Hood, CEO Maryland Association of Certified Public Accountants**

INTRODUCTION

Peter Frampton and Mark Robilliard

Two failed accounting students walked into a bar…

Sounds like an old joke, but it's not too far from the truth! Back in the 1990s, Mark and Peter—by then accomplished accountants working for the world's largest accounting firm—met and realized they shared a common conviction: there must be a better way to explain accounting.

Peter had to repeat Accounting 101 at university: such was his shock at the discovery of his first academic failure he fell down the stairs and sprained his ankle.

Mark signed up for accounting at university because marine biology didn't accept him. It didn't take long for his regrets to kick in. "Accounting 101 made me feel stupid. I memorized my way through college and then got a job at an accounting practice where I was soon in front of my boss, admitting that I didn't know what I was doing. He sat me down and showed me how to manually lay out the balance sheet and income statement accounts on a large pad. The proverbial lights started coming on and I 'got it.'"

This book is the result of a long journey of discovery, in which we have had the privilege of teaching—and being taught by—people like you.

We've come to love accounting, love the teaching of it, and deeply believe that accounting literacy improves the world.

As Toby York says in the foreword: accounting is amazing. It's everywhere in your life, enabling almost everything you do. Accounting is at the heart of financial accountability—in your personal life, in business, in politics, and in general society. Accountability is what makes the world go around.

Accounting enables trade and commerce and has facilitated the advance of civilization over the last five centuries. It's an art, a science, a language, an invention, and a technology that is exquisitely built upon simple and elegant principles. Accounting has a rich and consequential history. Humble bookkeeping spread the Arabic numeral system throughout Europe—a much better system than the Roman system that it displaced—thus enabling the Renaissance. Science, empirical thought, and rationalism benefited enormously. Accounting's history is woven, for good or bad, into the rise of nations, colonialism, and global trade. Colonialism… not so good. But trade? Well, as they say, "When goods cross borders, soldiers don't." Yes, free trade is a very good thing, and accounting is behind it all.

The United States itself began as a financial venture. The Mayflower Compact of 1620 had its own books of account to track expenses and profits. Later, the constitution of the new nation required in Article 1 that "Statements of Account of the Receipts and Expenditures of all public Money shall be published." And there it is: accounting at the very heart of the greatest experiment in democracy—the written constitution of those uniting states.

Accounting gives people a voice. And that's what we want for you, dear reader, learner, discoverer: a voice to express your own mission and purpose. So, thank you for picking up this book and allowing us to share our own journey of discovery with you. Accounting turns out to be simple and really easy to conquer when you clarify the language, draw a clear color-coded diagram, and follow a step by step explanatory sequence.

You're going to have a blast.

Welcome, thank you, and do stay in touch with us on easy@wealthvox.com with your feedback and ideas for improving *The Joy of Accounting*. We'd love to hear from you.

LEARN WITH YOUR HANDS

The explanations in this book draw on exercises and activities developed in hands-on workshops at universities, schools, and businesses. You can order the same materials used in those workshops to physically do the exercises as you work through this book. Includes: Color Acounting BaSiS Board™, highlighters, stickers, tickets and other props.

You'll get enormous value from the book even if you don't use the supplementary materials, but getting your hands moving adds another layer to your experience of developing accounting literacy.

For more information visit wealthvox.com/joy. Or point your phone camera at the QR code.

For bulk education orders and school curricula please email easy@wealthvox.com.

wealthvox

BOOST YOUR BUSINESS

**Do meetings with your accountant give you a sinking feeling?
Do you know what questions to ask finance experts?**

Discover the levers to boost profitability, cash flow and growth.
Enquire today about a tailored business finance workshop.
Contact: joy@wealthvox.com

PART 1

PRINCIPLES OF ACCOUNTING

1. WHAT IS ACCOUNTING?

I Want to Buy a Pineapple

I hear that you love pineapples. Couldn't agree with you more. Delicious. Love 'em. Prickly yes, but oh so juicy. An old symbol of hospitality too, going way back hundreds of years to a time when in Europe they were rare exotic imports. People would pass them around and display them on their mantles.

And here you are now, walking into our store, Lemonade & Laughter, for a fresh specimen.

Welcome! I'm so happy you're here. You've come to the right place to get one of those amazing fruits.

So here we are: you to buy a pineapple, I to sell a pineapple.

Now, enter Annie the Accountant. She's the business storyteller. She's going to tell the financial story of what happens in our mutually beneficial transaction. You giving me cash, me giving you a pineapple, me gaining cash, and you gaining a pineapple. Fine, but whose story will she tell? Yours or mine?

Let's hit pause for a minute on this playful and somewhat quirky start to what is, in truth, a wholly serious accounting book, because here comes the most important cornerstone of the linguistic construct that is accounting. An underappreciated point, a misunderstood distinction that almost everybody gets wrong. It's the source of myriad confusions, mistakes, misconceptions, and incorrect definitions in the world of finance and accounting.

The issue centers around this question of whose story is being told: Yours or mine?

And the answer is… neither. Insert long silence. The story that we'll tell about this pineapple exchange scenario is the story of Lemonade & Laughter itself.

Every accounting story is told about and from the point of view of a business entity. This business entity is undertaking the sale transaction, and it is always separate from its owner.

There's always a business entity, and there's always a separate owner of the entity. The business entity and the owner are never one and the same.

Sometimes it's obvious that the business is a separate thing. For example, the business may be called Lemonade & Laughter, Inc. "Inc." means "incorporated." As such, it's clear that there's a corporation, which is registered and which has a life of its own. But even if this isn't the case—if there isn't a separate registered corporation—for accounting purposes, there must exist a separate entity whose story is told.

Let's say I grow pineapples in my own backyard, and I sell them in my own name, as what's called a "Sole Trader." Accountants will still tell the story of a separate pineapple-selling business. The business is imagined, or as we say, the separate entity is "imputed."

I, the one who grows pineapples in my backyard, become the owner of the imputed separate accounting entity.

So, even in our little backyard scenario where Lemonade & Laughter is me, there are three parties: you, the customer; me, the owner of the enterprise and the worker in it; and Lemonade & Laughter, the business entity undertaking the financial activities about which Annie will tell the story.

THE BUSINESS

THE OWNER

THE CUSTOMER

Figure 1. **The separate business entity.**

This separate entity concept is so important for you to understand that we've given it a symbol. A pineapple, of course! From now on in this book, the pineapple symbol stands for "remember the separate entity" and "check your point of view." Whenever you see the pineapple map-pin image in this book, you are reminded to check whether you're thinking about the situation from the correct point of view.

One of the many teachers around the world who use the Color Accounting Learning System technology in this book to teach schoolkids is Anne Brown. Anne taught for years in high schools and ultimately became a national high school examiner of accounting. Anne said to us one day: "You know, after teaching accounting for forty years, I now reckon that getting the point of view right is the most important thing if you're going to understand the subject."

Figure 2. **Pineapple means "make sure you're thinking from the correct point of view."**

Welcome to Accounting

Welcome to accounting. We've gone and thrown you right in the deep end, so to speak. So, let's take a breath, step back, and ask ourselves a few questions about the context of what we're about to learn. Like, what actually is accounting? We said that Annie Accountant was standing by to tell the story of the separate entity, which we called Lemonade & Laughter. What is her job?

Financial reports describe the state of a business and how it has been performing. The purpose of accounting is to provide useful information for decision-making to the readers of these reports.

Useful information is what's key. If you simply list everything that a company has, then that's just data. To turn data into decision-useful information, accounting sorts and groups it.

By sorting similar assets and similar debts into groups and measuring them, the reader gets a much clearer picture of what the business is about. Data becomes information as long as you can understand the language.

After sorting, we can see what types of assets are used to run the business, how long they'll last, and what they're worth. With this information in hand, we may notice a shortage of some assets and an excess of others. When assets are sorted and sized, we can start comparing different groups to see whether we've got the right amount, and whether we should order more or cut back. We can check that we have enough critical assets like cash, and work out when we can expect to get more cash from people who owe us.

The assets are sorted, and so are the debts of the business. The debts of the business are grouped by type of debt and by when it must be settled. That'll give us even more useful information, such as our ability to settle the debts. Some must be settled soon, perhaps in days or weeks; for others, the business will have plenty of time to get the money together. We'll refer to the debts of the business by other names too, such as liabilities and obligations.

QUESTIONS, QUESTIONS, QUESTIONS

Readers of financial reports typically want answers to questions such as…

Assets:

- How much investment in assets is the company using? Now and previously?
- What sort of assets are they? For example, are they buildings, equipment, goodwill, cash, or goods for sale? Are they tangible or intangible?
- Are they liquid or not—can they be sold quickly or are they going to be around for a long time?
- How were the assets funded? Has the company borrowed assets from lenders, and how much did it get from the owners of the business?

Debts, Liabilities, & Obligations:

- By how much and to whom is the company indebted?
- How long does the company have to settle its debts? Are they short-term or long-term debts?
- What rate of interest are the liabilities incurring, and when is payment due?
- In what order must the company pay back its funders? Who's at the front of the repayment line and who would get paid last, especially if the business failed?

Performance:

- To what extent has the company managed to grow its assets organically by serving its customers?
- How much of these assets did the company have to consume in order to grow the assets?
- Given the size of the company's investment in assets, what level of return is being generated? How does this compare with other options?

That's quite a list of things we are interested in when reading financial statements. Yet it's not exhaustive. There are other questions to be asked. These ones above address just some of the main issues that readers want to know about.

TWO THINGS

Yet even though the list above has many points, it's still really about just two things: assets and how they are funded (by obligations).

If you pull finance apart to its elemental parts, that's all there is: assets and obligations. There's how the business acquires assets from funding providers, and then how it arranges them, grows them, uses them, and disposes of them. There's also how the associated obligations are arranged. That there are just these two things, assets and obligations, is good news. It's why accounting can be really simple. Yes, there are nuances that we'll explore, but we'll keep returning to the key ingredients: assets and obligations. These are the principle elements of what is often called "the language of business." Accounting literacy is the fluency to work with and speak that language. This book is going to give you access to accounting literacy.

The glue that holds civilization together

Big things are built with simple concepts. Ultimately, accounting is about accountability for all of society. Accountability is what advances civilizations, economies, enterprises, environmental stewardship, and personal prosperity. There can be no financial accountability without accounting. It's the glue that holds together the finances and lives of people, companies, communities, and nations.

Without accounting literacy, people make suboptimal decisions in their personal and business lives. They don't engage as constructively as they could with their advisors, colleagues, or even their spouses. We've met so many people whose careers and lives have been hamstrung through lack of accounting literacy, and from fear of engaging in the numbers of a business, budget, or project. So let's change that, starting with these first steps...

Separate Business Entity

We began by saying accounting always tells the story of a separate business entity. Let's look in further detail at what "separate" and "business" mean.

We said the business always has an owner. It always has a "master" whom it is serving. There's always, by definition, a separation between the business doing the serving and the master being served. By "serving," we don't in this instance mean serving the customer—we mean growing value for the owner. The business is trying to make itself more valuable for its owner's benefit.

That said, the term "owner" may not be strictly correct—there's an esoteric question about whether shareholders actually own a company, or just have some rights over it.[2] For some businesses, the master is not a shareholder but a stakeholder who benefits in a more general way from the company's work.

THE BUSINESS   THE OWNER

Figure 3. **Every business has a master.**

Accounting always tells the story of the separate business entity—not the story of its owner.

Figure 3 shows the separation between business and master. The diagram depicts a human as owner, but that doesn't have to be the case. The owner can be another business, as shown in *Figure 4*. The new owner of the original business will of course have its own owner.

---

2. *Salomon v. Salomon & Co.*, a famous British court case of 1897.

ORIGINAL BUSINESS   OWNER   OWNER OF OWNER

Figure 4. **The owner of an accounting entity can be a financial entity or a natural person.**

The Business of You

This applies to you too. The story of your finances is not actually told from your point of view. It's told from the point of view of—what we can think of as—The Business of You. To tell your financial story we impute a separate entity.

You can think of this business of you as "You incorporated," or "Financial Persona You," or your financial avatar. Accounting tells a story of this "Imputed Business of You". You the human being are the imputed business's owner. You own Financial You.

FINANCIAL YOU   REAL YOU

Figure 5. **Your personal financial story is told from the point of view of a separate financial entity.**

Being clear about whose story is being told is important. Confusing the point of view of the story is a source of a lot of confusion for accounting students, and it's easy to do. A lot of the real-life situations that accounting describes involve multiple parties. As we learn to describe the situations in accounting terms, we need to always first get clear on which party we are tasked with describing. Our job is to tell the story of just one of the many parties involved in the scenario. For example, if we're describing an investing scenario, there would be the investor and the company in which the investor is investing. If we're describing a sale of goods scenario in a shop, are we telling the customer's story as buyer, or the shop's story as seller?

> Accounting always tells the story of a separate financial entity.
> If we're accounting for your personal finances,
> we impute a separate financial entity.

Business Separate from Personal

It's not just for accounting reasons that we should think of the business as separate from the owner—it's also a good management practice. Think of the backyard grocery-selling business that we've imagined. Even if the assets and obligations of that business are legally part of your personal finances, you should regard them as belonging to a business that's separate in its own right. Of course, it's only a subset of your greater financial story.

SOLE TRADER BUSINESS   YOU

Figure 6. **Even a "personal sole proprietorship" business is accounted for separately from its owner.**

You will make different management decisions if you regard the business as separate from your personal finances. Imagine you take some of the money you made selling pineapples and then spend it to buy your friend a meal on the way home from a day at the local community market. If you don't separate the business-accounting from your personal-accounting, then you may get home and calculate that your grocery business made no money when it actually did. What happened was that you as the owner of the business drew money out of the business and then personally spent it on your friend. You'd come to a false conclusion about the business if you judged it by how much cash you had in your pocket when you got home.

SORRY, IT'S NOT MY MONEY

Seeing the business as separate from your personal finances is important for even more reasons. When we were teaching in a small rural community, one of the micro-business owners in the workshop told us she earned a living doing clothing repairs with a sewing machine. When we distinguished the concept of her business as a separate entity, she was thrilled due to an issue we hadn't thought of. She told us that in impoverished communities, it's hard to build up funds to grow a business and invest in new equipment, in part because relatives come asking for financial support for funerals, education, and other compelling personal needs. The business owner exclaimed that now that she saw the business as separate from herself, she could politely decline the requests for support, saying she didn't have any money to give. "Sorry, the money you're seeing me receive from the customers isn't mine—it belongs to the business!"

Legal Registration

That a business should always be seen as separate from its owner should now be clear. Sometimes this separation is obvious because the government allows for the incorporation of a nonhuman "person" to be the business. The word "incorporate" comes from the Latin word "corpus," which means "body." So, to incorporate means to give something form as a body. The authorities recognize the incorporated entity as a legal person. Accounting regards this incorporated entity as the financial entity whose story is told.

On the other hand, the law does not recognize a legal separation between the owner and a sole trader. The main relevance of this for the business owner is that the debts of the business are (for legal purposes) regarded as one and the same as the debts of the business owner. The owner of a sole trader is therefore responsible for settling the debts of the business if the business can't do so itself.

If a creditor who is owed money by the business is chasing the business for settlement of a debt, they can sue the owner for the payment. This may result in the owner's personal (non-business) assets, like their house or car, being seized under the authority of the law.

Limited Liability Companies

This risk to the owner of losing their assets because of the debts of their business leads to one of the most brilliant economic creations of modern civilization: the limited liability company. The fully paid-up (meaning they've fully paid for their shares in the company) owners of limited liability companies are not responsible for the debts of the company. If the company can't pay its debts, the lenders can't chase these owners for payment.

This form of company has unleashed the power of humans to collaborate economically on a scale that wouldn't otherwise be possible. Limited liability companies allow for enormous groups of people to band together, each contributing some money (or "capital") for a common purpose: to undertake massive and risky ventures to benefit humanity and generate wealth for owners, lenders, and stakeholders in the greater society.

How else would entrepreneurs marshal the funding and workers to create today's massive projects, like building new types of electric cars, digging a tunnel under the English Channel, or building a massive network of warehouses, trucks, and planes to deliver parcels to your door, as Amazon does? All of these mega-projects are possible because of the limited liability company, which allows for money in the billions to be pooled to invest in the assets that these projects require.

There's an irony in that by limiting the total amount of money the owners of a company must put into the company for their shares, much more money becomes available for companies to invest and undertake risky ventures. The owners of limited liability companies are prepared to invest money into the company because they know that their initial agreed investment is all that they are "on the hook for." The company or others who have lent it money cannot chase the owners for more money later.

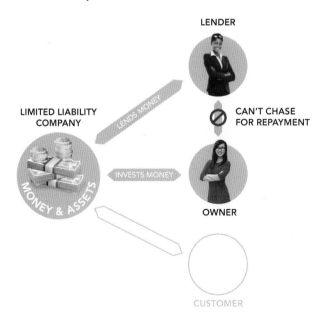

Figure 7. **Lenders to limited liability companies ordinarily can't chase owners for repayment.**

On the face of it, this isn't good for lenders because they've got more chance of not being paid back. Yet overall, everybody benefits because of the certainty that limited liability companies provide. Both lenders and owners know what their exposure is, especially if accountants do their job properly so that the financial position is clear. The lenders are comfortable with lending because they know how much money the owners have contributed, which money will help repay the lenders.

This is the brilliance of capitalism when it works smoothly and transparently. Even the lenders who cannot chase owners benefit because more companies are formed, and they therefore get more lending opportunities, choosing the best ones that give the best returns for the lowest risk. The genius of the free market gets to work. Everyone with a buck can decide where best to put it, consume it, lend it, or invest it.

> Limited liability companies limit what all the parties—
> the company, the lender, and the owners—are financially responsible for.

Think of what the word "limited" means to each of the parties in a company scenario: the company is limited from demanding more money from the owners, the lenders are limited to contributing what they agreed to lend, and the owners are limited to contributing what they agreed to invest into the company.

BREAKING BREAD TOGETHER

The word "company" also derives most appropriately from the Latin words *com* and *panos*, meaning "together" and "bread." A company is a group of companions who eat bread together.

And without accounting, no companionship would be possible!

A System for Telling a Story

Accounting is a system for telling a story about someone's assets and consequent obligations. In this book, that someone will mostly be a business, but it could also be the financial story of someone like you or a financial avatar.

In telling the story, accounting does more than just list those assets and debts. It tells us:

1) what the assets are
2) how they were funded, and
3) how they increased or decreased in value.

In *The Joy of Accounting*, we're going to build this three-part system from scratch. We'll work from first principles as we build the system, step by step. It's going to be easy and make sense.

WHAT DO YOU HAVE? HOW ARE YOU DOING?

Financial Statements

Accounting stories are told with two main reports that form part of a set of Financial Statements. Each one describes an aspect of the overall story.

- The balance sheet describes what assets the financial entity has and the obligations that funded them.
- The income statement describes the activities that grew and shrank the value of the assets and obligations.

A third report focuses on one particularly important asset: cash.

- The cash flow statement describes what caused cash to flow into and out of the company. It differs from the income statement both conceptually and in its format.

In a full set of public company financial statements, these three reports are joined by other narrative reports. The other reports give more detail about the three reports, express the opinion of the company management on how the business is doing, the opinion of auditors who check company accounts and confirm that they are true and fair, and so on.

Of all these reports that make up a set of financial statements, the most important are the balance sheet and income statement. They are called by many other names, such as Statement of Financial Position, Statement of Activities, or Profit & Loss Statement (or P&L). By any name, together they describe what the business has and how it's performing.

> Accounting is a system of describing and categorizing the nature and size of
> - a financial entity's assets,
> - the ways they were funded, and
> - what the entity did that grew and shrank them.

CHAPTER ROUNDUP

This chapter has looked at the question of what is accounting and whose story is told. We have explored how:

- Accounting is a storytelling system that describes the position a business is in with its assets and obligations. It also describes how the business has been performing.
- These two aspects of the business's financial story, position, and performance are told in the balance sheet and income statement reports that form part of a set of financial statements.
- The accounting story is always told about a business entity with an owner (or stakeholder in the case of a not-for-profit business).

- If you operate a business in your name, you impute a separate business entity and account for it separately from your personal finances.
- If we're describing your personal financial story, we impute a separate "business of you". You're its owner.
- Some businesses are legally incorporated. This means that the regulatory authorities recognize the entity as a separate legal person. This legal person becomes the separate entity that is accounted for by the financial story.
- We used a pineapple to remind us to always think from the point of view of the correct entity when accounting for a business scenario.
- Most legal corporations have limited liability. This means that creditors can only pursue the company for payment of debts owed. They cannot chase the shareholders of the company.
- Accounting has had a big impact on economic history and civilization. As a tool for accountability, accounting is an enabling technology for trade and the aggregation of capital for major projects.

2. ASSETS

Accounting is a system of describing and categorizing the nature and size of a financial entity's assets, the ways these assets were funded, and what the entity did to increase and diminish them.

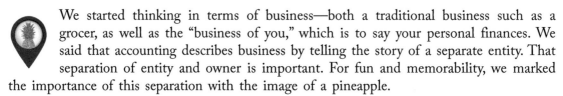 We started thinking in terms of business—both a traditional business such as a grocer, as well as the "business of you," which is to say your personal finances. We said that accounting describes business by telling the story of a separate entity. That separation of entity and owner is important. For fun and memorability, we marked the importance of this separation with the image of a pineapple.

We'll now take a closer look at the assets that the business entity has, starting with the question: what is an asset?

WHAT IS AN ASSET?

An asset is anything that's valuable.

So, if something you come across is valuable, then it's an asset. "Valuable" means "able to have value." If something is valuable, it means you, or someone, might pay for it. (Note: you might think the object has no value, but somebody else could think it does.) Being valuable is the defining characteristic of assets.

> Assets are anything valuable.

We're defining assets in a broad, universal way. We're not yet considering whether the asset is yours, or whether you'd count it and include it on a balance sheet. We'll get to that shortly. For the moment, assets are anything valuable.

Let's go one step further: not only are assets always valuable, nothing else besides assets is ever valuable. Assets have a unique claim to being valuable. If it's an asset, it's valuable. If something is valuable, we know it's an asset. It can't be anything else, because only assets are.

Assets Are Valuable

Delving deeper, what does "valuable" mean? Qualities that make something valuable include being desirable, sought-after, saleable, consumable, and convertible to cash. The best definition of "valuable" for our purposes is that something of value is, at least in principle, capable of canceling a debt.

This contrasts with another debt. You could never settle your debt to Jack by giving him the obligation to pay Jill, to whom you also owe money. You can't settle a debt with another debt.

Beware the pineapple when thinking about this. We're talking about our debt to another, not somebody's debt to us, which would be an asset rather than a debt.

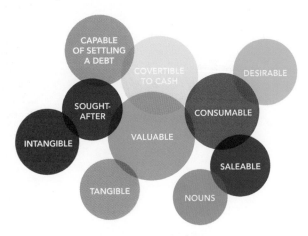

Figure 8. **Characteristics of assets.**

Examples of Assets

Here's a collection in Figure 9 of assets that you might find a company using. Some of the assets listed are the same thing, just described with alternative names. Note that some of these assets might never appear in the company's financial reports because they don't satisfy what is called "recognition criteria." We'll get to that momentarily.

For now, just look over the examples and think about how each asset might feature in your life or a business you know.

Figure 9. **Assets, including some not traditionally found on a balance sheet.**

Controversial Assets

If you know something about accounting already, you might be fretting at this point and saying, "Hey, you can't count things like talent, beauty, people, and reputation as assets!" So, let us reiterate: we're not saying you'd include these in a financial report. For learning purposes and for clarity, we want you to first think in a universal sense about what assets are. Let's start by getting clear on what an asset is (and is not), and then we can look at whether it would be recognized in typical company financial statements.

In a universal sense, is a talent or beauty valuable? Surely. Can a talent or beauty be used to generate revenue? Absolutely yes. There are many talented and beautiful people who use those qualities to generate revenue by giving advice in a boardroom or performing in a theatre, thereby earning themselves a living.

Similarly, people are also assets in a universal sense. Both human resource managers and military generals know that people make up the company, generate profits, and win battles. Famously, HR managers say that "people are our greatest asset": If you read the optional deeper dive discussion about assets below, you'll also see that people are physical, and all physical things are assets because they can't be anything else.

So, in conclusion: If an object is valuable or potentially valuable, it's an asset. Having value or potential value is the unique and defining characteristic of an asset.

Later, we will narrow our view of assets to include only those assets that qualify to be shown on a balance sheet according to accepted recognition rules—what are called "recognition criteria."

> - Assets are valuable
> - Only assets are valuable
> - If something is valuable it's an asset.

Optional Deeper Dive: Assets and Physicality

This optional shaded section is designed to stretch your thinking further, but only if you want to go there. It's not critical to the logic-flow or understanding of the book. Feel free to skip it for now if you prefer.

Physicality

Consider this: if something is physical, then it is valuable or potentially valuable; therefore, if something is physical, it must be an asset. This might surprise you, so let's think about it.

For starters, we're NOT saying assets have to be physical. There are plenty of things in the list above that aren't physical. Accounts Receivable (which is the right to receive money) and Intellectual Property (which are ideas) are not physical things. But they are assets. Which proves that assets don't have to be physical.

Rather, what we're saying is the other way around. If something is physical, it can't be anything other than an asset. Physical things must be assets.

You may have heard people say "my car is a liability." A liability is a debt to someone, a duty to pay, a promise, or an obligation. What people are often really saying is that they owe more money on the car than the car is worth, or that they are constantly spending money on it.

Similarly, people might think that way about their houses. When they know that the mortgage loan on the house is bigger than the value of the house, people talk about the house being "under water," or a "net liability." So, can the house be a liability?

The answer is: no. The car or the house is always an asset. The thinking error here is the collapsing of the two concepts of asset and liability into one. We conflate the concept of an asset with the concept of liability and call the result a single thing. We take the $10,000 car and the $15,000 debt on the car and say that the car is a liability.

That's impossible. You can't drive to work in a liability. A car is a car. Yes, it may be linked to and associated with a liability, but it cannot itself be a liability. A liability is always a non-physical thing—a debt or a promise to pay or serve. A liability can never be physical.

Later, we're going to learn that there are four accounting "elements" beside assets: liabilities, equity, revenue, and expenses. The same thing applies to them. None of them are physical things. Only assets can be physical.

So, if you come across something that's physical, you'll know that it's an asset.

How much you'll value the asset is another question! And whether you should show the asset in your accounts is also to be addressed. Not all assets are shown on a balance sheet.

We'll get to these issues momentarily.

> - Only assets can be physical
> - There are five accounting elements: assets, liabilities, equity, revenue, and expenses. Of the five, only assets can be physical
> - Assets can be physical or non-physical
> - Liabilities, equity, revenue, and expenses are never physical things. More on these later.

You may be asking yourself right now: what's the big deal about physicality?

There's nothing particularly special about physicality as far as accountants are concerned. We're not engineers or physicists who are very interested in physicality. The reason we have discussed physicality here is because, for one thing, holding concepts up to the light and exploring is a good thing in its own right. And secondly, it helps us get clear on the other four elements, which people often misunderstand. For example, later we're going to discuss how lots of people think that revenue is physical money. It's not and it never is.

Realizing that only assets can be physical, and therefore revenue can't be, helps people to avoid this and other mistakes.

Sorting Assets

Our definition of accounting says it's "a system of describing and classifying the nature and size of a business entity's assets." Accountants turn mere data about assets into useful information by sorting them into meaningful categories that readers can make sense of. Using logical groups, we create information that helps us make decisions. Different industries may use groups that are standard in that industry.

How, then, do we group assets? There are many ways to do so. We have a lot of choices. Pick any characteristic and you can classify the assets by that. Among many other examples, you can group your assets by:

- Longevity
- Color
- Purpose
- Size
- Location
- Origin

Let's think some more about the concept of sorting, using buttons as an easy example.

Figure 10. **Buttons to be sorted.**

What is the basis of the sorting into the two groups below? Are they sorted by shape, size, or color? Or perhaps some other characteristic? The learning point here is that in accounting you have choices as to how to sort assets. See the footnote below for the answer about how these buttons are sorted.[3] Hint: it's not what it might first appears to be!

Figure 11. **Sorted buttons.**

---

3. Button sorting answer: They're sorted by number of holes, two or four.

GROUP. SUBGROUPS. SUB-SUBGROUPS

We don't have to sort by just one characteristic. We can keep sorting into smaller subgroups. The extent to which you can divide assets into categories, subcategories, and sub-subcategories is called "granularity." Continuing the button sorting example, we can further sort the buttons into floral and non-floral. The two-hole buttons are shown below.

Figure 12. **Sorting: two-hole buttons, then further sorted into patterned vs. plain. (Four-holed buttons not shown.)**

We can then sort those patterned and plain buttons into round and non-round subgroups. A two-hole floral non-round button is at the bottom left in *Figure 13.* The two-hole non-floral round buttons are at the top right.

Figure 13. **Two-hole buttons sorted by pattern, then by shape.**

Chart of Accounts

Leaving buttons aside now but using the same logic of categorization, accountants define the groups they will use for record-keeping and reporting in a Chart of Accounts. In a chart of accounts you'll find some conventions that most businesses use to group their assets (and other elements like liabilities, revenue, etc.), but there is also a lot of room to sort your assets in a way that works for you. When deciding what groups and how much granularity to have, the manager thinks about what information they need in order to manage the assets. Do we need to know how many "chairs" we have, and how many "tables"? Or will it be enough to only know how much "total furniture" there is? Remember, it's all driven by the wish to have useful information for making decisions. The designer of the chart of accounts also considers what information other stakeholders need. For example, the tax authorities want certain categories of expense broken out and tracked separately, such as meals and entertainment, because they want to apply different tax rules to those expenses.

Companies' Assets Sorted

The general ledger is the database (in the old days, this was a big book/ledger) where all the accounting data is grouped into accounts. The computerized accounting system of a company like Amazon has thousands of "compartments" or "accounts." The narrowest compartments could be for each product sold. Those individual items for sale then aggregate through various categories to "all inventory." And all that inventory rolls up into the total short-term assets, and the short-term assets roll up into total assets. There are layers and layers of groups, subgroups, sub-subgroups, etc. The top-level groupings from the general ledger are then presented in the financial statements of the company with more detail and explanation shown in the notes to the accounts.

Global Retail, Inc.

Let's think about a true-to-life store called *Global Retail, Inc.*

[Note: We will use two businesses as the working examples in the *The Joy of Accounting*. "Lemonade & Laughter" is our made-up business that we have started in a backyard, and which we will grow with a series of journal entries in Part 2 of the book. We will also refer to "Global Retail, Inc.", a real-life business whose balance sheet and income statement we refer to when illustrating certain points.]

This is how Global Retail's recognized assets are grouped:

Figure 14. Global Retail Inc.'s asset-sorting categories.

The categories Global Retail uses, shown in the previous figure are generally accepted groupings that are widely used by preparers of financial statements. They are explained below.

TYPICAL CATEGORIES OF ASSETS

Category of asset	Explanation
Cash and deposits	Global Retail's cash and bank deposits are their notes and coins.
Receivables	Receivables are the right to receive money. Customers owe the company for products they've bought but not yet paid for. Receivables are Global Retail's right to be paid what they are owed. Visa and Mastercard, the credit card companies, also owe; that's included in receivables.
Inventories	These are the goods in shops and warehouses that are held to sell to customers or to be used in manufacturing other goods that are in turn sold to customers.
Property and equipment	These are the land, buildings, shelves, forklifts, trucks, conveyor belts, and so on, that the business entity owns.
Prepayments	Prepayments are the right to receive goods or services for which you've paid, but haven't yet received. Think of it like putting down a deposit on something when you order it.

Figure 15. **Typical asset categories explained.**

Measuring Assets

Accounting is a system of describing and categorizing the nature and size of a business entity's assets, the ways they were funded, and what the entity did to increase and diminish them.

Crucially, the second job that accounting performs, after sorting, is to measure.

Temperature is measured in units of Fahrenheit, Celsius, or kelvin. Electricity is measured in units of watts, amps, and volts. Speed is measured in miles or kilometers per hour. In accounting, the measuring unit is currency, like dollars, pounds, yen, euros, and rand. We'll talk about dollars mostly, for simplicity.

Valuation

Everything in accounting is compared with the value of an actual dollar. The value of a chair is measured by comparing it with the amount of dollars it took to buy it. To measure the size of a debt that you owe, the debt is compared with the amount of dollars you'd have to pay to settle the debt.

We're deliberately emphasizing this idea of comparison and how assets (and all the other accounting elements) are compared to actual dollars to measure them. It might seem like we're belaboring an obvious point, but the comparison with cash causes a lot of confusion.

Revenue, for example, is like everything else measured by comparison to an actual dollar. The problem is, people start to believe that revenue is the money itself. It's not. It's only compared with money. Revenue is never money. Money is always an asset.

MEASURE, MEASURE, TOIL AND TREASURE

In the world of cars, the car's power is measured by comparing it with the power of a number of horses to get horsepower. In the world of accounting, a car's value is measured by comparing it with the value of the number of dollar bills.

What we're seeing here is that a dollar in accounting can be two things: it can be an actual asset as cash, and it can be a currency unit used to measure the size of everything.

Actual physical cash dollars are also measured in dollars. You might have $50 worth of dollar bills, and, if you had a rare misprinted dollar bill or one that had Elvis's signature on it, you might have a dollar worth 1,000 dollars. When you looked at the single dollar bill, you would see a bank note worth one thousand dollars.

Global Retail's Assets

All of Global Retail's assets are measured and quantified in its financial statements. On a recent reporting date, the size of their assets was measured as follows.

GLOBAL RETAIL, INC

ASSET DESCRIPTION	Equivalent in value to how many dollar bills
Cash and cash equivalents	46 thousand
Receivables	128 thousand
Inventories	239 thousand
Land and buildings	502 thousand
Equipment	176 thousand
Investments	2 thousand
TOTAL ASSETS	1,093 thousand

Figure 16. Global Retail Inc.'s assets and size.

Quantification

The question still stands: How many actual dollars should an asset be compared to? Above, we said that the value of a chair is equivalent to how many dollars you paid to buy it, but that's not the full story.

Yes, we often choose to measure assets—the chair, for example—in terms of the number of dollars we paid to buy it. That is called the purchase price. But the chair could also be measured in terms of the number of dollars we would receive if we sold it.

What you compare the asset to is called the basis of measurement. Various bases of measurement, or "valuation methods," are listed in the following table. Which valuation method you use is a matter of choice, often governed by rules laid down by accounting regulators. The regulators prescribe (and proscribe) different methodologies for different asset-classes and circumstances.

Methods of Valuing Assets

METHODS OF VALUING ASSETS

Method	Description
Historical cost	This is the most common method of valuation. It looks at how much the business paid for an asset. It is factual and easy to prove.
Fair value	Fair value is the fair price that a reasonable buyer and seller agree on.
Market value	This is the price that other people are currently paying for the same asset, such as shares in a public company in an active market.
Realizable value	This is what you could sell the asset for, which may be lower than normal because of exceptional circumstances, like being in a hurry or closing down a business. The costs of making and completing the sale are usually deducted.
Current cost/ replacement cost	This is how much you'd pay to replace the asset.
Present value	For a cash flow over a number of periods, this is how much all the cash would add up to, factoring in that having money in hand today is better (worth more) than having to wait for it.

Figure 17. Asset valuation methods.

- Everything in a company's accounts are measured by comparison to a dollar (or other currency unit).
- The value of all assets on a balance sheet depends upon the valuation method used: acquisition price, going price, notional disposal price, or reasonable consensus price.

Recapping Valuation

This discussion about how to measure assets is an important theme you must be aware of. While accounting is in some senses a precise science, in others it isn't. You're going to learn about the principles of account-balancing, which means that one side of a balance sheet is always precisely equal to the other. This perfect balance can give the impression that accounting is a generally precise undertaking. In the narrow sense of perfect balancing where two numbers match, it is precise. But depending upon the assumptions you make, you can arrive at widely differing numbers that will then be made to perfectly match. This will make more sense when we've finished discovering the accounting equation.

As jesters down under in Australia ask when confronted with a difficult measurement question: "How long is a piece of string?" The answer (drumroll) is: "twice as long as half its length." Nice, mate. True, but not useful.

It's important to know that valuation in accounting is subjective. There are limits to what accounting can accomplish. The fact that there is no singular truth about the value of an asset is one of those limitations.

> There are many different values that could be ascribed to an asset. Regardless of what value is used, it will form part of a perfectly balanced financial statement.

Recognition of Assets

We've said that accounting sorts assets, obligations, and the other accounting elements into categories so that we can make more sense of them, turning mere data into useful information. We also looked at the principles of sorting.

With a focus on assets, we then saw that we measure them, choosing one of several possible measuring methods.

But what if some assets can't be measured at all? Perhaps we didn't buy them from anyone and have no reasonable idea as to what they could be sold for. Where this is going is that some assets are simply ignored in the financial reports of a company because they can't be measured with a reasonable degree of certainty.

Notice that the first-level heading of the collection of Global Retail's assets in *Figure 14* is "Recognized Assets." The implication here is that there's one higher sort-level of the assets, even before the current and non-current groups. The first two sort-groups of Global Retail's assets are Recognized Assets and Unrecognized Assets. The second group is not in the financial reports, so it's easy to forget about, but it's still important to keep in mind. Just because assets aren't described in the financial reports of a company doesn't mean that the assets aren't important or valuable to the company or a potential purchaser. They may, in fact, be the most important asset the company has.

NOW I SEE YOU, NOW I DON'T

Think of a hugely valuable asset like Coca-Cola's brand name and those unique trademarks the Coca-Cola Company has, such as the shape of the bottle and the ribbon motif that runs up the side of their cans. This brand collateral belongs to Coca-Cola, and nobody can use them without their permission. But how much are they worth? You can argue that they are the most valuable thing that Coca-Cola has. If the company lost a factory, it could build another one. But lose that name and their sales will dry up pretty fast. So, is the Coca-Cola brand worth, say, $100 billion? Or maybe $110 billion? There's no market price you can look to for comparison because there's no market where people buy and sell iconic soda pop names.

In theory, you could just pick one of those numbers, say $100 billion, and present an argument that it's reasonable and list the brand in the financial statements at your estimate. Unfortunately, your estimate would just be a guess. If I were another user of the financial reports and guessed that it's worth 10 percent more, then we're talking about a $10 billion difference between your guess and mine. That's a big difference.

Because we'd both be guessing, accountants don't go there. They avoid the guessing game altogether and simply leave the asset off the financial reports. Rather than include a number that is a subjective opinion that would introduce the storyteller's bias, the accountant leaves it up to the readers of the financial reports to decide for themselves what the brand is worth.

The investors and potential investors in Coca-Cola know that it owns its brand, that it's pretty well protected, and that it will keep on earning money for Coke in the years ahead. The investors decide for themselves how much the brand will earn and therefore how valuable they think it is today, along with the other unreported assets. In fact, the best indicator of the value of the unrecognized assets of Coca-Cola is the market value of the whole corporation, as judged by the stock market. In other words, not the value that the accounts of the company report, but the consensus value that all the myriad buyers and sellers of shares in Coca-Cola express through the intersection of supply and demand of those shares.

The market thinks the value of the unrecognized assets of Coke is equal to the market value of the whole company, minus the value of the recognized assets (and factoring in the company's debts). This market value goes up and down, of course, as the share price goes up and down, so it's not a useful reference point to put on the financial statements.

In summary, if an asset can't be measured reliably, then it isn't included in the financial statements of a company. It is just left out (as—by definition—an unrecognized asset).

> If an asset can't be measured reliably, it isn't shown in the accounts of a company.

Measurability

Measurability is therefore the first (but not the only) recognition criterion for assets. For an asset to be recorded on the balance sheet of a company, it must be measurable.

Control

The second qualification required for an asset to appear on a company's balance sheet is control. For an asset to appear on Global's balance sheet, it must belong to Global. It's what you'd expect. Intuitively, Global can't list other people's assets as their own. What if Global uses somebody else's asset for years, earning profits from the asset? Any store that rents its premises from a landlord does just that: the store is owned by the landlord but rented by the tenant with a right of occupancy that will last for the period listed in the lease.

And what if Global leases vehicles that technically and legally belong to a leasing company but are Global's to use, insure, maintain, and repair—and return at the end of the lease? Because Global might use such controlled-but-not-owned assets to run its business and generate revenue, accountants make the ownership test wider to include assets that are owned or merely controlled. Beyond that, any asset that is not controlled by the company is excluded from the financial reports of the company.

So, the second recognition criterion for assets is control. In order for an asset to be recorded on the balance sheet of a company, it must be controlled by the company.

> If an asset isn't controlled by an entity, it isn't shown in that entity's accounts.

Recognition Criteria

These two tests that require measurability and control in order for an asset to be shown in the financial statements of a company are called Recognition Criteria. They are important to keep in mind when thinking about a business and reading its financial statements. You should remember that the assets you're seeing aren't the full story. Other assets are being used by the business but aren't being listed.

We started this chapter with a list of random assets. Now that you know about the need for the recognition criteria to be satisfied in order to show the assets in the financial statements of a company, we can see that a number of these assets will rarely, if ever, be seen in the financials of a company.

NON-RECOGNIZED ASSETS

ASSET	Criteria: Reliably Measurable?	Control?
Beautiful view	No	Unlikely
Beauty	No	Unlikely
Branding	Possibly	Possibly
Customer list	Possibly	Possible
Exclusive rights	Possibly	Possible
Football players	No	No
People	No	No
Recipes	Possibly	Yes
Reputation	No	No
Right of access	Unlikely	Possible
Staff	No	No
Talent	No	No
Trade secrets	Possible	Yes
Trash	Possible	Yes
Unique location	No	No

Figure 18. **Non-recognized assets.**

Assets like **staff**, **people**, and **football players** will never appear in a set of financial statements because you can't own or control people. Even if you could, what is your star employee worth? Who can say?

You might be thinking "But teams buy and sell football players." Actually, they aren't buying and selling the person. Slavery being illegal, we can be sure of that. What a club is buying when they secure the services of a star soccer player is a registration right that secures their services to play exclusively for the club. Such rights do appear in the financial statements, but the asset isn't the actual player: it is the "right to services"—the player's contract.

Many of the assets like **right of access, recipes,** and **beautiful view** aren't measurable because they've never been bought. If something unique has never attracted a buy/sell price, then you can't say what it's worth with any degree of reliability.

Many beautiful people earn real money off their beauty. Some celebrities even insure their face or legs against disfigurement. If they get scarred, they'll be paid compensation for loss of earnings. Beauty is surely an asset to a celebrity, but what is it worth? Nobody can say with any certainty, so you don't see it as an asset on people's financial statements. The insurance company picks a value for their insurance purposes, but that number is not a value that satisfies traditional accounting recognition criteria.

Some accounting jurisdictions require that an asset must have been acquired in a transaction in order to be recognized. This disqualifies assets such as a **view** from recognition, which a company didn't acquire through a transaction.

Goodwill describes the reputation that a business has generated through its operations and the list of regular customers that it has grown—and never appears in the financial statements of a business. This is because you can't be sure of the value of that goodwill. However, when a business buys another business because of its reputation, that goodwill does appear as an asset in the buyer's accounts. This is because the purchase of the asset gave the goodwill a measured value. It is often referred to as "acquired goodwill" to distinguish it from "generated goodwill." Acquired goodwill is shown in financial statements. Generated goodwill isn't.

> Acquired goodwill is shown on the balance sheet of companies. Generated goodwill isn't.

We included **trash** in the original list of assets because—as discussed earlier in the Assets and Physicality section—anything physical must be an asset (because it can't be any of the other accounting elements Liability, Equity, Revenue or Expense, all of which are never physical). Most people's response to trash is probably "yuck." It doesn't seem like an asset at first blush, does it? Recall that an asset is anything valuable or potentially valuable, and trash can be valuable. Electronic goods that we throw away are often processed by salvage companies that reclaim the rare metals and plastics from them to sell for good money. As they say, "One person's trash is another person's treasure." So, trash is by definition an asset. Usually though, it doesn't show up on financial reports because it's considered to be worth zero, or less than the cost of disposing it. Zero-valued assets aren't shown in the financials. The learning point is that trash, having possible value, could in principle be shown as an asset.

Main recognition criteria

Measurability and control are the main asset recognition criteria that we want you to think about at the moment. The world's two main accounting regulatory bodies have more nuanced criteria for asset recognition. The two principal frameworks for company-accounting rules in the world are the Generally Accepted Accounting Principles in the United States, commonly known as US GAAP, and International Financial Reporting Standards in other countries, commonly known as IFRS. The two frameworks have somewhat different asset recognition rules from each other. Both go beyond the two main criteria that we've discussed (measurability and control).

Suffice it to say that control and measurability are at the essence of both. See the appendix on page 273 for more detail on the regulatory measurement and recognition rules.

Optional Deeper Dive Discussion: Financial Nature of Assets

The Joy of Accounting has started with a strong focus on assets. Assets are central to business, finance, and accounting, so it was always going to be important to explore them early and thoroughly. Before we move on to having a business source the assets, we're going to add one more layer to the definition of what an asset in a balance sheet is. Let's just do a quick review first...

Financial Story

The business entity is an accounting entity. Accounting tells a financial story about the finances of a business entity.

Since the accounting entity is financial in nature, it means that what it incorporates must also be financial in nature. Yet we've said assets can be physical. So how do we show physical assets in a non-physical financial entity?

The answer is that accounting doesn't strictly describe an entity's physical assets. It describes the entity's financial rights to the underlying assets. (Those underlying assets may themselves be physical or non-physical.) Global Retail's balance sheet describes Global's right to the physical buildings and equipment that Global owns, and the right to the non-physical assets that it controls, such as its accounts receivable.

It is the right to the asset that must be measurable and controlled.

Inspired by the famous painting by Belgian surrealist René Magritte called *The Treachery of Images* the diagram below makes the point that what you see is not a butterfly. It's a shape on a piece of paper or screen. In the Magritte painting the text below an image of a pipe reads "This Is Not a Pipe."

This is not a butterfly.

Figure 19. **An image of an object is not the object. Neither is the right to an object the object.**

The butterfly image is an abstraction from the underlying real butterfly. Similarly, a balance sheet describes a financial abstraction from the underlying objects, which could be chairs, tables, or rights to receive money.

A balance sheet being a financial paradigm, everything inside it is financial in nature.

We will continue to talk about assets on a balance sheet and may describe the underlying physical or non-physical assets themselves. Strictly speaking though, when we speak about assets, we will usually be meaning the rights to the assets. We'll use the concepts of assets and the right to assets somewhat interchangeably.

CHAPTER ROUNDUP

The goal of this chapter has been to have a thought-provoking investigation of assets, the entity that owns the assets, the nature of assets, what an asset is and is not and how it's defined, how they are described in financial statements, how they are measured, and when they are shown in financial statements and when they aren't.

We've explored how.

- Assets are used by businesses to generate revenue and achieve their purpose.
- Assets are anything that is valuable or potentially valuable.
- The quality of being valuable is associated with desirability, saleability, convertibility to cash, and capacity to generate revenue. Valuable things are uniquely capable of canceling obligations.
- Grouping and categorization are used to create decision-useful information.
- The accountant can choose what and how many groups and sub-groups to use in describing the assets. Using many groups gives a finer "granularity," but comes at an administration cost.
- Assets and other accounting elements are measured in currency units.
- There is no one true value of any asset. The measurement of value is subjective.
- Assets can be measured by what they were bought for, what they could be sold for, what reasonable people would agree they are worth, and what similar assets are judged to be worth.
- Businesses use recognized and unrecognized assets. Only the recognized assets are reported in the accounts of the company.
- The principle recognition criteria require that assets can be measured and are controlled by the entity.
- Assets can be physical or non-physical things, tangible or intangible.
- While physicality isn't inherently significant in accounting, the potential for physicality distinguishes assets from all the other accounting elements.
- Because accountants describe a financial entity, the assets in it must be financial in nature. Therefore, the assets being described on a balance sheet are, strictly speaking, the rights to the underlying physical and non-physical assets—not those assets themselves.

3. SOURCING ASSETS

Funding the Business

We've talked a lot about assets. Nothing can happen in business without assets. They are central to the story of any business. So, the question of how a business acquires assets is important. The short answer to the question is by incurring obligations. The only way that a business can increase the total assets it has is by getting them from someone and being obligated in return.

To explore this, we'll start by going back to the creation of our backyard business, Lemonade & Laughter. As accountants, we imputed a business entity. Lemonade & Laughter, the entity, is the financial vessel that holds the rights to all the assets. Needless to say, at the moment of its creation, the Lemonade & Laughter entity was empty. It had no assets at its inception, nor any obligations. In *Figure 20* below, we represent the Lemonade & Laughter entity as a rectangular box.

ENTITY REPRESENTED BY A BOX

Now assume that the business goes ahead and acquires an asset that it will use to operate the business. Since the entity started empty, this asset must have come from a provider of the asset. We call that person or entity the "funder" or "contributor."

The next critical principle to grasp is that the entity has an obligation to return whatever it receives from a funder. The entity never holds an asset for itself. It always holds the assets it has for the funders who provided them.

So, whenever an entity acquires an asset, it also acquires an obligation to return an asset.

Figure 20. **Whenever an entity acquires a right to an asset, it also acquires an obligation.**

The entity has a matching obligation for any asset it receives, which means that if the business ever decided to close, it would be obliged to return all the assets it has. It would never have any assets left over that it didn't have to return.

Furthermore, the business is only obligated to return what assets it has. It is never obligated to return assets it doesn't have. Therefore, the business never has more obligations than it has assets.

Another way of saying this is the net worth of the entity is always zero! Net worth is how many more assets you have than obligations. People can have a net worth, but accounting entities never do. They never have more assets than they have obligations. They always have the same amount of assets and obligations.

NET WORTH OF ZERO

This is critical to appreciate. Every right that the reporting entity has is matched by an obligation to return the asset. All assets in the box are held on behalf of funders to whom the entity is obligated.

Note: especially if you are already somewhat familiar with accounting and business terminology, this assertion that a business's net worth is zero may surprise you. The statement is somewhat provocative and being made here in a very literal sense. In day to day practice, you will hear reference to the net worth of a business being equivalent to the amount of equity the business has, rather than zero. This is understandable in ordinary common usage of the term "net worth". What we must remember is that the casual statement is really saying "the net worth of a business *to the owner*" is equivalent to the equity. There's an assumed point of view change from the business to the owner. To the owner, yes, the business is worth the amount of the equity. But overall, when all the funders of the business are considered, both owners and non-owners, the business has nothing that is not obligated to those funders.

Obligations

What then is an obligation? Unlike assets (though not unlike rights to assets), an obligation is a concept distinguished, or "invented," by humans. It's a jurisprudential concept, which is to say it's a legal and financial concept that exists within the realms of law and finance. (Jurisprudence is the theory and philosophy of law.)

An obligation is:

- a commitment
- a duty
- a responsibility
- a burden
- the owing to another
- a debt to another
- a liability[4]
- an intangible thing that can be eliminated ("settled") by contribution of an asset or a service
- something you can't see

---

4.   Later we'll distinguish between liabilities and another kind of obligation. Not all obligations are liabilities, but all liabilities are obligations.

THE JOY OF ACCOUNTING

- something you can't touch
- not money, and
- not even "money you owe."

You can't see, touch, or show someone an obligation. It's an idea that exists in the ether. You might be thinking that you can point to a piece of paper that represents the obligation. Indeed, you can, but that piece of paper is not the obligation. It's an asset that evidences the size and nature of the obligation. The paper will, for example, enable you to prove the limitation of your obligation—that it's not bigger than was agreed.

> An obligation is a duty to pay or perform that could
> be cancelled by handing over an asset.

The reason we're emphasizing that obligations are intangible and are not money is because people often look at a balance sheet, see obligations (such as liabilities), and think that they are money owed to someone else. Many dictionaries expressly define liabilities as "monies owed." This implies that a liability is money. A liability is not and can never be money. A liability is only measured in relation to money, but it is not itself the money.

OBLIGATION IS NEVER MONEY

The words "obligation" and "liability" both come from the Latin and French words meaning "to bind." The root word is *ligare*, the same as in "ligament." The sense of the word is that when you get an asset from someone, your obligation binds you to them.

While an obligation is never money or tangible or physical, it's still a good idea to see it in your mind's eye as a virtual object. That way, you'll clearly see that when you put an asset into your reporting box, you must put in an obligation too—like the two virtual objects shown in *Figure 20*.

CHAPTER ROUNDUP

This Sourcing Assets chapter introduces the idea that a business funds all assets with obligations. All assets are sourced from funders to whom the business becomes obligated.

We've explored how:

- The business starts with no assets and no obligations.
- When a business acquires an asset, it also acquires an obligation that funds the asset.
- Obligations are duties and responsibilities that can be settled by contributing an asset or providing a service.
- In other words, you can pay a lender with an asset to cancel your debt to them.
- An obligation is never money. It is not "money you owe someone." It is measured by comparison to money, in currency units, but it is never itself money.

- The business never has more assets than it has obligations.
- Strictly speaking, the net worth of a business is always zero.
- In casual conversation people say the net worth of a business is equivalent to the equity of the business. This is understandable because the statement assumes that the point of view is the owner rather than the business itself. From the point of view of the business, the net worth is always zero.

4. ACCOUNTING DUALITY

Rights and Obligations

So, now we have an entity with two (and only two) types of things in it. There is nothing else in the entity except assets (specifically rights to assets) and obligations.

BOX IS NOW TWO-SIDED

Because there are only ever two types of objects in the entity, we show it as a two-sided box. One side to put all the rights, and the other side to put all the obligations.

Figure 21. **Rights and obligations - a two-sided box.**

To emphasize this two-sidedness, we think of a butterfly with its two wings. This butterfly won't fly unless both wings are firmly in place! The butterfly represents what we call the "Accounting Duality."

Figure 22. **Balance sheet box shaped like a butterfly, emphasizing sides.**

The accounting duality is the double-ness that says there is always both a right and an obligation in the accounting entity. The butterfly shape of the entity-box captures the symmetry of rights (to assets) and obligations.

BUTTERFLY BOX

The duality is a truly beautiful thing, a profound truth at the core of accounting and the accountability that accounting gives us. There is an elegance and a perfection to the duality, like so many things in nature. It is yin and yang, matter and antimatter.

Our butterfly splits rights from obligations in an act of perfectly symmetrical creation. When rights and obligations emerge in our accounting entity, they describe the finances of our business. "Rights = Obligations" is the highest possible form of the famous accounting equation that we'll be exploring in detail soon.

> The accounting duality describes the division of the accounting entity into rights and obligations.

The accounting duality is profound and beautiful, and it is also the source of a lot of the confusion that people have about accounting. The fact that there are two aspects to be considered in any accounting situation means that people can confuse one aspect for the other, or collapse the aspects and think about them as one thing instead of two.

You won't do that! You'll always have a strong awareness that there is an underpinning double-ness in any financial situation you are analyzing, and you'll be on the lookout for that confusion.

Measuring the Objects

We explored in Chapter 2 how assets are measured. They are quantified using currency as the unit of measurement and by reference to one of a number of values, such as the amount of currency required to purchase the asset.

It's not only assets that are measured. Obligations are measured too.

MEASURED

So, how do you measure an obligation you incur? You look at how much value you got by incurring it.

And how do you measure an asset you acquire? You look at how much obligation you incurred (and possibly immediately settled through payment) to acquire it. Assets and obligations are measured in terms of each other.

Where this gets us is that you always have the same amount of assets and obligations. This is why a balance sheet balances.

To illustrate this, we show the butterfly balancing on a see-saw with currency symbols.

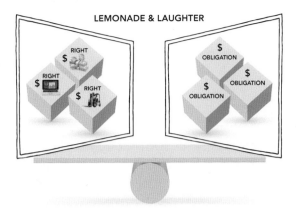

Figure 23. **The assets in the entity are the same total size (measured in currency) as the obligations.**

Equivalence

From this inherent equivalence of the amount of assets and the amount of obligations comes the name **balance sheet**. We're going to spend a lot of time on this report in the chapters ahead.

In terms of size, both sides of the entity are always the same. Size-wise, the assets and the obligations on the balance sheet always balance. The quantum of assets is always equal to the quantum of obligations.

SAME SIZE, DIFFERENT NATURE

We're being careful to specify that it is the size of the assets and obligations that are equivalent. Their natures are not equivalent. They are quite different beasts when it comes to what they are, rather than how big they are. Only their size is the same. This is a thinking error that people make, believing that they are the same in all respects. They definitely are not.

> Only the total size of assets and obligations are the same. Their natures are never the same.

You may well ask yourself, "Does a balance sheet always balance?" The answer is yes. Not because it's a rule that someone laid down. Not because it should or it would be bad if it didn't. By definition, a balance sheet balances.

As explained above, each side is measured in the same currency, in terms of the other.

You may well ask yourself, "Does a balance sheet always balance?" The answer is yes. Not because it's a rule that someone laid down. Not because it should or it would be bad if it didn't. By definition, a balance sheet balances. As we like to say, a balance sheet cannot not-balance! (Short of an addition error, that is.)

> A balance sheet cannot not-balance.

CHAPTER ROUNDUP

This Accounting Duality chapter introduces the idea that the financial reporting entity is divided into two halves.

We've explored how:

- The financial entity contains rights to assets as well as obligations to return those assets.
- The rights and the obligations are each shown on a side of the entity box.
- The two-sidedness is emphasized by showing the entity in the shape of a butterfly.
- The accounting duality describes the split of the financial reporting entity into rights and obligations.
- The duality is represented by the two wings of a butterfly.
- The rights and obligations are both measured.
- Their size is defined by cross-referencing each other.
- Assets are measured by referencing obligations, and obligations are measured by referencing assets.
- By definition, the rights and obligations in the financial entity are therefore equivalent in size.
- The butterfly diagram represents the balance sheet.
- The balance sheet always balances.

5. ACCOUNTING EQUATION

There are only two things in the accounting entity: rights and obligations. We've seen that they are, in total, the same size by definition.

When we express this as a mathematical equation, we say that rights are equal to obligations. In math notation, it reads *Rights = Obligations*.

RIGHTS $=$ OBLIGATIONS

We have rights to assets. So we often find the same equation worded in various ways, such as *Rights to Assets = Obligations*, or as *Assets = Obligations*. They all amount to the same thing.

> Alternative ways of expressing the accounting equation:
> Rights = Obligations
> Rights to Assets = Obligations

Regardless of how the equation is expressed, it does not mean that "assets are the same as obligations." Assets are most definitely not the same as obligations. In most respects, they are entirely different. For example, assets themselves can be physical, while obligations cannot be. Rights are valuable, obligations are not.

In math, there's another symbol that looks like an equal sign with three lines. It looks like this: $\equiv$

This three-stripe symbol means "is identical to." Assets and obligations are never identical to each other, so the symbol is crossed out. **Assets $\not\equiv$ Obligations**. Assets are not identical to obligations.

RIGHTS $\not\equiv$ OBLIGATIONS

Because it is the total size of the assets and obligations that is equivalent, as measured in currency, it's a good reminder to think of the equation as **\$Rights = \$Obligations.**

\$RIGHTS $=$ \$OBLIGATIONS

In accounting, assets can never become obligations, and vice versa. They are permanently distinct concepts, on a balance sheet equivalent in amount only. The only change that can happen to assets and obligations on a balance sheet is to increase or decrease. They can't turn into something else.

> Assets can't turn into obligations, nor vice versa.

When thinking about these ideas, remember to keep the point of view constant. You shouldn't, for example, think about turning an asset into an obligation by switching the point of view. Yes, my liability may be your asset, but I must stay consistent in telling my story.

This chapter marks the introduction of the famous accounting equation that underpins all of accounting. There's nothing mysterious or hard about it at all. Soon, we'll give it more detail by splitting the obligations into two types.

CHAPTER ROUNDUP

In this chapter, the duality we discovered earlier is now expressed in simple math via the accounting equation, which in its simplest form is expressed as Rights = Obligations.

We explored how:

- By definition, as measured in currency, the total size of the rights to the assets on the balance sheet is the same as the total size of the obligations.
- This is expressed in the equation Rights = Obligations.
- The rights described are rights to assets. So, the accounting equation can also be expressed as Rights to Assets = Obligations, and Assets = Obligations.
- To emphasize that the equivalence is the size as measured in currency, we also expressed the accounting equation with currency symbols: $Rights = $Obligations.
- The equation is not saying that "assets are the same as obligations." In most respects, they are different.
- Assets cannot turn into obligations. Obligations can't turn into assets.

6. ACCOUNTING EQUATION: BALANCE SHEET

We saw in the previous chapter that the accounting equation is expressed variously as

- Rights = Obligations
- Rights to Assets = Obligations, and
- Assets = Obligations.

We're going to use the third form now because assets and obligations are what people are used to seeing on balance sheets.

The accounting equation for Global Retail, Inc., shown on the butterfly diagram, looks like this.

Figure 24. **Corporate balance sheet showing the funder of the business.**

As discussed in Chapter 1, your personal financial story is told from the point of view of Financial Persona You. It might look like this.

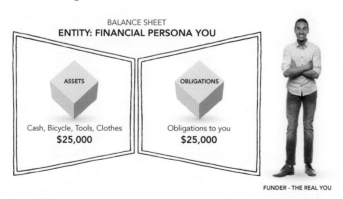

Figure 25. **Personal balance sheet showing real person and financial persona.**

The separation of the storytelling entity from the owner and funder of the entity means there is always an obligation within the entity to the funder. This applies for both legally incorporated as well as unincorporated entities. The accounting equation therefore always applies: Assets = Obligations.

For your personal balance sheet, if there wasn't a separation between you and the separate financial persona, then there wouldn't have to be an obligation in your story. You wouldn't be obligated to yourself, so to speak. Having a separation between you the human and the financial persona that we nicknamed "You incorporated." means it remains true that there are always obligations on a balance sheet.

> Your financial persona that captures your financial story has an obligation to the real you.

There are some psychological advantages to thinking of your financial persona as separate from the true you. Money worries can get us down, but it's easier to keep them in perspective when we objectify our financial personas. You are much more, and much more wonderful, than your financial persona. Keep your money worries in perspective.

> You are much more wonderful than your financial persona.

Two Kinds of Obligation

We're clear now that there are always contributors of funds to the entity: those who provide the assets to it. Those funders are shown below as the people to the right of the butterfly diagram. The entity is obligated to them. Until now, we've been assuming they are all owners, but they don't have to be.

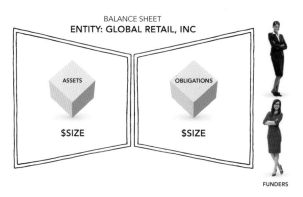

Figure 26. **Two distinct funders of the entity.**

We now introduce a new concept to our unfolding accounting model: the funders can contribute their assets to the business entity in two different ways. They can either lend the assets to the business or invest them. The difference between lending and investing has to do with the funders' expectations of getting the assets back and their reward for providing them.

LEND OR INVEST

Depending upon whether the funders lend or invest assets into the business, the business in return acquires different forms of obligation to the funders. When the funder lends assets to the business, it results in a liability-obligation in the business's accounts. When the funder invests assets into the business, it results in an equity-obligation in the business's accounts.

We will explore the difference between liability-obligations and equity-obligations in the next chapter.

Butterfly: Three Parts

After establishing that there are just two elements on a balance sheet—assets and obligations—we're now seeing that there are two kinds of obligation. The obligations of a business are divided into liability obligations and equity obligations. In the diagram below, the right-hand wing of the butterfly now shows Liabilities and Equity. Liabilities are the obligations of the entity to people who have lent assets. Equity is the obligation to the shareholders who have invested assets, and therefore become owners or shareholders.

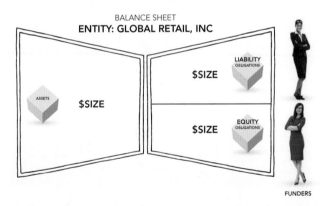

Figure 27. **Two types of obligation on the balance sheet butterfly.**

Accounting Equation: Three Parts

Recall that the accounting equation Assets = Obligations is saying that the size of the total assets is the same as the size of the total obligations, as measured in currency.

Now that we've distinguished that there are two types of obligation, we show the additional detail in the equation by splitting the obligations on the right-hand side into two different types. This creates the equation Assets = Liability Obligations + Equity Obligations. This is usually written as: Assets = Liabilities + Equity

ASSETS = LIABILITIES + EQUITY

This is the most common expression of the accounting equation.

It is also expressed to focus on Equity by writing it as ***Assets - Liabilities = Equity***. Mathematically, this is achieved by subtracting liabilities from both sides of the equation. This form of the equation puts equity on its own, making it equivalent to the amount of assets minus the amount of liabilities. This is done because the purpose of the business is to grow equity, and the equation and accounts are often prepared for the principle benefit of owners. This following expression of the equation focuses on what's of interest to the owners.

ASSETS - LIABILITIES = EQUITY

For our true to life example, Global Retail, the balance sheet butterfly looks like this. Note that while we have shown the funders as people, they could be corporate entities rather than real individuals.

Figure 28. Global Retail, Inc. showing balanced assets and obligations to funders

The word "net" in accounting is used when something has been taken away from something else. When the quantum of liabilities has been deducted from the quantum of assets, we call the result "net assets." Therefore, the balance sheet equation can also read: **Assets - Liabilities = Net Assets**.

> All of the accounting equations are saying the same things in different ways. The quantum of assets is equal to the quantum of obligations.

ASSETS - LIABILITIES = NET ASSETS

Particularly when speaking about individuals' personal balance sheets (and also when describing nonprofit corporations), the term "Net Assets" is commonly used instead of the term Equity.

Notice, however, that we're being careful not to say that net assets are leftover assets. ("Leftover" in the sense of what assets you'd be left with for the shareholders if you settled all the debts and liabilities.) Many books do say this, but they're wrong. Saying this would be collapsing the duality and conflating the two sides of the butterfly. Net Assets aren't assets. They're obligations, albeit the same size as the leftover assets. The leftover assets are always on the left of the butterfly. The Net Asset obligation is on the right of the butterfly.

> "Net Assets" aren't leftover assets.
> They're equivalent in size to the leftover assets, but they are not them.

It's interesting to consider where the word "equity" comes from. It derives from Middle English and the Old French word *equité*, which means "equal." That French word in turn derives from the Latin *aequitas*, also meaning equal. So why should Equity in the accounting equation come from the sense of "equal"? The answer is that it's the equity figure that changes to make sure the equation balances. When assets are given and liabilities are given, equity changes to make the equation balance and be equal. We'll explore this much more in the chapters ahead.

Money vs. Currency Units

Let's remind ourselves that in the preceding *Figure 28* above, the "$" sign in front of the numbers 1,093,428, 824,399, and 269,029 does not mean that those numbers describe money. Liabilities are never money, and neither is equity.

Thinking that, for example, the $824,399 is "money owed" would be to confuse money with monetization. The accounting equation is monetized because all measurement happens in monetary terms. There is no money on the right side of the butterfly, and not all assets are money either. They're all measured in money, but only actual money is money.

Even money is measured in currency. Dollars are measured in dollars—by which we mean that actual dollars are measured in currency-unit dollars. Think about when a business is holding other currencies, like Japanese yen or British pounds, in which case that foreign money would also be measured in dollars on the balance sheet. Global might hold $1M pounds—British pounds in an amount worth say 1.45 million USD.

MONEY VS. MONETIZATION

> Dollar signs ($) don't mean there's money there.

> Both sides of the accounting equation are monetized, but money only appears in assets.

Sources and Uses of Funds

Another way to think about the accounting equation is to see it as the story of funding a business. The equation describes how the business has sourced funding to operate the business, and what it used for that funding. You can think of funding as energy.

To source funds for the business, the business incurs obligations. So, obligations are a source of funds. And how do the funds show up, or manifest? In what form does the energy appear? It shows up as money in the bank or in the form of other assets. So, assets are a use of funds. They are funds "in use."

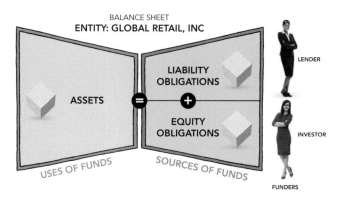

Figure 29. **Balance sheet butterfly showing sources and uses of funds.**

In the Color Accounting Learning System, we have chosen the color orange to represent sources of funds and the color green to represent uses of funds. As you can see above, the colors make it very easy to differentiate visually.

Later, you'll see how this ties into the concept of debits and credits (which you might have heard about).

Why green and orange? Orange reminds us of sunshine, which is the ultimate source of our energy. Coloring obligations in a shade reminiscent of sunshine is a reminder that you can't touch them—just as you can't touch sunshine. They are abstract in nature—intangible. Green, on the other hand, reminds us of physical things, like plants in the garden, and cash.

In the 1860s during the Civil War, the United States government printed paper currency, the back of which was printed in green. From then on, US paper money has been known as "greenbacks," setting up an association of cash with the color green.

Another reason we use green and orange for coding concepts in Color Accounting is that they are vivid colors that highlight numbers and text well. Also, a color like red would not be wise to use. Red would be misleading because it carries historic connotations of danger. In accounting specifically, red indicates a loss or a deficit. We wouldn't want to add that confusion to the mix.

From now on, whenever you see orange in this book, you can think "sources of funds," and when you see green, you can think "uses of funds."

> Green represents uses of funds.
> Orange represents sources of funds.

Figure 30. **A green and radiant world.**

Vertical Balance Sheet

Figure 31. **Butterfly rotating.**

The report below, in Figure 32, is how the balance sheet is laid out in its traditional, vertical format. The numbers are for example only.

This is the traditional layout in the United States. In Europe and elsewhere, the layout used for external reporting is slightly different. For example, long-term assets might go above short-term assets, but these are formatting conventions. The information is the same.

Reporting Entity Balance Sheet at Period End

ASSETS	
Total short-term assets	111
Total long-term assets	222
TOTAL ASSETS	**333**

LIABILITIES	
Total short-term liabilities	50
Long-term loans, leases and tax obligations	150
TOTAL LIABILITIES	**200**
TOTAL EQUITY	**133**
TOTAL OBLIGATIONS	**333**

Figure 32. **Traditional vertical balance sheet layout (arbitrary numbers).**

You can see the accounting equation in the above report: Assets = Liabilities + Equity.

Global Retail, Inc. Balance Sheet

The balance sheet of our real-life company looks like this:

GLOBAL RETAIL, INC
Balance Sheet at 31 December Year End

$

ASSETS	
Current Assets	
Cash and Deposits	46,083
Accounts Receivable	128,178
Inventories	238,885
Total Current Assets	**413,146**
Non-Current Assets	
Land and Buildings	502,425
Equipment, Fixtures and Fittings	176,273
Investment in Other Companies	1,584
Total Non-Current Assets	**680,282**
TOTAL ASSETS	**1,093,428**

LIABILITIES	
Current Liabilities	
Borrowings	63,566
Payables	182,475
Provisions and Accruals	29,593
Total Current Liabilities	**275,634**
Non-Current Liabilities	
Borrowings	548,765
Total Non-Current Liabilities	**548,765**
TOTAL LIABILITIES	**824,399**

EQUITY	
Issued Capital: 192,160 shares	192,160
Retained Earnings	76,869
TOTAL EQUITY	**269,029**

Figure 33. Global Retail Inc.'s balance sheet for the year ending December 31.

Did you confirm the accounting equation?

Balance sheet commentary

You can already start to easily read the Global Retail balance sheet in *Figure 33*, just by applying the simple concepts that we've covered.

Here are some things to notice...

- The balance sheet is always headed up with the name of the reporting entity and the date at which the balance sheet is describing the business. In this case, it is December 31.
- The balance sheet is, analogously, a snapshot of the company at the moment of the reporting date—in this case, midnight at December 31. It's like the value of all the assets and consequent obligations were frozen for one second before the entity continued on again.
- There are only two elements on Global's balance sheet: its assets and its obligations. They both amount to almost 1.1 million dollars.
- The obligations are split into the two subtypes of obligation: liabilities of $824,399 and equity of $269,029.
- Liabilities are the contractual obligation to repay creditors who have temporarily provided cash, goods, or services with the expectation of timely repayment. "Creditors" as used here means "those to whom we owe."
- Equity is the obligation and commitment of the company to hold and return
  - assets equivalent to what the owners put into the company as investments on a permanent basis, and
  - assets equivalent to those that were earned by the company on behalf of the owners. We'll look thoroughly into how equity works momentarily.
- As is the convention on many "classified balance sheets," the assets are divided into short-term and long-term assets. The short-term or "current" assets, like cash and inventory, are expected to be used up or turned into cash within twelve months. The long-term or "non-current" assets will remain in use beyond twelve months.
- The table below explains the assets and liabilities on Global's balance sheet.

CATEGORY	EXPLANATION
Cash & deposits	Money at the bank. Or strictly speaking, the right to access the money held at the bank.
Accounts receivable	The right to be paid money by customers, usually within a short period such as 14, 30, or 90 days.
Inventories	Goods that the business has that it intends to sell to customers.
Land and buildings	Just that.
Equipment, fixtures, and fittings	Equipment and also property that has been attached to the buildings.
Investment	Ownership stake in another company. Probably measured based on the amount of money put into it originally.
Current borrowings	This is the part of the loan obligation that will be repaid within 12 months.
Payables	The obligation to pay Global's suppliers, mostly for goods but also for services like electricity and security that those suppliers have provided. Accounts Payable are sometimes also called Trade Payables or Trade Creditors. They are an important category of obligation because they are typically due within 30 or 90 days. Global must make sure to have enough available cash to settle these debts when they are due.
Provisions and accruals	Sometimes you have incurred an expense but haven't received an invoice from the supplier saying that you owe them. When this happens, you recognize anyway that you owe something. That uninvoiced obligation is called an accrual. Sometimes you don't even know for sure when you'll have to settle up for an expense that happened, or how much it will be. In that case you recognize the obligation as a provision.
Non-current borrowings	This is the part of the loan obligation that will be paid beyond 12 months.

Figure 34. **Explanation of balance sheet items for Global Retail, Inc**

> "Current" refers to elements expected to be used or sold
> or settled within twelve months.
> "Non-current" refers to elements expected to be used
> or sold or settled beyond twelve months.

Statement of Position

One of the main challenges when learning about finance and accounting is getting to grips with the terminology. There are often a lot of different names for the same thing—not to mention the problem of the same word being used for different things. Accounting is synonym city!

There are many names for our faithful storytelling butterfly:

- Balance sheet
- Statement of position
- Position statement
- Statement of financial position
- Statement of assets, liabilities, and owner's equity
- Statement of net worth

Regional Terminology

There are two principle bodies that govern corporate accounting. These are the Financial Accounting Standards Board (FASB) in the United States, and for everyone else, the International Accounting Standards Board (IASB), headquartered in London.

These boards issue guidance and mandates on various aspects of formal financial reporting, including terminology. This means that terms or practices used in one country may differ from those used in another. For example, the IASB has encouraged the use of the term "statement of financial position," whereas in the US, the traditional term "balance sheet" is still prevalent.

FASB AND IASB

Universal Principles

The principles we focus on in *The Joy of Accounting* are universal. They apply everywhere. The principles are sometimes applied differently depending on the particular issue, but the underlying principles are all the same. For example, the inventory that is shown in Global's balance sheet is an asset wherever you are in the world, even if different names are used.

But whereas the process for measuring the value of inventory differs between countries, inventory itself is always an asset. And that's true everywhere.

TRUE EVERYWHERE

Almost all of what we cover in this introductory accounting book is universal. You don't need to be concerned that you're learning a different kind of accounting in this book than is used in your country. Some terms may be used differently, but they refer to concepts that are the same wherever you go. We'll refer to alternative terms throughout the book—all the better for you to recognize them when you come across them in the wild.

CHAPTER ROUNDUP

This Accounting Equation: Balance Sheet chapter on the expanded accounting equation introduced us to the balance sheet.

We explored how:

- The butterfly diagram presents the Assets = Obligations duality for companies as well as for people's personal finances.
- The obligations are divided into two types: liability obligations and equity obligations.
- Liability obligations result from receiving assets lent to the business by funders.
- Equity obligations result from receiving assets invested in the business by funders (more detail follows in the next chapter).
- The expanded accounting equation is: Assets = Liabilities + Equity.
- The equation can be restated to read: Assets - Liabilities = Equity.
- In this form, equity is sometimes referred to as "net assets."
- Monetization is distinct from money. Money is one form of asset. All assets and obligations are monetized, meaning they are measured in monetary terms indicated by a currency sign such as "$."
- Obligations are sources of funds.
- Assets are uses of funds (funds in use).
- It's helpful to think of funds as energy, which is a broader concept than "money."
- In the Color Accounting Learning System, sources of funds are coded orange. Uses of funds are coded green.
- The butterfly diagram is a representation of the balance sheet.
- The modern balance sheet is traditionally laid out vertically.
- By convention, "current" means that the asset or liability is expected to be used up or settled within twelve months. "Non-current" means the asset or liability is expected to be used up or settled after twelve months.
- The principles described in this book are universal and apply to all accounting jurisdictions.
- Some application of the principles and terminology differs from region to region.
- The Financial Accounting Standards Board and the International Accounting Standards Board regulate accounting in the US and elsewhere, respectively.

7. EQUITY: A DEEPER DIVE

What Is Equity?

Equity is one of the most widely misunderstood concepts in accounting. It's vital that we are crystal clear about equity.

As we've already stated: equity is the business's obligation to its shareholders (also known as stockholders in the US).

Both lenders and shareholders have claims over the assets of the business. They stand outside the business looking inwards at the value of the assets in the business. Standing from the point of view within the business, all assets are obligated by the business to the funders of the business. That is, the business obligates all its assets to either lenders or shareholders. Equity represents the residual obligation by the business of the portion of the total asset value attributable to shareholders.

OBLIGATION TO SHAREHOLDERS

Equity represents the duty and commitment of the business to hold and put assets to work for the shareholders. For example, it represents the duty to:

- attribute earned assets to shareholders,
- give control to shareholders, and
- prioritize creditors above shareholders, among other obligations.

People often say that equity is the "leftover assets" of a business. Take the assets, pay off the debts, and what you're left with is equity. While that seems to make sense, what they are really doing is collapsing the accounting duality and mixing up the two wings of the butterfly. Equity cannot be and never is an asset.

Beware the pineapple here. We must think of equity from the point of view of the entity we are accounting for, and not from the funder's point of view.

Many texts poorly define equity. Here's a sample of definitions from various accounting books that are inadequate, misleading, or just plain wrong.

"Amounts invested by the owner of the company [together with] the sum of all net income…"

This definition is saying that equity is an "amount" and a "sum." That confuses *what* equity is with *how much* equity there is. Not only that, but assets and liabilities also have amounts associated with them. The first definition "Amounts invested by the owner… etc." isn't answering the question "the amount of what?".

"The share of a company's assets that are due to the shareholders."

This second definition is saying that equity is a "share of assets." That's saying that equity is an asset.

"Ownership, especially in terms of net monetary value, of a business."

This third definition is saying that equity is "ownership." Ownership is a quality, like sportsmanship or brinkmanship. Perhaps the intent was to describe a type of asset, which would make the definition wrong because equity isn't a type of asset. Equity is never an asset. Equity is something other than an asset.

"The owner's interest in the business, which is the total assets minus the total liabilities."

This fourth definition is making a classic pineapple error. It's speaking from the owner's point of view instead of the company's point of view. It's saying that equity is an interest. If I have an interest in a business, then that's a valuable right I have. The "interest" is an asset. The definition goes on to remind us of how we calculate the size of equity, but that's not a definition of the meaning of the word equity. It's a way of quantifying equity.

Even the accounting regulators don't do well at defining equity—see the appendix at the back of the book. They say equity "is the residual interest in the assets of an entity that remains after deducting its liabilities."

Equity is the residual obligation of the business, not the residual assets.

> Equity is the residual obligation of the business.

Here is one reason that people confuse assets and equity: assets are nice, we're trying to grow them and we'd like more of them. Equity is also nice; we're trying to grow it and we'd like more of it. Therefore, assets must be equity! That, of course, is a logic error and not correct. It collapses the accounting duality.

Assets and equity are on the opposite sides of the accounting equation. They're on different sides of our butterfly box. They are not the same thing.

> Equity is not the "leftover assets."

Multiple Points of View

Consider a company shown as "The Business" in the diagram below. Its balance sheet is shown in the form of our familiar butterfly, with its assets shown in the green left-hand wing and its two forms of obligation in the orange right-hand wing: Liability obligation to lenders and Equity obligation to investors. All the assets on the left are obligated on the right to the funders, per the accounting equation. Nothing new there.

Now consider the two types of funder. The lender has their own balance sheet, as does the investor. Each is shown as a butterfly too, named "Lender" and "Owner."

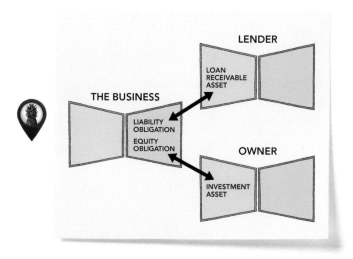

Figure 35. **A kaleidoscope of butterflies.**

Remember how the word liability came from the same root word as ligament, those bands in our body that bind our bones together. You can think of the double-headed arrows between the entities as ligaments that define their relationships with each other.

- The Business has a Loan Obligation to the Lender, whereas the Lender has a resource (the right to be repaid) in the form of a Loan Receivable Asset. As an asset, it's shown on the green left-hand side of the Lender's butterfly as a use of funds.
- The Business also has an Equity Obligation to the Shareholder and that entity has a resource (the right to investment returns, and a share of any available distributed assets in the event of liquidation) in the form of an Investment *Asset*. As an asset, it's shown on the green left-hand side of the Shareholder's butterfly as a use of funds.

Because The Business is beholden to and works for the Lender and Shareholder, it's very easy to slip into thinking and speaking about the business from their points of view—but we mustn't. It's essential that we keep in mind that the descriptions and definitions pertaining to The Business are done from its point of view.

One of the collective nouns for butterflies is a "kaleidoscope." Always keep in mind the kaleidoscope of butterflies as you analyze an accounting scenario. A lot of the mistakes about equity stem from standing in the wrong place. For example, describing equity as the interest of the shareholders is to stand in the shareholder's butterfly. That's the wrong point of view when telling the story of the business.

Debt vs. Equity

We now explore the specific differences between the two forms of obligation: the first to the lender-funders, and the second to the investor-funders.

The differences between liabilities and equity are in six main areas:

- Quantum: how you calculate the amount of the obligation,
- Priority: the order in which the obligations must be settled if the company is dissolved,
- Remuneration: how the entity remunerates the lenders and borrowers,
- Settlement: the requirement to settle the obligations,
- Duration: the lifespan of each, and
- Obedience: who does the business have to listen to, or who controls the business.

Quantum, or amount

How do you know how much debt the business has, and how much equity? Liabilities are contractual and the amount is specified. If the business borrows $100 for a year, and the agreed interest rate with the lender is 10 percent, then after a year, the size of the liability will be $110. That's the contract between the business and the lender.

The equity obligation to the owners is calculated differently. The owners are not promised an agreed amount. The equity is the residual obligation, calculated by establishing how many assets the business has and how much is owed to lenders; the arithmetic difference is the amount of equity.

So, while the amount of liabilities is contracted, the amount of equity is derived.

Priority

Assets are the only valuable thing the business has. Assets are what the funders have entrusted to the business and are what those funders eventually want returned. So, what happens if the business loses some assets? What happens if there are not enough assets to settle all the contractual obligations to lenders or meet the hopes and expectations of the owners to have what they contributed returned? How do the assets get divvied up?

The answer is, when a business is shut down and the assets are returned to the funders, lenders get paid first and owners get paid last. The business has a priority obligation to lenders and a subordinate obligation to shareholders. From their points of view, lenders have a priority claim and owners have a subordinate claim on the assets of the business.

Remuneration

Both shareholders and lenders contribute assets to the business in the expectation of getting more back than they put in. When the business rewards lenders and shareholders, it does so differently. Lenders are typically rewarded with interest. Shareholders are rewarded with growth of the equity obligation to them and with distribution of dividends.

Interest payments are made to lenders according to a contracted agreement. Dividend payments to shareholders are made at the discretion of the company.

Settlement

When a business borrows money from a lender, there is usually an expectation of repayment and a settlement date. The settlement date might be a month later or years later. There may be installments that pay down the loan steadily, or maybe only interest is payable during the life of the loan with the full capital portion of the loan repayable at the end. The loan might be at call, where the lender can demand repayment at any time.

When a business receives money from a shareholder, on the other hand, there is no expectation of repayment. Investors—that is, shareholders—cannot demand repayment. If they want to get their money back, they sell their stake to another investor (if they can). The company itself isn't returning any money.

Sometimes the business can reserve the right to buy back equity from its shareholders. This is called "redeemable equity." Public companies frequently buy back their own shares on the open market, but these actions are always at the discretion of the company, not the investor.

Duration

When a business seeks financing, it may arrange a short-term loan or a long-term loan. Loan financing is therefore both short- and long-term as a source of funds for the business.

Equity financing, on the other hand, is used as long-term financing for the business. It's unlikely that the business would sell shares to obtain cash from investors in what's sometimes called an Initial Public Offering, only to repay those funds in the short term. Equity financing is long-term financing.

Obedience

Who controls the company, you may ask? Or, from the point of view of the business, who does the business listen to and take instructions from?

Usually, the company listens to shareholders, who have a say in how the company is run by voting to elect members of a board of directors, who in turn appoint a Chief Executive Officer who executes the business's strategy.

Lenders do not automatically get a say in the running of the company. They don't get votes to select the board of directors. In practice, however, lenders who provide large amounts of money to a business will demand a say in the running of the business, such as negotiating internal controls that the business must adhere to, like not borrowing more money in addition to the lender's loan.

Conclusion

These six characteristics are where we find some key differences between debt obligations and equity obligations.

Obligations are necessarily legal in nature, and a thorough discussion of the subject quickly becomes academic and intellectual. Some injections of money into a business fall into a gray zone, hard to classify clearly as debt or equity as they may have characteristics of both debt and equity. Accountants can easily find themselves struggling to classify corporate obligations as one or the other. And yet, it's an important matter because whole industries are regulated around the differences. The regulation of banks is in large part about controlling how banks use debt and equity, the specific natures of each, and the amount of each that the banks use.

From a business's point of view, debt is riskier because it has to be paid back, whereas equity does not. From the funder's point of view, it's the opposite. It's riskier to invest in a company than to lend to it. The loan must be repaid with priority, whereas the equity investment doesn't have to be repaid and does not have priority.

All of this discussion about equity prepares us for the main significance thereof. That is, assuming the business is a for-profit business, the business exists to grow its equity. It exists to further obligate itself to its owner.

CHAPTER ROUNDUP

This Equity chapter has looked at what equity is and how it differs from liability obligations. This chapter is important because equity is widely misunderstood.

The discussion has stayed at a fairly summary level.

We have explored how:

- Equity is the business's obligation to its shareholders.
- The obligation is residual, because it comes after the business's obligation to its lenders and creditors.
- Equity is not "leftover assets" or "residual assets."
- When thinking about equity, it's very important to remember whose point of view is being described.
- The "kaleidoscope of butterflies" reminds us that there is the business, the lender, and the investor, each with their own point of view.
- The difference between debt and equity obligations is not always black and white. Some debt may have characteristics of equity, and vice versa.
- The main differences between debt and equity involve how their size is determined, the priority with which they are settled, how funders are remunerated, responsibility for settlement of the obligation, duration of the obligation, and the duty to respond to the wishes of the lenders and shareholders.
- Debt is riskier to the company; equity is less risky. The reverse is true from the funder's perspective.
- The purpose of a for-profit business is to grow its equity—which is to say, grow its obligation to its owner.

8. JOURNALING THE NEW BUSINESS

Lemonade & Laughter

To see how we go about creating a balance sheet from the daily operations of a business, let's start an imaginary one. We'll loosely continue with the theme and scenario that we began in our backyard in Chapter 1. The business will sell goods and also provide consulting advice on retailing.

Figure 36. **Lemonade & Laughter storefront.**

We'll use a series of imagined business events to learn how to account for classical business transactions, such as borrowing money and incurring expenses. Our aim is not to make a fully realistic business situation. What we're after is the essence of business, not the details of the myriad administrative and other tasks needed in reality. We'll give ourselves license to simplify as we bring to mind a series of events and keep our attention focused on the key issues and principles as they relate to accounting.

Journal and Framework

As we know, the cardinal discipline of accounting is to be very clear about the point of view from which we are telling the story. The first thing we'll do, then, is create our separate entity. We'll tell the business story from that entity's point of view. We'll continue to call it Lemonade & Laughter.

Using our butterfly analogy, we can show our virgin entity as in Figure 37. It's all set to source and use funds with its orange and green wings.

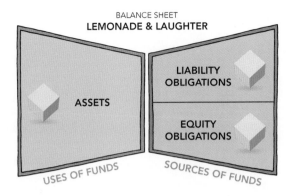

Figure 37. **Balance sheet of Lemonade & Laughter business.**

Since we're going to be doing a number of transactions, we'll square up the butterfly and make it look like a geometrical framework. Think of it as our square butterfly. It's a balance sheet framework.

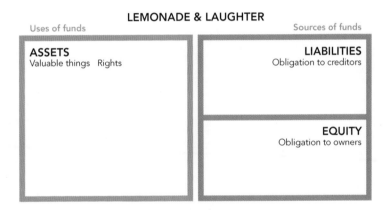

Figure 38. **Geometric butterfly.**

To capture what happens financially in the business, we're going to do what are known as "journal entries." For every event that happens in the life of the business, we'll capture the financial effects. And then we will reflect those effects on the balance sheet framework.

Everything with a financial impact on the business is first captured in a journal, which is where we first record whatever happens. It's called a book of prime entry.

Just as you might keep a personal journal of your life, the accounting journal is an ongoing linear description of everything that happens in the business. Where you might write "Met with the president and first lady today," we'll write more prosaic activities like "Borrowed money from the bank."

For each of our three elements of the balance sheet, we are also showing our educational definitions distinguished so far. For liabilities, we have replaced "lenders" with "creditors," which is a broader legal term and simply means "those to whom we owe."

Now recall that when we deduced the concept of a balance sheet, the logic went something like this:

Double Entry

Because all of accounting happens inside of a duality of assets and obligations as described by the accounting equation, it follows that whenever we enter an event into our journal, each journal entry will have not one but two effects, and they will be equal in amount.

This is famously called "Double Entry." Every time you capture a financial event in the business, you will reflect not one but two financial effects.

> The balance sheet duality gives rise to the "double entry" principle. Each business event causes two financial effects.

First Event: Borrowing Cash

The first event in our business is the borrowing of cash. The event has two effects: The entity gets cash, and it gets a liability to give cash back to the funder.

In our journal, we record it like this: Event: Borrow money from lender

Effects:

Increase cash	30,000
Increase liability obligation	30,000

This is reflected on our balance sheet framework like this:

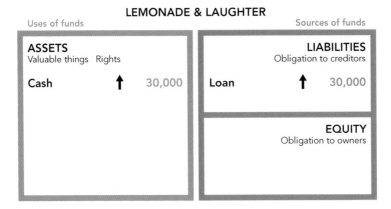

Figure 39. **Balance sheet framework showing cash asset and loan obligation.**

Our business now has cash of $30,000, and it has an equivalent obligation to eventually give all those assets back to its creditor.

You can ask yourself at this point "What is the business worth to the lender and to the owner?" That is, standing in their shoes, from their points of view outside the business, what do they have? The answer is respectively, $30,000 and nothing. The lender has a $30,000 claim on the business (which is to say, an indirect claim on the assets.) Whereas the owner has no claim on the business–because there's no equity yet. Another way of saying this is "The net-worth of the business to the owner is zero."

Looking at the diagram, the existence of the two sides of the framework reflects the accounting duality. The fact of writing down the two numbers, in this instance one in assets and one in liabilities, is what we call double entry. Double entry is a natural consequence of the duality.

The direction arrows, in this case at least, both indicate an increase in that element. For example, the business had zero assets and now it has $30,000 in assets, so assets must have increased. Same for its liabilities.

Second Event: Owner Invests

So far, the owner of Lemonade & Laughter hasn't put any assets into the business herself. As we often informally say, "She doesn't have skin in the game." Now the company issues ownership shares to her and receives cash from her in return.

In our journal, we record it like this:

Event: Receive investment from lender

Effects:

Increase cash	20,000
Increase equity obligation	20,000

This is reflected on our balance sheet framework like this:

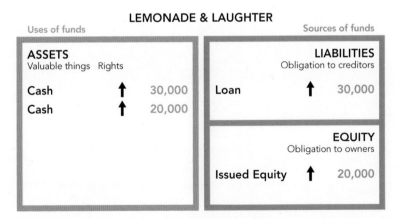

Figure 40. **Balance sheet framework showing cash, loan, and equity.**

Now the business has assets of $50,000 and obligations of $50,000. Those obligations are in the form of liabilities of $30,000 and equity of $20,000.

Leverage

If you look at the total assets of the business, you notice that 60 percent were funded by borrowing. We say that the business is 60 percent leveraged. $30,000 of the $50,000 in assets is debt financed (30,000 ÷ 50,000 × 100 = 60%). The owners contributed $20,000 of assets, but now have a business that is using $50,000 of assets to achieve its purpose. The $20,000 was leveraged up to $50,000. Just as a physical lever magnifies force, the financial lever magnifies the amount of assets that the company works with, compared with only using assets funded by the owners.

> Leverage means the company has magnified the assets it has and is using compared with how much it would have if it only used funding from the owner.

In Britain, people use the term "gearing" instead of "leverage." It comes from the same notion of multiplying what you are working with. As the gears on a bicycle multiply the speed of the pedals to make the wheels go faster, financial gearing multiplies the amount of assets the owner contributes.

The vertical balance sheet of the company would look like this now:

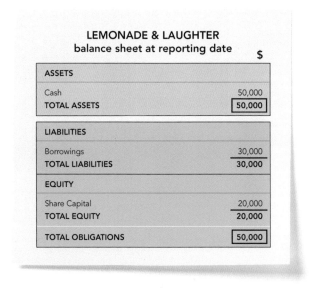

Figure 41. **Balance sheet showing debt and equity funding.**

Purpose of the Business

Our business has $50,000 of assets now, but to what end? As a for-profit business, the reason it exists is to get more assets, assets being the only valuable thing that the business can have! The business wants to grow the $50,000 assets, but not by borrowing more assets or even by getting more from the owners as investment. The business wants to generate more assets by operating. It wants to do so not for the lenders' benefit, but for the benefit of the owners. The business exists for the benefit of its owners.

The business "wants" to increase its residual obligation to its owner. The business likes being obligated to its owner because that is its very purpose. Being obligated to its owner is its "raison d'être," as they say in French—its "reason for being." What we're emphasizing here is that an obligation isn't inherently a bad thing.

RAISON D'ÊTRE

Movie analogy

If you've seen the Harry Potter movies, you'll remember Dobby, the house elf who is deeply loyal to Harry Potter until the end. You could say that Dobby eagerly wants to serve and be obligated to Harry. Our company is like Dobby in that it wants to serve and be obligated to its master, the shareholders.

Growing its equity through its operations is the purpose of a for-profit business. This will often be associated with growing the assets, but it doesn't have to be. In the balance sheet above, the assets could remain at $50,000, and if the business—through its efforts—reduced or "worked off" the $30,000 liability to the creditors, reducing it down to say $15,000, then the equity would have increased to $35,000. The balance sheet would then read:

Assets $50,000
Liabilities $15,000
Equity $35,000

The owners are now wealthier because the business owes them more. The residual obligation of the business to the owners is greater. The owners own a company that is the same size, but they enjoy a claim to a greater share of its assets.

The assets might even decrease while the equity grows. The balance sheet might read:

Assets $45,000
Liabilities $5,000
Equity $40,000

Third Event: Earning Cash

Without further ado and ignoring all the real-world setup and logistics it takes to form a business, from registering the company to arranging furniture, our business starts operating. It's a retailer selling goods and providing advice.

You now go out on behalf of the company and visit a client for whom you provide a few hours of advice. It's your first consulting engagement. You personally aren't earning a salary yet, so we're ignoring any salary expenses the company might be incurring. The client is, of course, very grateful for your pearls of wisdom and pays the company for the consulting service by handing you an envelope with $1,000 cash in it. You return to the office and ask yourself what—in financial terms—just happened for the company. What two financial effects has this consulting event caused?

The company clearly has $1,000 more cash than it used to have. So, assets have increased from $50,000 to $51,000.

Then, remembering that all assets are obligated to a funder, you ask yourself: is the loan effected or the equity?

You may at this point be tempted to recall the conversation in the previous chapter about the differences between debt and equity and the priority of liabilities over equity. You'll remember how you must pay back lenders before you pay shareholders when liquidating a company. You may think we must pay back the $1,000 cash to the lenders. That's a thinking error and is not correct.

The issue here is not about the order in which we must pay the funders back. Rather, the issue is about rights and obligations. It's about which funder gets to say that the company is now holding more assets for them. In other words, after the business has earned $1,000, is it obligated $31,000 to the creditors or is it obligated $21,000 to the owners?

The correct answer is the company is now obligated $21,000 to the owners. The bank that lent the $30,000 to the company doesn't get richer because the company did some consulting. They'll get the amount of their loan plus any interest that is due to them later, but they don't get to claim the $1,000 that showed up in the company because of the hard work. The company has no additional obligation to the lenders arising from the consulting.

To illustrate the issue of rights to the assets, here's another zany movie analogy: *Finding Nemo*, the movie about the cute little lost clownfish. In Wealthvox finance workshops, we like to ask what the seagulls in the movie said. And we're always surprised by how many people know. When little Nemo is in the beak of the pelican and being chased by a flock of seagulls who want to eat him, their squawks can be heard shouting "Mine, mine, mine."

Apologies for this pop-culture digression, but it's analogous to what's going on with the $1,000 cash that showed up as a result of the consulting that the company did. Of the two funders of the business (the lenders and the owners), who gets to put up their hands and say of the $1,000 that's just made its way into the company's coffers, "Mine, mine, mine! Hold that $1,000 on my behalf!" From their point of view outside the business, both the lenders and the owners would like their claim on the business to grow by $1,000, but only one can benefit. So who is it to be? The lenders or the owners? Of course, the answer is the owners. The consulting activity does not affect the lenders' claim on the business.

From the company's point of view, the company is obligated an additional $1,000 to the owners. It's grown the equity to $21,000 and is pleased to be further obligated to its owner. Doing that is why it exists.

In our journal, we record the transaction like this:

Event: Do consulting for client and get paid cash.

Effects:

Increase cash	1,000
Increase equity	1,000

This is reflected on our balance sheet framework like this:

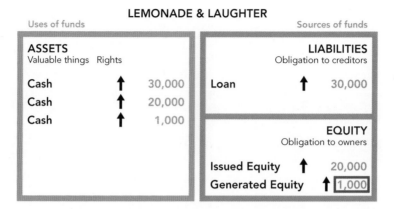

Figure 42. **Balance sheet framework showing cash, loan, and two types of equity.**

Our traditional balance sheet looks like this now:

LEMONADE & LAUGHTER
balance sheet at reporting date
$

ASSETS	
Cash	51,000
TOTAL ASSETS	**51,000**

LIABILITIES	
Borrowings	30,000
TOTAL LIABILITIES	**30,000**

EQUITY	
Contributed Equity – Share Capital	20,000
Generated Equity – Retained Earnings	1,000
TOTAL EQUITY	**21,000**

TOTAL OBLIGATIONS	**51,000**

Figure 43. **Balance sheet showing two types of equity, contributed and generated.**

We've now divided equity into two types: contributed equity and generated equity (profit). Generated equity is the best kind. From the owner's point of view, their claim over the business has grown by 1,000 with no further contribution from them. They've gained as the company has gained. On the other hand, they also could have lost if the company lost. That's the risk they're taking.

The traditional name for generated equity in the balance sheet is Retained Earnings.

Fourth Event: Sacrificing Cash

To get to the client where you provided the consulting service, you caught a taxi. It was a very long ride, and they waited for you while you did the consulting, so the total fare came to $250 including the tip.

When you got back to the office, you paid the taxi driver $250 of the company's money for the ride. The business logic is: you had to sacrifice this $250 in order to generate the $1,000.

In our journal, we record the event like this:

Event: Incur travel expense and settle by paying taxi driver cash.

Effects:

Decrease cash	250
Decrease generated equity obligation	250

This is reflected on our balance sheet framework like this:

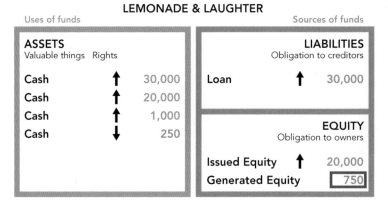

Figure 44. **Balance sheet framework showing profit cash reduction and profit impact.**

The traditional balance sheet looks like this now:

LEMONADE & LAUGHTER
balance sheet at reporting date

$

ASSETS	
Cash	50,750
TOTAL ASSETS	**50,750**

LIABILITIES	
Borrowings	30,000
TOTAL LIABILITIES	30,000

EQUITY	
Contributed Equity – Share Capital	20,000
Generated Equity – Retained Earnings	750
TOTAL EQUITY	20,750

TOTAL OBLIGATIONS	**50,750**

Figure 45. **Balance sheet showing generated equity reduced by the travel expense.**

The retained earnings have decreased to $750 from $1,000.

The net cash gained from the consulting job is $750 after taking into account the travel cost. With a gain of $1,000 and a loss of $250, at the end of the day, the business is up $750 cash. On the other side of the balance sheet, in equity, that extra cash is earmarked for the owners, shown by the $750 increase in retained earnings.

The retained earnings are the incremental obligation to the owners. for the incremental assets. It's the generated obligation to hold the generated assets for the owners.

> Retained Earnings is the accumulated incremental obligation to the owners.

Position of the Company

Recapping where the company is at, let's remind ourselves what the balance sheet is now telling us. We can articulate the story like this:

The business has 50,750 dollars of cash. All that cash is obligated to the funders of the business—that is, the creditors and owners. 30,000 dollars of it is obligated to lenders who lent cash to the company, shown by the total liabilities figure. 20,750 dollars of the cash is obligated to the owners of the company because they put in, and left in, that much cash, shown by the Total Equity figure of $20,750. They put in 20,000 dollars of cash, which the company recognizes by showing 20,000 dollars' worth of Contributed Equity, and they left in 750 dollars of cash. The company recognizes that the earned cash is attributed to the owners by showing 750 dollars' worth of Generated Equity or Retained Earnings.

PUT IN. LEFT IN.

The idea of "leaving in" the money and matching obligation in the company is where the name Retained Earnings comes from. The money is retained in the company, versus being distributed as dividends.

Note how in articulating the balance sheet like this, we're being careful to talk about "dollars of cash" but "dollars' worth of equity." This is because cash takes the form of actual dollars, but equity is only *compared* with dollars. Equity does not constitute actual dollars; it's only measured in dollars.

The common thinking error people make here is looking at the Retained Earnings figure of $750 and thinking that it is actual money. It isn't. It's an obligation that's equivalent in size to 750 dollars. It's probably because people have a deep sense that retained earnings is a good thing, and cash is definitely a good thing, therefore retained earnings must be cash. But as you know, that's fallacious reasoning.

> Retained earnings isn't money.

The most we can say is that retained earnings is a "good" or "desirable" obligation. The company "wants" to be obligated to its owner because the owner is its source of existence. Its purpose is to grow its obligation to its owner as much as it can. It's the whimsical Dobby factor we talked about, where the house elf loves being of service to his master.

Profit

Growing retained earnings through the efforts of the company is why the company exists, and it goes without saying that we want to measure it. That measure is called profit.

Profit is the amount of obligation to the owners that the company has generated during the reporting period. On the balance sheet, profit is an obligation to the owners.

> Profit is the amount of obligation to the owners that the business has generated during the reporting period.

Profit is a subset of retained earnings. It's the amount of owner-obligation generated during just the current period. Retained earnings is the cumulative obligation arising from this period as well as all the previous periods.

> Profit is part of Retained Earnings.
> Retained Earnings is part of Owners' Equity.

Note: We deliberately use the term Equity in place of Owners' Equity, while knowing that Owners' Equity is widely used. Equity, by its very nature, can only be for the owners—there is no other type of equity. So there's an element of tautology in the term "Owners' Equity."

CHAPTER ROUNDUP

This "Journaling the New Business" chapter has looked at how we account for cash injections into the business, as well as earning and consumption activities of the business operations.

We explored how:

- The butterfly duality is presented as a balance sheet framework.
- We record events using journal entries.
- Because of the accounting duality, journal entries always capture two effects on the business.
- This phenomenon of two effects for each event gives us the term Double Entry.
- Borrowing cash impacted the assets and the liabilities of the business.
- Raising investment funds from the owner impacted the assets and equity of the business.
- Earning fees from services provided impacted the assets and equity of the business.
- Equity was divided into two types: contributed equity and generated equity.
- Earning fees increased generated equity.
- Incurring a taxi expense reduced cash and reduced generated equity.
- The purpose of a for-profit business is to increase its obligation to its owner.
- Profit is the incremental obligation to the owner, generated during the accounting period.
- The traditional term for generated equity is Retained Earnings.
- Retained earnings is not money. It's only measured in monetary terms. Money is always an asset.

9. UNPACKING PROFIT

Telling the Story of Profit with the Income Statement

We will now discover why accounting needs an income statement.

Lemonade & Laughter's financial position is shown on our framework like this:

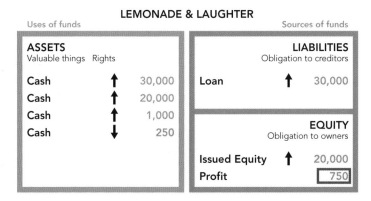

Figure 46. **Balance sheet framework with Generated Equity renamed Profit.**

We have a problem, though. All our information is correct, but we've lost some detail, and that's the problem. It's true that the business has $50,750 of cash, has $30,000 of liability to lenders, and has $20,750 of obligation to the owners (because of what they invested, and an additional $750 of obligation to the owners because of what the business earned on their behalf). That's all true, but with just this information we can't answer a very important question, which is: how did the business manage to generate that $750 of obligation to the owners? Since generating a profit is the very purpose of the business, it's a pretty important question that warrants a more detailed explanation.

We're not showing the details of how the $750 was generated. The gross amounts were lost when we recorded both the gain and the loss into the single profit line, and now all we're able to see is the net-gain of $750.

The information that's been lost is what's called the *profit margin*.

In our one consulting job so far, we made a profit of $750 that came from the gross earnings of $1,000. As a proportion, $750 is 75 percent of $1,000. So we say that the profit margin is 75 percent.

LEMONADE & LAUGHTER Profit Margin		
Sale	1,000	100%
Expense	250	25%
Profit	750	75%

Figure 47. **Profit margin calculated.**

The formula for Profit Margin is:

Profit ÷ Sales × 100 = Profit Margin%

> Profit Margin% is calculated as Profit ÷ Sales × 100.

Infinite number of ways of getting to the profit

Lemonade & Laughter's profit result was $750, but there are an infinite number of other combinations of gaining and losing to arrive at the net result of $750, as shown in *Figure 48* below.

- You could earn $760 and incur expenses of $10, to end up with $750 as in Business A,
- You could earn $7,500 and incur expenses of $6,750, to also end up with $750, as in Business B, or
- Any other Example C where Sales "S" less Expense "X" = $750.

In all cases you've made profit, but the profit margin in the first example would be 99 percent and in the second case would be 10 percent.

When people are reading financial statements and comparing companies, how they make their profit and their profit margins is very important information.

	Lemonade & Laughter	Business A	Business B	Business C
Sale	1,000	760	7,500	S
Expense	250	10	6,750	X
Profit	750	750	750	750
Profit Margin %	75%	99%	10%	

Figure 48. **Numerous ways of getting to the same profit figure.**

For two businesses that had similar sales potential, you'd rather have the one with the greater profit margin. If one can grow much bigger than the other, you'd be happy to accept a lower profit margin to get higher total profits. In *Figure 49* below, Business D has a higher profit margin at 25 percent than Business E at 20 percent, but Business E has more total profits at $2,000 versus $250 for Business D. As they stand, you'd rather own business E than Business D.

	Business D	Business E	
Sale	1,000	10,000	*Better total profit!*
Expense	750	8,000	
Profit	250	2,000	
Profit Margin %	25%	20%	

Better margin!

Figure 49. **Profit and profit margin.**

Inventing the Income Statement

A place to tell the story of profit

All this discussion is to show that we need a place to tell the detailed story of how we got to the profit figure shown under Equity in the balance sheet. We've distinguished the need for the income statement.

We need a way to show how we generated assets by providing consulting services (which made $1,000 of cash come into the business). We also sacrificed assets by taking a taxi ride (which caused $250 of cash to leave the business), the combined actions of which caused a net gain of $750 in assets.

In our framework, we need to open the $750 profit to show how it was the result of the $1,000 gain and $250 loss.

Figure 50. **Double-click opens the folder.**

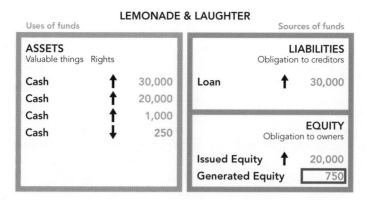

Figure 51. **Let's "uncollapse" the generated equity number.**

Play along

On Figure 51 above, take a pen or some other solid pointing object and imagine that the $750-profit figure is in a folder on your computer screen. Pretend that your pen is the computer mouse and double click the profit folder. Tap your pen on the table so that it makes a "double-click" sound. Make sure you actually hear a double-click sound. You're creating what's called an "auditory anchor" to remind you of this opening up of the profit account. Go on, do it!

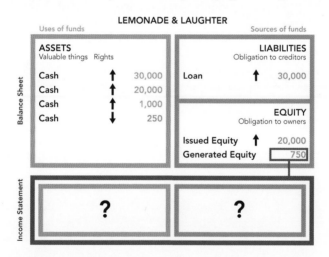

Figure 52. **Framework showing balance sheet and income statement sections.**

Imagine how the profit folder opens to reveal two folders within it. We now show these folders as the bottom right-hand and left-hand boxes in the newly expanded framework shown in Figure 52.

Our framework above now has five boxes instead of three. The bottom two, within the purple line, are there to explain effects upon the profit folder. They represent the very important accounting report traditionally known as the income statement, or profit and loss statement. Like the balance sheet, it also has many names.

As we saw with the consulting job, the effect of a transaction can increase profit or decrease profit. The job of the income statement is to capture and describe these two types of effect.

Let's continue our color scheme for each side of the expanded framework—the income state-ment. The box on the right will be orange, and the left one will be green. We have already determined that the income statement will provide additional details on the profit figure within equity on the balance sheet. Recall the double-click. Profit is calculated as revenue less expenses. Therefore, one of our new boxes will be Revenue and the other will be Expenses—but which is which? Let's start with revenue—will that be the orange box or the green box? What do you think?

In our workshops and classes around the world, about a third to a half of each group will say that revenue is the green box—did you? If you did, you would be wrong! Let's go back to first principles—is revenue a source of funds or a use of funds? It is a source of funds to the business and therefore it goes on the orange side. That leaves expenses as a use of funds (funds used up), which will be on the green side.

Why do such a high percentage of participants think revenue should be green?

Perhaps their reasoning is that "the green side is the good side, while the orange side is the bad side." Maybe they think this because assets are green and they are "good," so the green side must be the good side.

Sources and uses of funds

The left-hand and the right-hand side of the framework are not defined around the ideas of good and bad. Rather, they describe sources and uses of funds.

The three boxes on the right-hand side of the framework are all sources of funds. The two boxes on the left-hand side of the framework are both uses of funds. We show this by making the whole right-hand side orange and the whole left-hand side green.

In the Color Accounting Learning System, orange means sources of funds, and green means uses of funds.

By thinking in terms of sources of funds and uses of funds, it's intuitive that

- profit-increasing effects like the consulting revenue are sources of funds, and
- the taxi travel expense that decreased profit is a use of funds.

Two types of profit effect: income/revenue and expense

The two possible types of effect on profit have their own special names in accounting: increase-effects are called income or revenue, and decrease-effects are called expense. You've no doubt heard those terms before, but we're going to define them in a way that's likely dif-ferent from what you might expect.

Notice in the framework below how we've gone ahead and labeled the bottom right-hand box "Revenue/Income"[5] and colored it orange. We've labeled the bottom left-hand box "Expenses," and color it green.

---

*   We'll explain why we are using the combined heading 'Revenue/Income' soon.

BaSIS Framework™

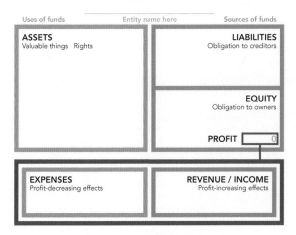

Figure 53. Five-box BaSIS Framework™.

The framework in the figure above has a heading for each side: Uses of Funds and Sources of Funds. It has a label for each of the five boxes: Assets, Liabilities, Equity, Revenue/Income, and Expenses. Profit is shown as a source of funds to the business, which is why it's an orange account. The profit folder lives within equity, and that profit "folder" is connected with the bottom two boxes of the framework, now named Revenue/Income and Expenses. Those two elements are what make up profit. Revenue/Income increases profit, and expenses decrease profit. The connection between the profit and revenue and expenses is shown by the purple line.

The top three boxes of the framework represent the accounting report traditionally known as the balance sheet. The bottom two boxes of the framework, as we've said, represent the income statement. As a nod to these two reports—the **Ba**lance **S**heet and the **I**ncome **S**tatement—Color Accounting calls this diagram the BaSIS Framework™.

You can download and print out at home a letter- or poster-sized BaSIS Framework by visiting wealthvox.com/joy

Redo the consulting job transactions

Now that we've got a five-box all-encompassing framework, let's use it to account for the consulting service that the business provided and the travel expense that it incurred. Together, these activities generated a profit of $750. We'll rerecord those transactions, but this time we won't make the mistake of losing the detail of how we got to the $750 net gain. We'll keep the generative and consumptive effects separate by recording them in the respective bottom two boxes. We'll still end up with a net $750 in the profit box, but we'll be showing the detail of how we got there.

Calculation of profit

Profit is calculated as revenue/income less expenses, or $1,000 - $250. On the framework, the profit folder in the balance sheet Equity box will be equal to the Revenue/Income box minus the Expenses box.

> • Profit is calculated as Revenue/Income less Expenses.
> • In the BaSIS Framework, profit is calculated as the bottom orange box less the bottom green box.

Revisiting the third event: earning income

We went out and completed a few hours of consulting for the client, for which they paid $1,000 cash. In our accounting journal, with the availability of the bottom two boxes, we now record this as follows:

Event: Do consulting for client and get paid cash.

Effects:

Cash increases	1,000
Revenue increases	1,000

This is shown on the full framework below.

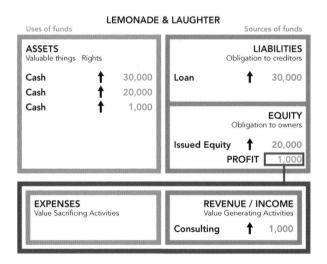

Figure 54. **BaSIS Framework showing consulting revenue/income.**

Revisiting the fourth event: incurring an expense

As before, you now incur an expense by using the services of a taxi, for which you hand over $250 of the company's money as payment. In our accounting journal, with the availability of the income statement, we now record this as follows:

Event: Incur travel expense and settle by paying taxi driver cash.

Effects:

Increase expense	250
Reduce cash	250

This is reflected on our full framework like this:

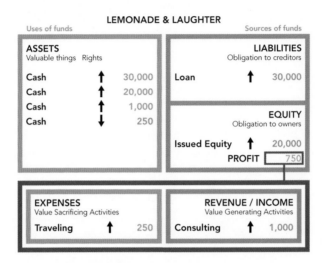

Figure 55. **BaSIS Framework showing expense.**

You can see in the framework above that we've landed in the same place as we did with the three-box balance sheet framework in *Figure 51*. Assets total $50,750, liabilities total $30,000, and equity totals $20,750.

We now see a more complete story: equity comprises $20,000 of contributed equity and $750 of generated equity/profit. Furthermore, we can see that the generated $750 equity was the result of $1,000 of revenue and $250 of expenses.

Definition of Revenue, Income, and Expense

Revenue, income and expense don't mean what we usually use them to mean in casual day-to-day conversation.

The BaSIS Framework is serving us well. It's describing the assets and obligations that our business has. It does this in the top three boxes that represent the balance sheet. Now we've seen how it also captures the story of the business growing the assets and obligation to the owners through its operating activities—the framework is telling that part of the story in the bottom two boxes, which represent the income statement.

Meaning of the income statement elements

The most misunderstood concepts in all of accounting are the terms revenue, income, and expense. They cause more confusion than anything else. Pay a lot of attention to the following discussion about definitions. We're going to precisely define what the terms mean. We'll also get explicit about what they don't mean.

Revenue/Income

In the BaSIS Framework in *Figure 55* above, we accounted for the consulting transaction by showing $1,000 in the assets box at the top left of the framework, and we showed $1,000 in the Revenue/Income box, which we said was the source of the money.

What, then, does the $1,000 number in the Revenue/Income box measure? We know that it can't be describing cash, because cash is in the green Asset box. You can't have cash in more than one place. It would be nice to have $2,000 of cash by counting both the Assets box and the Revenue/Income box! But clearly we don't. All the cash is shown only in the Asset box.

What the Revenue/Income box describes is the consulting itself. It's measuring the activity of doing consulting. The consulting is what gave rise to the $1,000 cash that flowed into the business. The consulting activity is the source of the money. By doing the consulting we generated the received-money. The money appeared because the consulting happened. If the business hadn't done the consulting, it wouldn't have received the cash.

The words "revenue" and "income" therefore describe an activity. That's why another name for the income statement is the "Statement of Activities." Revenue is, in a sense, more of a verb than a noun. It's not what you get, but what you do.

In a consulting business, the revenue is the consulting, talking, or whatever the consultant is doing when they are running the clock and charging the client. In a lawn-mowing business, the revenue is the pushing of the lawnmower and the cutting of the grass. In a law firm, the typing and negotiating is the revenue. In your own life, if you are an employee, your revenue is the showing up at work and working at your desk or on the shop floor or on the building site.

We know that dictionaries don't list revenue as a verb, but perhaps they should. If not an actual verb, revenue is at least a "verb concept." A lot of dictionaries define revenue and income as money. For accounting purposes, that's wrong.

In everyday conversation, we talk about "receiving" income. We don't talk about "doing income" and "doing expenses." It would sound strange, but you could. Revenue and income are activities that you do that give rise to assets. In our example above, the business did consulting; that activity generated cash. The cash is the asset and the consulting is the revenue.

The educational definition of revenue (and income) is therefore: value-generating activity.

VALUE-GENERATING ACTIVITY

VGA

We normally try to avoid acronyms. But to mark the importance of the definition of revenue, it deserves its own acronym: VGA! Sear these letters into your brain. A lawyer in a Wealthvox finance fundamentals seminar once memorably exclaimed "You've blown a fuse in my head" when presented with this definition and the idea that revenue is a verb concept. We want you to rewire your brain to always be conscious that revenue isn't cash. As we've said, people thinking that revenue means cash is the biggest cause of confusion in business finance, but never forget *VGA*. When you're speaking with a colleague and they talk about a business's revenue, knowing that people confuse revenue with cash, you will check if they mean the cash that the business received or the value-generating activities that it did. You'll be on the lookout for the mix-up.

VGA is the third source of funds for any business.

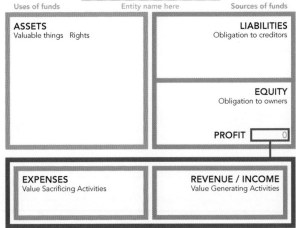

Income and Revenue mean "Value-Generating Activity"

Figure 56. **BaSIS Framework with explanatory subtitles for Revenue/Income and Expense elements**

Casual vs. financial communication

You've no doubt heard people say things like "I put all my income into the bank." What they mean, of course, is "I put all the money I received from my job into the bank." But if income is a verb, then the sentence doesn't make sense. You can't put your income in the bank because income is not money.

Perhaps we should concede that defining income as money is okay for casual, informal, and nontechnical conversation. But in the realm of accounting, finance, and technical conversation, and when reading financial statements, we need to be more precise in how we use the terms. In formal settings, it's wrong to think of income and revenue as money.

Shocking lack of agreement among accountants

You may have been wondering why we've been referring to both income and revenue, and sometimes writing "revenue/income," or sometimes "income/revenue."

Both words mean value-generating activity—sort of.

The problem is that income has different meanings in different places. In the United States, income mostly but not always means profit. In the United Kingdom, Australia, and other English-speaking countries, income means revenue.

The shocking fact is that accountants globally don't agree on what some of the main words in accounting mean. Worse, they often don't realize they don't agree. No wonder people are confused if we accountants aren't even clear ourselves! The fault is with us accountants who haven't got our linguistic house in order.

With the internet, people are increasingly exposed to journalism and financial information that crosses international borders. So, we need to cover all the bases here.

Defining the BaSIS Framework boxes

Let's flip the task here and instead of trying to define income and revenue, let's start by defining the VGA bottom right-hand orange box of the BaSIS Framework.

In the United States, two words are needed to capture the meaning of the bottom right-hand box of the BaSIS Framework: "revenue" and "gains" (see *Figure 57* below.). There's no single word synonymous with value-generating activity.

Revenue is like the consulting activity in our example above. Gains are activity that increases the value of investments, a sort of passive generation of value. Together these words make up the bottom right-hand BaSIS Framework box that we are calling VGA.

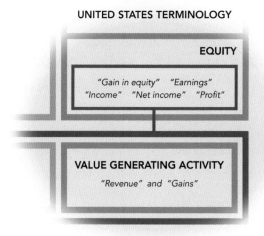

Figure 57. **Definition of VGA in the USA.**

So, what does the word "income" mean in the United States? It is not officially defined by accounting regulators. In common practice in the US, income is often used to mean profit, which is also net income, i.e., revenue less expenses. There is also the related and officially defined term "comprehensive income," which describes a form of profit that doesn't come from the main activities of the business. So in the US, "income" appears in the Equity box, whereas elsewhere in the world (as shown in *Figure 57*), "income" appears in the VGA box.

> • In the USA, the terms used to describe Value-Generating Activity are revenue and gains, but usually not income.
> • Elsewhere, the terms used to describe Value-Generating Activity are both income and revenue.

Outside of the USA, such as in Great Britain and Australia, the word "income" alone captures the meaning of the bottom right-hand box of the BaSIS Framework.

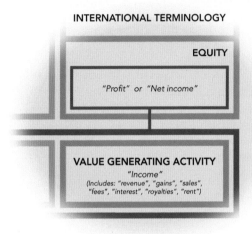

Figure 58. **Definition of VGA outside the US.**

Problematic word: income

So, in the USA, income usually means profit, whereas in Australia, income means value-generating activity. Down under, income is mostly synonymous with the terms sales and revenue, and includes the USA's gains.

Figure 59. **Income as used in the USA and Australia.**

But to futher complicate matters, in the USA, the word income doesn't only mean profit. People sometimes also use income in the sense of revenue. For example, "rental income" is the gross value generation of renting out your house, and "interest income" is the gross value generation from your savings account. In this usage, income does not describe the profit after expenses of renting out your house or the net interest after bank charges.

Ironically, in the USA, "income" and "net income" usually mean the same thing: profit.

Educational and transitional definitions

We refer to Value-Generating Activity as an educational and transitional definition. This is because it will help you to get your head around the meaning of the common terminology and later be better able to make sense of the official regulatory definitions of these commonly used terms.

As mentioned previously, the Financial Accounting Standards Board defines official accounting terminology in the US. For the rest of the world, the defining authority is the International Accounting Standards Board, based in London, UK. Each of the Boards publishes a concept paper that defines the fundamental principles and elements that make up commercial accounting.

For the purposes of this book, we will integrate the pronouncements of both boards. For example, we've titled the box that describes value-generating activity "Revenue/Income."

So, when you read "income" in this book, we are referring to value-generating activity, not profit.

The Appendix "Regulatory Definitions and Recognition Criteria" on page 273 includes the official definitions of the accounting elements as laid down by the two accounting standards boards.

Having gotten all that confusion out of the way, let's get back to the heart of the matter and ask ourselves some fun and interesting questions. For starters: what's the proverbial sound of income?

Sound of income

Think of a local business near you and imagine the employees going about their work. Perhaps a hair salon. What's the sound of the income of the business?

When we ask students this question—and we've had fun asking it in Vancouver, New York, Johannesburg, Stockholm, Singapore, Sydney, Mumbai, and many other places—we inevitably hear "ka-ching." We've never had a miss. It's up there with "mine, mine, mine" as a famous sound-bite! Ka-ching, of course, is the sound of the cash register in the hair salon receiving the money that all those groomed and coiffed customers pay for their treatments.

But it's a trick question. At a hair salon, the sound of income is more "snip-snip" and "buzz-buzz" than "ka-ching." That's because income and revenue are the value-generating activities that the business does. The notes and coins going into the cash register are the assets that result from the hair cutting. The income that gives rise to those assets is the hair-cutting service itself. As we've said, income is the doing verb-concept; cash is the noun-concept.

VSA

We've defined the terms revenue and income as value-generating activity. So now we ask: what's an "expense"?

When they hear the term "expense," many people immediately think "cash out" or "spend." It's understandable. Incurring expenses and spending cash often go together. You get a shoeshine, you pay cash for it, and presto, shoeshine expense. We think of the payment to the shiner as the expense, but it's not. The expense is the consumption of the shoe-cleaning services. Cash going out was the payment for the expense, but not the expense itself. This is the accounting duality at work again. There are two aspects of the transaction: the consumption and the payment for it.

If revenue and income are Value-Generating Activities, then expenses are the opposite: Value-Sacrificing Activities. The expense is the consumption of the shiner's service and shoe polish. An expense is the burning gas in your car and the wearing and tearing of the tires. When a business hires staff, the use of the staff's time and labor is the expense that the business incurs daily when the staff clock in.

Expenses—like Income—are verb-concepts. Cash is a noun. Expense is the verb-type action that often results in you paying cash to settle the obligation incurred.

You can fill in the word you like instead of "sacrificing": Value-_____ Activity:

- Destroying
- Obliterating
- Consuming
- Annihilating
- Depreciating
- Eroding
- Reducing
- … you name it.

VALUE-SACRIFICING ACTIVITY

Do this…

The following is quirky, but serious. Let's physically illustrate the idea of an expense. Grab something like a piece of paper near you. Maybe it's a business card, a Post-it Note, or a napkin.

What you've got in your hand is an asset. It's not a very significant asset. It doesn't have much value at all. Maybe a few cents or a fraction of a cent, but it's still an asset. It certainly isn't a liability, nor is it equity, revenue, or an expense. It's an asset even though it might not be recorded on a balance sheet as an asset because it's worth too little to worry about. When something's too small to worry about, in accounting, we say it's "immaterial."

Assuming you've got a Post-it Note, when was it paid for? It could have been yesterday. It could be while you are holding it that your colleague is next door paying the stationer. Or maybe it hasn't been paid for yet. Perhaps you have an account with a stationery shop, and you pay them for your supplies at the end of each month. The point is that when thinking about an expense, it's irrelevant when the payment happened. What determines the expense is when the value of the note is lost.

Now tear up the note. Yes, rip it in half, and in half again. Now it's not useful as a notepad. Your action of tearing up the paper is the expense in this scenario. You've just "expensed" the asset.

TEAR IT. RIP IT.

We said the real sound of income in a hair salon was "snip-snip." Here, the sound of the expense is the tearing of the paper.

We'll leave it as this for now. You're getting the very important point: that an expense is not "cash out." It's a value-consuming activity that appears on the second main accounting report, called the Statement of Activities.

> An expense is a value-sacrificing activity.

We'll further refine the definitions of revenue and expense later in the book. For the moment, let it sink into your consciousness that in the realm of the accounting duality versus casual conversation, revenue/income means value-generating activity, and expense means value-sacrificing activity.

Income Statement

The Equity box of our framework in *Figure 55* comprises obligations to the owners of the business that come about in two ways.

Firstly, the business is obliged to the owners because the owners contributed assets to the business when they invested. In our Lemonade & Laughter example, the owners invested $20,000 cash into the business; in return, we recorded the business owing the owners $20,000 as Contributed Equity.

Secondly, the business then generated a net $750 of cash by doing consulting and the associated traveling. This cash was generated on behalf of the owners. This gave rise to additional equity for the owners, which is reflected in a folder called Profit as a subset of the total equity.

To show the detail of how the $750 profit was generated, we "exploded" the profit folder into the bottom two boxes of the BaSIS Framework. The two elements that give rise to profit are now shown separately in those new boxes. Asset-generating activities are shown on the Sources of Funds side. Asset-sacrificing activities are shown on the Uses of Funds side.

The bottom two boxes make up the traditional accounting report titled the income statement. As you know, the top three asset, liability, and equity boxes of the BaSIS Framework make up the traditional balance sheet report.

> There are many names for the income statement.
> Statement of Activity reminds us that revenue and expenses are activities.

The income statement is always dated "over" a period because the activities happen over time. So, for example, an income statement may be "for the twelve months ending December 31, 2027." This contrasts with the balance sheet, which is dated "at" a moment in time, such as "Balance Sheet at December 31, 2027."

There are many other names for the income statement. These include:

- Statement of activities
- Statement of operations
- Statement of financial performance
- Statement of income and expenditure
- Income and expenditure statement
- Statement of earnings
- Statement of financial results
- Profit and loss statement
- Statement of profit or loss
- P&L

The report, regardless of which name is used, takes the information presented in the BaSIS Framework's bottom two boxes and presents it vertically.

Value-generation activities go to the top, and value-sacrificing activities go underneath. The difference between the value generated and sacrificed shows at the bottom as profit (or loss if more value was sacrificed than generated).

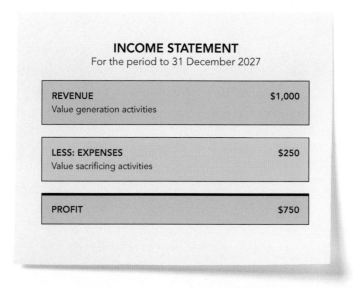

INCOME STATEMENT
For the period to 31 December 2027

REVENUE Value generation activities	$1,000
LESS: EXPENSES Value sacrificing activities	$250
PROFIT	$750

Figure 60. **Structure of the income statement.**

Notes on the presentation of the income statement:

- The colors orange and green are not traditional. Rather, they represent Color Accounting Learning System coding to show sources of funds and uses of funds. Later, we'll see how the colors also represent the traditional terms "credit" and "debit."
- The net value generated in this statement is shown as "profit" in orange because it's a new source of funds. This is also referred to as "net income."
- If the expenses had been, say, $1,100 rather than $250, giving a loss of $100 (calculated as sales of 1,000 less expenses of 1,100), then instead of a profit of $750, that loss would have been shown in green.
- In this statement, because there was more orange ($1,000) than green ($250), the net result was an orange $750.
- Later, we'll see that in traditional income statements with multiple expenses, the various expense activities are often subdivided into subgroups of similar type. Direct expenses may be grouped together with a subtotal, indirect expenses grouped with their own subtotal, and taxes listed on their own. Beneath each expense group, a sub-profit figure may be calculated with names such as Gross Profit, Operating Profit, and Profit After Tax. In the end, the final profit remains the same, recorded as we have done here, at the bottom.
- In some income statements, income may also be shown in parts. For example, unusual value-generation activity might be shown toward the bottom of the income statement as "Other Income."

BaSIS Framework™

This is an important moment on our learning journey—a journey to build from scratch–from first principles–the system that is accounting. Building the accounting system from the bottom up ensures that we really understand it. If you build a machine for yourself, you know what all the parts are, why they are there, and how they interact.

The way we are presenting accounting is with a diagram called the BaSIS Framework. It's got five boxes, or elements, being revenue, equity, liabilities, assets and expenses. It seems appropriate and fun that this can give us the mnemonic "RELAX".

You can indeed relax because there is no sixth box. Everything that happens financially in a business (or in your personal financial life) can be described using just these five elements. They are all you need. As a learner, this should be reassuring. All you need to learn is five elements. When you understand those, you understand accounting.

Figure 61. **There are only five elements in accounting.**

CHAPTER ROUNDUP

This "Unpacking Profit" chapter has been all about the income statement.

We explored how:

- There is a need for the income statement because recording profit alone on the balance sheet loses margin information.
- There are an infinite number of ways to arrive at any one profit figure. The same profit number could have been arrived at in different ways, via different profit margins.
- Margin information is an important management metric and we must track it.
- Value consumed is compared with value generated to arrive at profit.
- Profit is the net value generated.
- If more value is sacrificed than generated, the net profit becomes a net loss.
- Double-clicking the profit figure like opening a folder on a computer to reveal two folders inside is analogous to how the income statement reveals the details of profit.
- The bottom two boxes of the graphical framework, one orange and one green, represent the income statement.
- The combination of the top three balance sheet boxes and the bottom two income statement boxes gives us the name "BaSIS Framework."
- There are many names for the income statement, including Statement of Activities.
- Revenue/Income is the third source of funds of a business.
- Expenses are the second use of funds of a business—these funds are used up.
- For the moment, we are defining revenue and income as value-generating activity. Expenses are value-sacrificing activity. We will expand on these definitions later.
- Revenue/income and expenses, being activities, are verb-concepts.
- We use the acronyms VGA and VSA to emphasize these definitions.
- VGA is referred to as revenue and gains in the USA. Outside the US, it's referred to as income.
- Revenue and income are not money, nor money received.

- Lightheartedly, but illustratively, we distinguished that "ka-ching" is not the sound of income. Rather, the sound of income is the sound of the business activity being performed for the client.
- Quirkily, but with serious intent, tearing up a piece of paper illustrated how the consumption of an asset is an expense. Payment for the piece of paper is not the expense.
- The vertical income statement presents value-generating activities and value-sacrificing activities with the net value generated or consumed at the bottom.
- There are only five elements in accounting, represented by the five boxes of the BaSIS Framework.
- The five boxes represent **r**evenue, **e**quity, **l**iabilities, **a**ssets and e**x**penses. This gave us the mnemonic RELAX.
- There is no sixth element so you can relax.

10. ACCOUNTING EQUATION: INCOME STATEMENT

The Final Accounting Equation

We discovered the balance sheet equation when we pictured a business entity as the butterfly. We saw that for any asset, there is an equivalently-sized obligation to the funder of the asset.

This led us to the initial balance sheet equation:

Assets = Obligations.

We then saw that there are two fundamental types of obligation: liabilities and equity. This led to the next expression of the accounting equation:

Assets = Liabilities + Equity.

We then saw the need for the income statement to explain the profit component of equity. We saw how revenue/income and expenses explain how value was generated and sacrificed to generate the profit. We represented this on a complete schema we call the BaSIS Framework.

BASIS FRAMEWORK

We saw that this financial framework shows the funding of a business, with sources of funds and uses of funds. The right side of the framework, the orange side, shows all the sources of funds of the business. And the left side, the green side, shows the uses to which the funding is put.

The equivalence of the two sides gives us the BaSIS Framework equation:

Uses of Funds = Sources of Funds

Expressed in detail, in terms of all five elements of the Framework, this gives us the accounting equation:

Assets = Liabilities + (Opening Equity + Revenue/Income - Expenses).

The reason the Opening Equity is shown in the equation rather than all Equity is, of course, because the total Equity is made of the opening equity (the equity we had before we started earning the new profit) plus the new profit. The new profit is the revenue/income less expenses.

ACCOUNTING ON A PAGE

Another way to write the expanded accounting equation is by moving the expenses to the left-hand side so that all the Uses of Funds are on the left, like in the BaSIS Framework. The equation reads:

Assets + Expenses = Liabilities + Opening Equity + Revenue/Income

The full accounting model is now complete.

We're now done creating a complete storytelling model that we can use to describe any financial situation. We've reinvented accounting for ourselves from first principles. The BaSIS Framework is a complete model. It's accounting on a page. What we need to do now is practice using the Framework. And that's what we're now ready for, coming up in Part 2 of *The Joy of Accounting*.

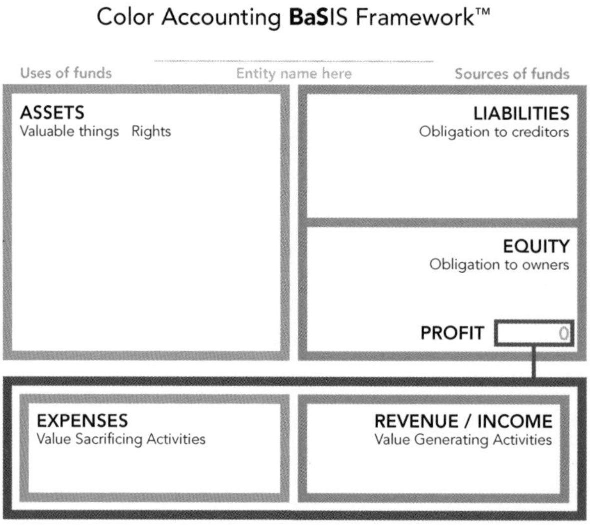

Color Accounting **BaS**IS Framework™

Uses of funds	Entity name here	Sources of funds
ASSETS Valuable things Rights		**LIABILITIES** Obligation to creditors
		EQUITY Obligation to owners
		PROFIT [0]
EXPENSES Value Sacrificing Activities		**REVENUE / INCOME** Value Generating Activities

Figure 62. **Color Accounting BaSIS Framework captures the principles of accounting on a page.**

CHAPTER ROUNDUP

This "Accounting Equation: Income Statement" chapter has completed the various expressions of the accounting equation.

We explored how:

- The purest form of the accounting equation is Rights = Obligations.
- All assets in a financial paradigm are financial rights. The rights are to the physical and nonphysical operational assets.
- The equation is also expressed as Assets = Obligations.
- Because obligations are divided into two fundamental types, the equation is expressed in the next level of detail as: Assets = Liabilities + Equity.
- These above forms of the equation are also called the Balance Sheet Equation.
- The equity element of the balance sheet equation can be unpacked to its parts: Opening Equity + Revenue - Expenses.
- This leads to a full expression of the accounting equation: Assets = Liabilities + Opening Equity + Revenue - Expenses.
- To match the format of the BaSIS Framework, which puts all uses of funds on the left and all sources of funds on the right, the equation can be expressed as: Assets + Expenses = Liabilities + Opening Equity + Revenue/Income.
- The BaSIS Framework is a complete graphical model of accounting.

PART **2** CLASSIC TRANSACTIONS

YOUR LEARNING JOURNEY, SO FAR

Let's pause for a moment. You're well into *The Joy of Accounting*. How are you doing? You may be surprised at how much we've talked about concepts, principles, relationships, words, and even grammatical ideas like verbs, nouns, and adjectives. Perhaps you're surprised at how little we've talked about numbers.

You might be wondering where it's all headed, and perhaps you're concerned that it doesn't seem to be about reading financial reports and making sense of how a business is doing, or how what we've covered is relevant to your personal finances.

It may not all make sense yet, and that's OK. It's fine. You're exactly where you're meant to be. Remember, this process we're going through has been tested hundreds of thousands of times.

So far, we've developed a one-page schematic diagram of how accounting works called the BaSIS Framework. You need to know three things about the diagram. We call them the three key aspects of accounting literacy:

- Structure
- Language
- Mechanics

When you understand these three aspects, you'll be accounting-literate.

Structure Language Mechanics

Figure 63. **Aspects of accounting literacy: structure, language, and mechanics.**

Structure

Structure refers to how the BaSIS Framework is laid out and how the boxes interact. For example, why the framework has two sides (to reflect the accounting duality) and how the income statement explains one number on the balance sheet—profit. These are structural concepts.

Language

Language is what the words mean. You need to be very clear on the definition of the five elements. We've distinguished the top three boxes as noun-concepts and the bottom two boxes as verb-concepts. Assets are valuable. Liabilities and equity are obligations. Revenue is value-generating activity, and expenses are value-sacrificing activity. There is more work to do on language as we learn more about how accounting works.

Mechanics

Mechanics refers to the logic of how the boxes and the accounts within them increase and decrease to reflect what's happening in the business. We've started to see how this works, like when cash increased and liabilities increased, or when cash decreased and profit decreased.

When you get on top of these three aspects of accounting, you'll be accounting-literate. They all need to be in place, like links in a chain. It's quite straightforward.

So far, we've made good progress on Structure and Language. Now it's time to see how they work in practice and to further explore Mechanics.

This is where it all comes together.

We're going to exercise the principles we've covered so far by doing fifteen classic transactions.

By "classic transactions," we mean we will put on our accountant-hats to tell the story of a business scenario with fifteen archetypal events that happen in any business. We'll account for the events on the BaSIS Framework. It's easy and fun, and you'll gain a profound understanding of and deep insights into accounting, finance, and business.

WAX ON. WAX OFF.

Do be patient as we work through the transactions. They may be for you like the "wax on, wax off" practice in the famous movie *The Karate Kid*. In that memorable film, when the student began his apprenticeship, he was told by his master to wax the floor and paint the fence. The student thought the tasks were menial and felt he was going too slowly. Little did he know that he was learning the essential moves of karate. Doing those simple tasks, he very quickly built up a solid foundation of skills that he later used to great and dramatic effect. You too will very quickly be able to use your learning foundation to understand complex business events and use financial statements to great effect.

CHAPTER ROUNDUP

This "Your Learning Journey, So Far" chapter took stock of where you're at on your journey to accounting literacy.

We explored how:

- In *The Joy of Accounting*, we've focused a lot so far on words, concepts, and principles.
- You might be questioning your learning progress and concerned that it doesn't all make complete sense yet.
- You're invited to trust the process.
- There are three aspects of accounting, the grasp of which will make you accounting-literate: Structure, Language, and Mechanics.
- We will entrench all three aspects by using the BaSIS Framework to model a business scenario. With just fifteen events, it captures the essence of any business.
- Recording the transactions will create a solid foundation of skills that will serve you well.

1. BORROWING CASH

Classic Transaction One

In this first of the classic transactions, we'll start our business scenario over.

We will be using the BaSIS Framework as a working model of the accounting general ledger. Although the images you will see might remind you of a board game, it is not a game. Rather, it is a scenario-modeling exercise.

The business, Lemonade & Laughter, will borrow cash from a lender and put it into the company's bank account.

You'll recognize this transaction from before. It's the same first event we accounted for on page 60 when we began deducing the BaSIS Framework. Recall that we did four transactions to reveal the five boxes of the framework. The company first borrowed cash, then it received invested cash from the owners. It then generated revenue before incurring an expense. We'll revisit all four of those transactions again in the classic transactions.

Accounts

Instead of writing a line on the framework for each transaction as we did previously, we'll create subgroups within each of the five boxes on the framework. That is, we'll create accounts, just like in a real accounting general ledger.

As discussed in Chapter 1, deciding how many accounts to have and what to call them is done with a Chart of Accounts.

Buckets

In the Color Accounting Learning System we represent accounts with buckets. The buckets live within the five Framework element boxes. The buckets take on the same color as the element they belong to. The liability, equity, and revenue/income buckets are orange because they are sources of funds. Asset and expense buckets are green because they are uses of funds.

Every bucket is either green or orange.

Color Accounting **BaS**IS Framework™

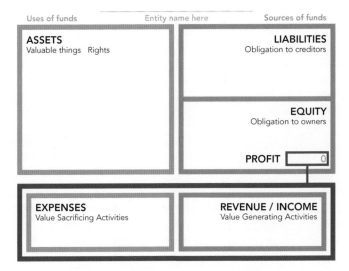

Figure 64. BaSIS Framework—five elements.

As we account for each of the fifteen classic transactions, we'll ask ourselves two vital questions:

1) Which of the five elements will be impacted by the two effects?
2) Will those impacts be an increase to that element or a decrease?

> Every bucket is either green or orange.

Tickets to Show Effects

In addition to the buckets, the Color Accounting Learning System has another storytelling device: tickets. When we want to change the balance of a bucket—which is to say, increase or decrease its net total—we do so with tickets. We put a ticket into the bucket. The tickets have an amount on them, reflecting the size of the change. The tickets also have a color, either green or orange.

As we account for each of the fifteen classic transactions, we'll ask ourselves, "What two buckets are impacted?" Every transaction has two effects, represented by the two tickets, and will impact two buckets.

> Every transaction has two effects on the Framework, represented by the two tickets, and will impact two buckets.

Not money

Think of the tickets as green effects and orange effects. It's easy to start thinking of the tickets as money, but it's better not to. You're not dropping money into a bucket when you put a ticket in it. Tickets aren't money—they are simply effects. When you put a ticket into a bucket, you are affecting that bucket; the impact will be either an increase or a decrease.

> Tickets are effects.
> A ticket changes the balance (the net total) of a bucket.

The size of the effect is measured in monetary terms, but it's not money. If you think of the tickets as money, you'd be thinking that revenue or loans are money too. There's only one bucket that could represent money, and that's the asset account "Money," or "Cash." Everything else is only measured in monetary terms, but isn't money.

In the BaSIS Framework, the buckets and the tickets are storytelling devices, representing what is happening to the actual assets in the business in terms of the five elements

> Tickets don't represent money.

Here's a picture of a student putting an orange ticket into an orange bucket. By doing this, she's increasing the total balance of the account represented by this bucket. She's also increasing the total amount for the element within which this account is situated, and the whole source of funds side of the Framework is increased. We'll show you how this all works momentarily.

Figure 65. **Affecting a bucket with a ticket.**

Every transaction involves two tickets: a green one and an orange one.

> Every transaction has at least one green and one orange ticket.

When we record Lemonade & Laughter borrowing cash, we can show the transaction using two tickets and two buckets as follows:

Classic Transaction 1—January 2

The business borrows $30,000 of cash from a lender.

To record the business borrowing cash, the first thing we do is ask ourselves how this transaction impacted the business. Don't try and "think accounting" yet. Just ask yourself what actually happened in the real world. In your mind's eye, see the business getting $30,000 of cash that it did not have before. See the business getting a liability obligation that it didn't have before: to pay the money back. The business acquired two things: an asset (cash) and a liability (loan).

Now you're ready to think accounting! We represent those two impacts using buckets in Lemonade & Laughter's BaSIS Framework below, shown circled in blue.

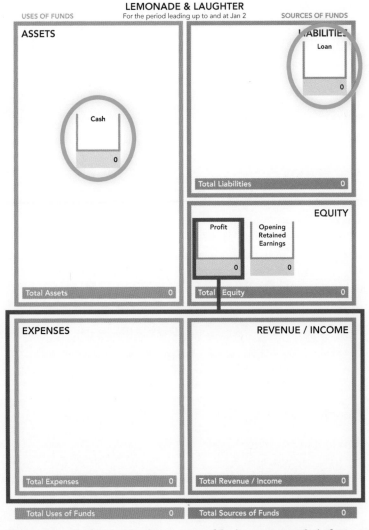

Figure 66. **BaSIS Framework showing buckets impacted by borrowing cash, before posting of tickets.**

The Loan bucket represents the liability the business acquired. It is the source of the cash and is therefore an orange bucket on the Sources of Funds side of the framework. Filling up Lemonade & Laughter's bank account with cash is the use to which the funding was put. So, the Cash bucket is green and lives on the green "Uses of Funds" side of the Framework.

We've named the asset bucket "Cash," but we could also have called it something like "Bank," or "Cash in Bank." The exact naming of the bucket is not that important. What's most important is that the two buckets we use to reflect the transaction are located within the correct element in the framework. The cash received is valuable, so it's in the Asset box. The loan is an obligation with the expectation of repayment to the lender, so we show it in the Liabilities box.

Now that we've decided what buckets (accounts) to use to reflect what happened in the real world, we need to make sure that the values of the buckets are reflective of reality too. The business had no cash and no liability before the transaction, and it now has $30,000 of each.

To increase the buckets from zero to $30,000 we put a green and orange ticket into each bucket respectively (i.e., same color ticket and bucket).

The effects are recorded in the accounting journal like this:

	Green Effect	Orange Effect
January 2	Cash	Loan
Get cash from lender	30,000	30,000

Traditional term: *posting*

The accounting jargon for putting the tickets into the buckets is *posting*. You post the journal entries to the general ledger accounts. The BaSIS Framework is the Color Accounting name for what's traditionally known as the "general ledger." The journal above with the green and orange tickets is one row of the general journal that you can think of as an endless scroll. It's got a row for every transaction and keeps going and going as long as you have transactions to record. Large companies like Amazon add millions of rows to their computerized journals each day.

In years gone by, the general ledger was a big book where each account had its own page. Where Color Accounting has buckets, a traditional general ledger would have a page for cash and a separate page for the loan. These days, of course, the ledger is usually an accounting system on a computer.

We'll talk more about journals and ledgers later.

BaSIS Framework: Borrowing

The green and orange journal tickets are posted into the buckets on the BaSIS Framework as shown in *Figure 67* below.

Think carefully about this and each of the following Frameworks as we go through the classic transactions. Read each of the blue speech-bubble commentaries and make sure you understand the points they are making. By repeatedly reading the Frameworks and the matching Financial Statements, you'll become comfortable with their formats and the stories they tell.

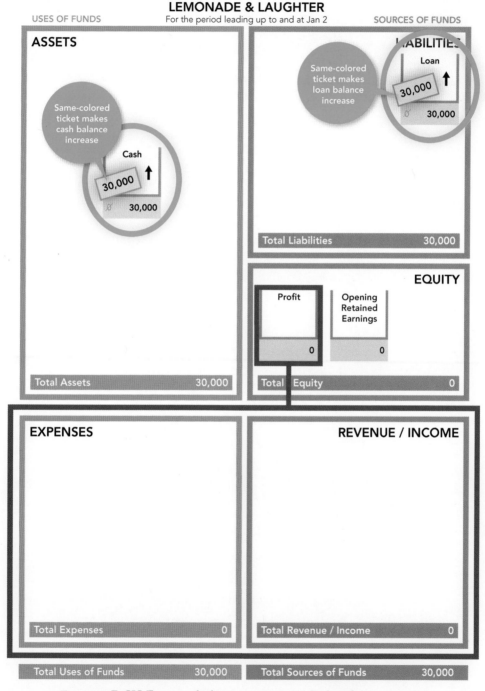

Figure 67. BaSIS Framework showing increase in Cash and increase in Loan.

Nothing happened in the Revenue/Income and the Expense boxes. The Profit account in Equity is therefore not impacted either. As you can see, its balance is zero, like the Total Expenses and the Total Income/Revenue.

The Opening Retained Earnings bucket is where the profits from previous years are shown. Because this is the first year of operation for Lemonade & Laughter, that bucket is empty and will remain so as we do the fifteen classic transactions. It will only have a balance in it for the second and subsequent periods of operation.

Financial Statements after Borrowing Transaction 1

After Borrowing Transaction 1, the balance sheet and income statement of Lemonade & Laughter look like this:

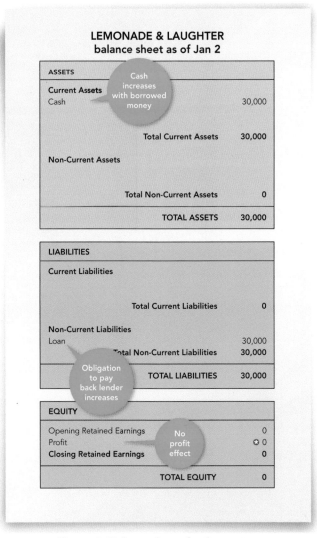

Figure 68. **Balance sheet after borrowing.**

Note: You can see that both Assets and Liabilities have been split into current and non-current - more on this soon.

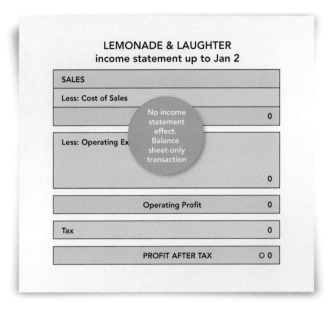

LEMONADE & LAUGHTER
income statement up to Jan 2

SALES	
Less: Cost of Sales	
No income statement effect. Balance sheet-only transaction	0
Less: Operating Ex	
	0
Operating Profit	0
Tax	0
PROFIT AFTER TAX	⟳ 0

Figure 69. **Income statement after borrowing.**

The business now has total assets of $30,000, all of which is funded by debt. There is no activity on the income statement because the business is still in its setup stage and has not yet commenced sales operations. Which is to say, it hasn't started earning revenue or incurring expenses.

Remember, the classic fifteen transactions have been carefully designed to build your accounting literacy in a systematic way. They are only loosely based on a startup scenario and are not meant to be comprehensive.

Discussion: Borrowing

Our imaginary business, Lemonade & Laughter, has just sourced funds through borrowing. In reality, the lender would likely want to see the owners put money into the business first before they lent money to the business. Lenders want owners to have skin in the game. They feel safer if owners have put in money and are behind them in the repayment line; lenders rank above owners for repayment if things go wrong in the business. You might have expected to see an investment transaction first, but for learning purposes, we wanted to start out with a borrowing transaction.

In our personal lives, we often think of debt as a bad thing. We dislike that our credit card debt hangs around our neck and that we will have to use cash to pay it off. While the credit card liability remains unpaid, it can be subject to exorbitant rates of interest. Of course, it would be wonderful if we could wave a magic wand to make our debts miraculously disappear. In that sense, yes, debt is undesirable.

But a liability is a source of funds, and that's not a bad thing. In fact, it's an incredibly powerful tool. It's a source of funds that our business can put to good use. Lemonade & Laughter now has $30,000 of cash that it can productively use to get (earn) even more cash to benefit the owners. Imagine that the business can triple the money through trading. It will then have

$90,000 cash and still just $30,000 of liabilities (ignoring interest and charges associated with the borrowing, to keep it simple). If the business then paid back the original $30,000 that was borrowed, it would be left with $60,000 all for the owners. The owners' claim on the company would have grown to $60,000 without putting any money down. They would have made money out of thin air.

This concept of making money using other people's money is called *leverage* or sometimes gearing. It's an enormously important concept at the heart of modern free enterprise. It's what drives capitalism. Businesses are expected (especially by shareholders) to incur liabilities by borrowing other people's money to use in the business. Shareholders will insist that companies use borrowed funds as well as their own. A business that only used shareholders' funds would not be operating to its maximum potential.

Getting the right balance between borrowed money and shareholders' money is important—that is, how much of each to use. Too much of one source or the other is not a good thing—the mix must be right. The proportion of debt to assets is called the *leverage ratio*. The leverage ratio expresses how much of the total assets of the company is funded by loan obligations.

In our Lemonade & Laughter company, the leverage ratio is 100 percent right now. The company has $30,000 of cash, all of it from loans. No funds have been contributed by the shareholders yet.

Managing the ratio is the job of the Chief Financial Officer of a corporation. What the right ratio is for the company depends upon a number of factors. An appropriate ratio for one company may not be right for another. The factors may include the company and the owners' appetite for risk, the type of business conducted, the nature of the assets that are being funded, the prevailing interest rates, and so on. Manufacturing companies might have about half their assets financed through debt, whereas banks often have 90 percent of their assets financed through debt.

Corporate bonds

For big corporations, the process of getting cash through borrowing, as we've seen here in classic transaction 1, often takes the form of selling bonds. The company takes lenders' money and gives them a certificate in return. The certificate is proof that the company owes the lender. In the hands of the lender, the bond is an asset. The certificate also specifies the interest rate (called the "coupon rate") that the loan pays and when the debt must be paid back, or "falls due" in the jargon of finance. What makes these corporate bonds special is that they are transferrable. That means that the owner of the certificate can sell the bond to someone else. This happens in what's called the "secondary market." The company doesn't know who it will ultimately have to pay back. In the hands of the lender, the value of the asset (the bond) can change. For example, if the bondholders start to be concerned that the business might not be able to pay the money back, the value of the bond will fall. Since the coupon interest that the bond pays is a fixed amount, the interest rate relative to the new value of the bond (versus the original face value) changes. This new interest rate is called the "yield rate." The yield and change in value of the bond affects the lender more than the company. The company will continue to pay the fixed interest rate that it agreed to when it borrowed the money by issuing the bond. The company will, of course, keep an eye on what is happening to its bond value outside in the marketplace. It is a signal as to what the market thinks about the company and its prospects. And it will inform and affect any future borrowing that the company may want to make.

Recall the pineapple and the kaleidoscope of butterflies when thinking about bond value. Which is to say, remember whose point of view we're talking about when we talk about people buying and selling the bond in the secondary market. From the company's point of view, nothing changes in its accounts when other parties buy/sell this asset. The original obligation remains unchanged in the liabilities section of the balance sheet. The company as borrower still has to pay back the original agreed amount, known as the "face value." It's from the lender's point of view that the value of the asset changes.

From a language point of view, what can be a bit confusing is that lenders who buy corporate bonds are often referred to as *investing* in bonds. They use the word "invest" to describe a loan situation. Until now, we've used (and will continue to use) the word "invest" to refer to people putting money into the business permanently, as owners, in contrast to loaning money to the business temporarily, as lenders or creditors, as in this Transaction 1.

In your personal life, borrowing may be something you want to do more of. We're not suggesting you borrow to pay for a holiday in the Caribbean. The holiday will be over, and you'll be left with the debt. Bad idea. What we're suggesting is that if you borrow to buy a productive, cash-generating asset like an investment property, that might be a very good reason to leverage up your personal balance sheet. Needless to say, this book doesn't give financial advice. Speak to a trusted financial advisor whose fees are not linked to the advice they give you or the product they sell you.

For learning purposes, our intention is to make it clear that debt isn't simply bad.

2. RECEIVE INVESTED CASH

Classic Transaction Two

In the second of the classic transactions, the business also receives cash—but unlike the previous transaction, the obligation that the company acquires with the cash is not a loan obligation. Rather, it's an equity-type obligation to the owners who contribute the cash.

Classic Transaction 2—January 3

The owners invest $20,000 cash into the business.

As always, the first thing we must do is establish the two impacts on the BaSIS Framework to reflect what happened. Always ask yourself: What are the two impacts? Then we'll ask of each: increase or decrease? Finally, we'll reflect those changes with a green and an orange ticket.

Figure 70. **What will be the two impacts on the BaSIS Framework?**

1) Where on the BaSIS Framework will the two impacts land?
2) Will each impact be an increase or a decrease?

We know that the business now has an additional $20,000 of assets (cash) that it didn't have before, and we know that it has an equity obligation to the owners that it didn't have either.

We'll use the existing Cash bucket we created in Transaction 1 to show the new cash received. We'll need to create a new bucket to show the obligation to shareholders. We'll call that bucket Contributed Equity. So those are our two buckets: Cash and Contributed Equity.

In answer to the question increase or decrease, we know that the balances of both accounts have increased. We (the business) have more cash and more contributed equity.

To reflect those two impacts, we use the accounting journal like this:

	Green Effect	Orange Effect
January 3 Business receives cash as investment from owners	Cash	Contributed Equity
	20,000	20,000

To record the increases in both buckets, the tickets are posted to the BaSIS Framework, impacting the buckets as shown by the blue up or down arrows. The green ticket makes the green Cash bucket increase from $30,000 to $50,000, and the orange ticket makes the Contributed Equity bucket increase from zero to $20,000.

BaSIS Framework: Incurring Equity

Look carefully in *Figure 71* at how the journal posts onto the BaSIS Framework, noting which elements are impacted and the increases in the impacted accounts shown by the blue arrows.

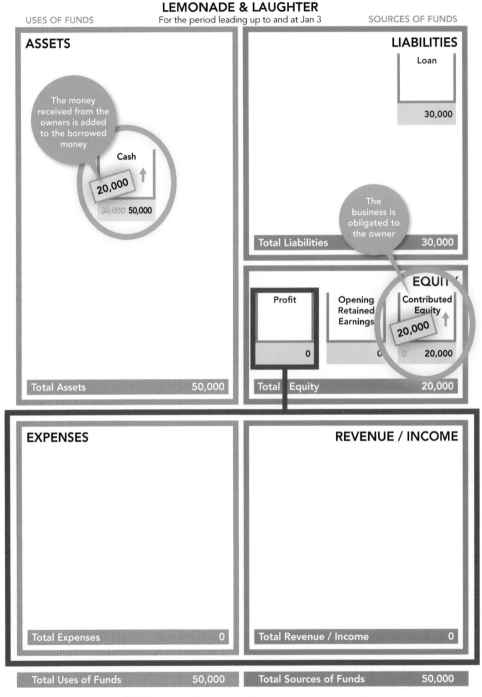

LEMONADE & LAUGHTER
For the period leading up to and at Jan 3

USES OF FUNDS

SOURCES OF FUNDS

ASSETS

The money received from the owners is added to the borrowed money

Cash

20,000

30,000 **50,000**

Total Assets 50,000

LIABILITIES

Loan

30,000

The business is obligated to the owner

Total Liabilities 30,000

EQUITY

Profit

Opening Retained Earnings

Contributed Equity

20,000

0

0 0 20,000

Total Equity 20,000

EXPENSES

Total Expenses 0

REVENUE / INCOME

Total Revenue / Income 0

Total Uses of Funds 50,000

Total Sources of Funds 50,000

Figure 71. **BaSIS Framework showing business incurring equity investment.**

Financial Statements after Investing Transaction 2

After Investing Transaction 2, the balance sheet and income statement of the business are as shown below.

Read and think about each of the speech bubbles on the BaSIS Framework, the balance sheet, and the income statement. The bubbles highlight the pertinent points in each transaction.

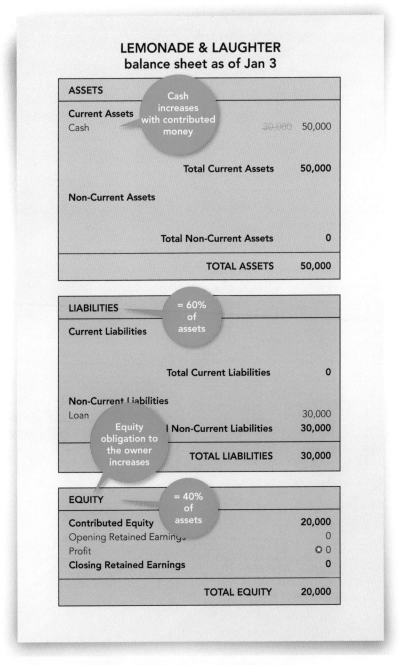

Figure 72. **Balance sheet after cash investment.**

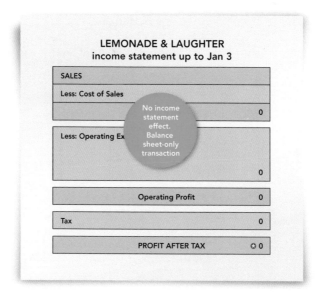

LEMONADE & LAUGHTER
income statement up to Jan 3

SALES	
Less: Cost of Sales	
	0
Less: Operating Ex	
	0
Operating Profit	0
Tax	0
PROFIT AFTER TAX	0

No income statement effect. Balance sheet-only transaction

Figure 73. **Income statement after cash investment.**

The business now has total assets of $50,000, total liabilities of $30,000, and total equity of $20,000.

The equity value is sometimes referred to as the book value or net book value of the business. In other words, presuming to speak from the point of view of the owners, that's how much they are "owed" by the business according to the books of the business.

The assets are funded 60 percent with debt (30,000 ÷ 50,000 × 100) and 40 percent with equity (100% - 60%).

What we have called Contributed Equity has many names in practice, including Issued Capital, Paid-Up Capital, Share Capital, Ordinary Shares, Paid-In Capital, Common Stock, and more.

> Other names for Contributed Equity include Issued Capital, Paid-Up Capital, Share Capital, Ordinary Shares, Paid-In Capital, and Common Stock.

Discussion: Equity Investment

This gray shaded box is a more in-depth discussion that you may want to come back to later.

Various Methods of Expressing Leverage

Lemonade & Laughter is now less leveraged because only some of the assets have been funded with debt. Of the $50,000 of assets that the business has, $30,000 was sourced from lenders and the rest from owner-investors. Because 30,000 is 60 percent of 50,000, we say the business is 60 percent leveraged.

Debt/Asset Ratio

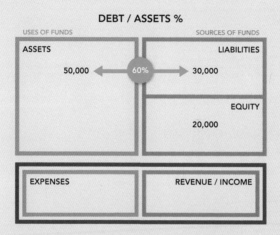

Figure 74. Debt/Assets ratio shown on BaSIS Framework.

We call this expression of leverage the Debt/Asset Ratio.

> It is calculated as:
> Debt ÷ Assets × 100 = leverage %
> 30,000 ÷ 50,000 × 100 = 60%

Because of the balance sheet equation (Assets = Liabilities + Equity), the three elements will always move in tandem with each other. If one element changes, at least one of the other elements must change too. Notice the upper portion of the BaSIS Framework with the three ALE elements. The proportion of leverage can therefore be expressed using any two of the three elements of the accounting equation. Compare any two elements and you'll be expressing a ratio of leverage.

Asset/Equity Multiple

The Asset/Equity Multiple starts with equity and shows how much that funding was "multiplied" by using borrowed funds. It focuses on how much total assets were "built on the equity foundation." For Lemonade & Laughter, after Transaction 2, the company now has 50,000 from its foundation of 20,000 of equity. The leverage multiple is 2.5 times. In other words, $1 of the owner's money turned into $2.50 of assets being used by the company.

ASSETS / EQUITY MULTIPLE

USES OF FUNDS   SOURCES OF FUNDS

ASSETS	LIABILITIES
50,000	30,000
2.5 TIMES	EQUITY
	20,000

EXPENSES	REVENUE / INCOME

Figure 75. **Asset/Equity multiple shown on the BaSIS Framework.**

The Asset/Equity Multiple is calculated as:
Assets ÷ Equity = Multiple
50,000 ÷ 20,000 = 2.5×

Debt/Equity Ratio

Debt/Equity directly compares the amount of debt to the amount of equity. After Transaction 2, Lemonade & Laughter has 30,000 of debt compared with 20,000 of equity. This debt to equity ratio is saying that the business is using 1.5 times more debt than equity.

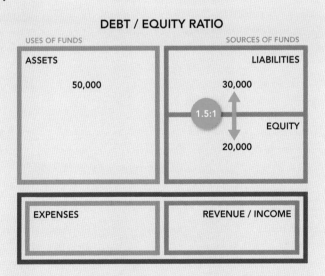

DEBT / EQUITY RATIO

USES OF FUNDS   SOURCES OF FUNDS

ASSETS	LIABILITIES
50,000	30,000
	1.5:1
	EQUITY
	20,000

EXPENSES	REVENUE / INCOME

Figure 76. **Debt/Equity ratio shown on the BaSIS Framework.**

The Debt to Equity Ratio is calculated as:
Debt/Equity = Ratio
30,000/20,000 = 1.5:1

Leverage shown graphically

The diagram below compares two financial structures of an entity with $100 of assets. One structure has less leverage, and the other has more. The liability and equity boxes have been sized proportionally to the amount of each source of funds that finances the $100 of assets.

$100 Leverage Comparison

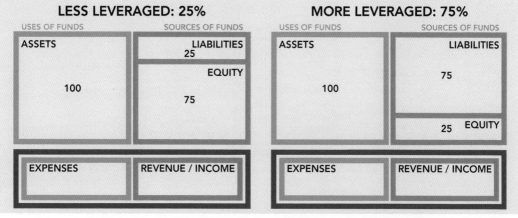

Figure 77. **Leverage shown with scale drawing on BaSIS Frameworks.**

Equity buffer

The lenders to our Lemonade & Laughter company are happy that the owners have contributed equity financing because it makes their loan to the company safer. In Chapter 7 ("Equity: A Deeper Dive"), we explored the nature of debt versus equity. One of the most important differences we saw is the fact that if the business is being shut down and doesn't have enough assets with which to pay back its creditors for debts that are due, it must use what assets it does have to pay back as much as possible to the liability-funders before it pays anything to the equity-funders. Only then can it distribute any assets to the owners. On winding up a company, if there's not enough to pay everybody back in full, then lenders must get paid before owners.

This means that from the lenders' point of view, the equity is a safety buffer, protecting them from losses. All the equity of the company must be erased before the lenders start losing out and being paid less than they are owed. The more equity the company has, the more losses it can sustain before the lenders start losing out.

As Lemonade & Laughter stands now, if the company suddenly had $15,000 of its assets stolen so that it had $35,000 total assets left, and it then decided to shut its doors, it would pay back the lenders $30,000 and the owners $5,000.

If the company had $21,000 stolen and $29,000 total assets left, it would pay back the lenders $29,000 and the owners nothing. The lenders would have lost $1,000 out of their $30,000 loan and the owners would have lost their whole $20,000 investment.

Issuing and Pricing of Shares

The following section on issuing and pricing of shares is not critical to your understanding of accounting. It talks about an issue that is more relevant to the owners of a company, rather than to the company itself. It's for your interest and is parallel to the main accounting themes and lessons in this book. The next core lesson is in the following chapter, "Loan Repayment." You can skip there now if you want to.

By talking about "owners," plural, we're assuming that there is more than one shareholder. Collectively, the owners contributed $20,000 for 100 percent of the ownership of the company. The ownership is typically divided into shares, each of which represents a portion of the ownership of the company—hence the term "shareholders." You can think of the ownership as a pizza divided into slices.

In the diagrams below, we assume there are two shareholders of Lemonade & Laughter, Dave and Sally. There are four "issued" shares in the company, shown by the four slices of the pizza. At a public company, you'd usually have thousands or millions of slices. Walmart had 2.85 billion shares outstanding at one recent period end. This number fluctuates because the company frequently issues and buys back stocks.

Shareholding Scenario 1

In the Shareholder Initial Contribution Scenario 1 diagram below, Dave is shown by the light blue and Sally is the dark blue. When they formed the company together, Dave and Sally each paid $5,000 for their shares. Dave bought three shares and Sally one. He contributed $15,000 to the company and she contributed $5,000. All the shares are of the same type and therefore have equal voting power, though companies can have different classes of shares with different attributes, such as more votes per share. Dave can control the company with his shares because he has 75 percent of the shareholder votes. Barring a special agreement otherwise, he can unilaterally select who sits on the board of directors, which controls the company by appointing the CEO.

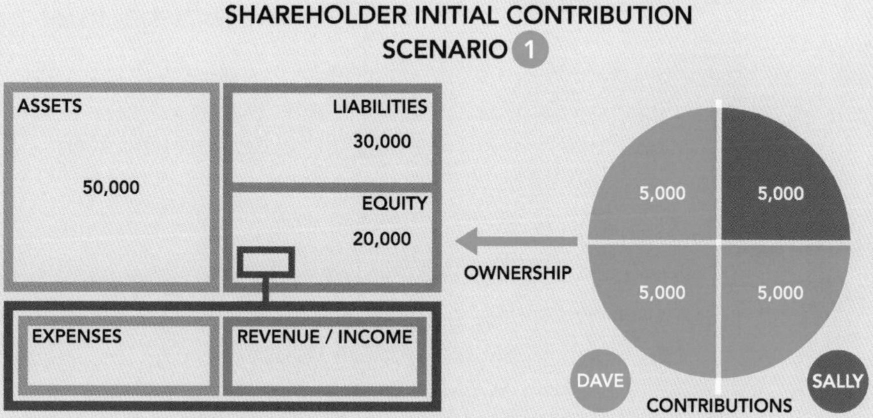

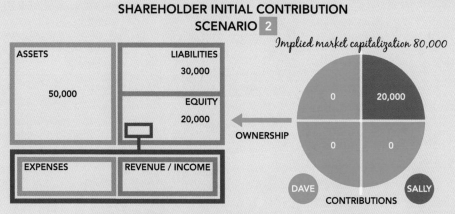

Figure 78. **Equal cash contributions by shareholders.**

Shareholding Scenario 2

In Shareholder Initial Contribution Scenario 2 below, it was Dave's idea to form the company and he did all the paperwork and organization to incorporate it. He invited Sally to invest into the company, offering her 25 percent of the company for an investment of $20,000, which she accepted. Sally knows that she contributed more cash than Dave (i.e., her shares cost more than his), but she believes it's a good investment.

Sally's equity share of the company is $5,000, being a quarter of the $20,000 Contributed Equity account. That means that in terms of book value, she's overpaid, but she believes that the market value of the company is or will be higher. She thinks that her 25 percent of the company will be worth more than the $20,000 she paid for it. In fact, she thinks the total market value of the company will be more than $80,000. It will have to be for her quarter to be worth more than $20,000.

Book value is what the balance sheet says the company owes the shareholders. It's an internal measure.

Market value is what the owners could sell their shares for. It's an external measure.

Figure 79. **Differing cash contributions by shareholders.**

Book Value vs. Market Value

In Share Price Scenario 1 below, the book value of the company is the same as the market value of the company—both are $20,000. The Contributed Equity account is $20,000 because that's how much cash was contributed by Dave and Sally. With no profits yet to boost the Total Equity, the Net Book Value of the company is $20,000. Net Book Value is another way of saying Total Equity.

Book Value and Market Value are the same

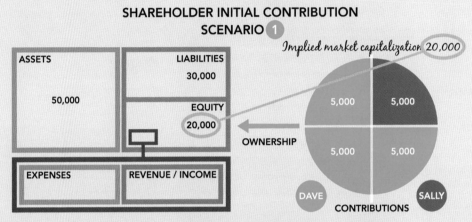

Figure 80. Market value and book value of the business are the same.

The total value of the "blue pizza," known as the *market capitalization* of the company, is also $20,000. This is because there are four shares and each is valued at $5,000, giving a total "market cap" of $20,000. For such a small company as our Lemonade & Laughter example (and for companies not listed on a public stock exchange), determining the share price is a very subjective exercise. With no active market in the shares, we don't know at what price buyers and sellers would exchange their shares.

Different book value than market value

In Share Price Scenario 2 below, the share price is assumed to have increased to $20,000 per share based on Sally buying in at that price. The market value of the company is therefore $80,000. Dave has three shares representing $60,000 of that total market value, and Sally has one share worth $20,000.

Note that when the company increased in value to $80,000 from the initial "launch value" of $20,000, there was no accounting effect within the company. The changes within the blue ownership pie don't affect the accounting within the company, as shown by the BaSIS Framework.

In Dave's and Sally's own accounts, they might revalue their investment assets, but that's another story. Think of the kaleidoscope of butterflies. We're concerned with the company's balance sheet, not the shareholders' balance sheets.

The only changes recorded by our company have happened not within the accounting system, but in the company's Shareholder Register. This register is separate from the accounting ledgers; it is used for the company to track who owns what shares. This can be a big job for a public company with constant share turnover. Large public companies often outsource the job to a share registry that works in conjunction with stock exchanges.

Stock price

The management of a public company will keenly track the stock price. It gives them an indication of what the market thinks of the company's performance and prospects. If the share price is very high, the company might consider issuing new shares, which would bring a set amount of money into the company with less dilution of existing shareholders than a lower share price would have required. If the share price is very low, the company might buy shares back from the existing shareholders and then cancel them. This reduces the book value of the company, but it also concentrates the ownership in the hands of the remaining shareholders. With less total shares outstanding, each individual remaining shareholder gets to enjoy ownership of a bigger proportion of the company.

Book Value and Market Value Are Different

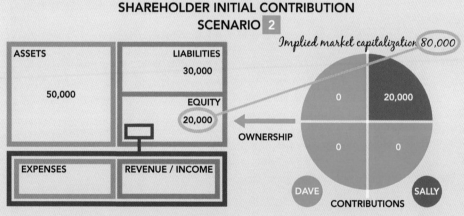

Figure 81. **Market capitalization based on 25 percent share sale.**

3. LOAN REPAYMENT

Classic Transaction Three
Including the Mechanics of Increases and Decreases

In the third of the classic transactions, the business decides to pay back some of its $30,000 loan. In reality, you might say "But we've just borrowed it, why repay it now?!" Point taken. Whatever the case, for learning purposes, there's a great new lesson for us in this repayment.

Classic Transaction 3—January 4

The company repays $5,000 of the loan with cash.

To record this, as always, let's ask the standard "two impact" questions: where (which of the five elements) and how (increase or decrease)?

Money Out

In Wealthvox introductory finance workshops on campuses and in businesses, we often see people reaching to record an expense at this point. They instinctively think: because money's gone out to pay down the loan, there must have been an expense.

Wrong. Money going out does not mean an expense has been incurred. No value has been sacrificed. That becomes clear when we think about which of the five elements have been impacted by this event.

We know that $5,000 cash went out to repay the lender. So, the Assets (cash) must be impacted, and we also know we've paid down the loan. So, where we previously owed the lender $30,000, we now owe them $25,000, which means the Liabilities (loan) must also have been impacted. Both elements have decreased.

And there you have it. Those are the only two buckets affected. It is possible to impact more than two buckets with one transaction, but that's not what happens here. There are just two buckets impacted, and neither is an expense. We have less assets, and less liabilities, so no value has been sacrificed. The equity, revenue, and expense elements are unaffected.

The buckets that are impacted are the same as those that were impacted by Transaction 1, shown below circled in blue.

BaSIS Framework (1): Loan Repayment

The two buckets impacted by the loan repayment are shown on the BaSIS Framework.

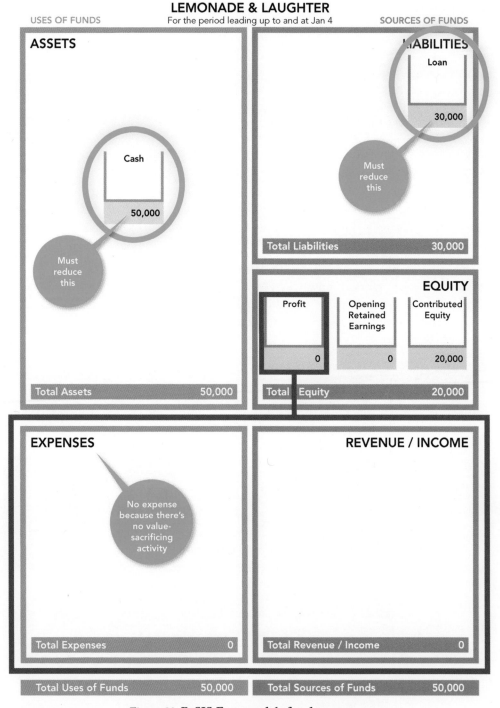

Figure 82. BaSIS Framework before loan repayment.

The difference, however, between this transaction and Transaction 1 is that now the totals of the buckets are decreasing instead of increasing.

The Logic of Increasing and Decreasing Account Balances

The next question you need to ask is: how are we going to make the $50,000 cash account and the $30,000 loan account decrease? You might say that instead of putting tickets into the bucket as we have done until now, we should take them out. There are two problems with that: firstly, we didn't put a $5,000 ticket in that we could now remove. And secondly, we'd destroy historical information (audit trail) if we removed tickets.

OK then, so let's add a negative, you say. That's doable. Last time we added a green ticket to the cash account with "$30,000" on it. That made the bucket increase by $30,000. Now let's alter the green ticket with "-$5,000" on it. Yes, that arithmetic approach would work. It would reduce the balance of the bucket to $45,000 because $50,000 plus negative-five thousand gives $45,000.

But there's a much easier and more elegant way that accountants use.

Let's use the color of the tickets as an indicator.

Where previously we put a **green** ticket into the **green** cash bucket to indicate an increase (account becomes "more green"), now let's put an **orange** ticket into the **green** bucket. And because we've put the opposite color into the bucket, that will have the effect of reducing the total of the bucket rather than increasing it ("less green").

We'll do the same for the loan account. Where we previously dropped an orange ticket into the orange Loan bucket to increase it, now we'll drop a green $5,000 ticket into it, which will reduce it by $5,000.

The green and orange effects are recorded in the accounting journal like this:

	Green Effect	Orange Effect
	Loan	Cash
January 4 Business repays part of loan		
	5,000	5,000

Note how the word Cash is now written on the **orange** ticket that's headed to the Cash bucket. Contrast that with Transaction 1, where the word Cash was written on the green ticket. Similarly, Loan is now written on the **green** ticket because that's the bucket the ticket's headed to, whereas before, the word was written on the orange ticket.

On the BaSIS Framework in *Figure 83*, we can see the two buckets with a contrasting (opposite color) ticket in each.

The balance of the cash account has decreased to $45,000, and the balance of the loan account has decreased to $25,000.

BaSIS Framework (2): Loan Repayment

Notice the colored tickets posting into the buckets on the BaSIS Framework in *Figure 83*. The business now has $45,000 of cash, which is financed through $25,000 of loan obligation and $20,000 of equity obligation.

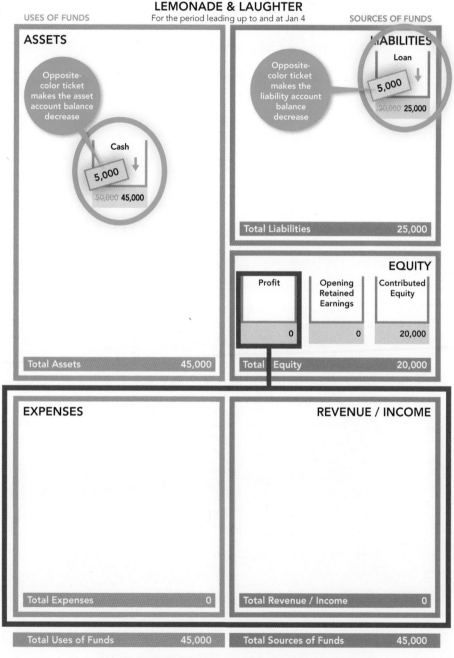

Figure 83. BaSIS Framework showing loan repayment.

De-Leveraging

The business has been de-leveraged because a lesser proportion of the assets at 56 percent (25,000 ÷ 45,000 × 100) is now financed by debt, down from 60 percent (30,000 ÷ 50,000 × 100).

SAME UP. OPPOSITE DOWN.

Recapping on the Mechanics of Movement

Green tickets can have one of two impacts upon a bucket: they can increase it or decrease it.

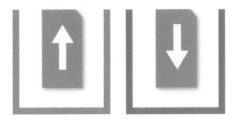

Figure 84. **Logic of movement: Greening a green account up, greening an orange account down.**

When the ticket is the same color as the bucket, the impact is to increase the net balance.

When the ticket is the opposite color to the bucket, the impact is to decrease the net balance.

Ticket and bucket the same color:

Ticket and bucket different color:

Relational

Notice that the color of the ticket on its own doesn't determine the increase or decrease impact of the ticket. The impact depends upon the relationship between the color of the ticket and the color of the bucket. Same causes an increase. Opposite causes a decrease.

This logic applies to both green and orange tickets. Orange tickets increase orange buckets and decrease green buckets.

You can't say that a ticket on its own means increase or decrease. Tickets on their own don't mean anything.

Language of Effects & Impacts

The impact of the tickets depends upon the account to which they are posted. If they go into a same-colored bucket, they cause an increase. And if they go into an opposite-colored bucket they cause a decrease.

In classes or workshops, we ask the group "What does a green ticket mean?" and almost always someone will say "Increase," which is incorrect. Now you know that the color of the ticket (green or orange) only acquires meaning when it is contextualized by the color of the destination account. Then it has meaning.

When expressing these concepts, we generally use the word "effect" to describe the color of a ticket. So, there are green effects and orange effects. When the ticket is posted, we talk about impacts. There are increasing impacts and decreasing impacts. You only know what an impact will be when you know the color of both the ticket and the bucket.

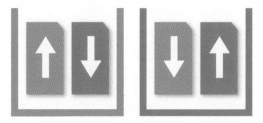

Figure 85. **The logic of movement.**

Debits & Credits

What we're talking about here is debits and credits. The Color Accounting Learning System takes the traditional concepts of *debit* and *credit* and represents them with color. We aren't changing the underlying concepts at all. We're just representing them in a way that makes them intuitive to grasp. In Chapter 10 we explain how the terms debit and credit are used. For the moment, we'll continue to use color without also referring to debit and credit. If you want to skip ahead to that chapter now and then come back, go ahead.

Financial Statements after Repayment Transaction 3

The balance sheet of the business after the loan repayment is shown below. The speech bubbles highlight key points you should think about.

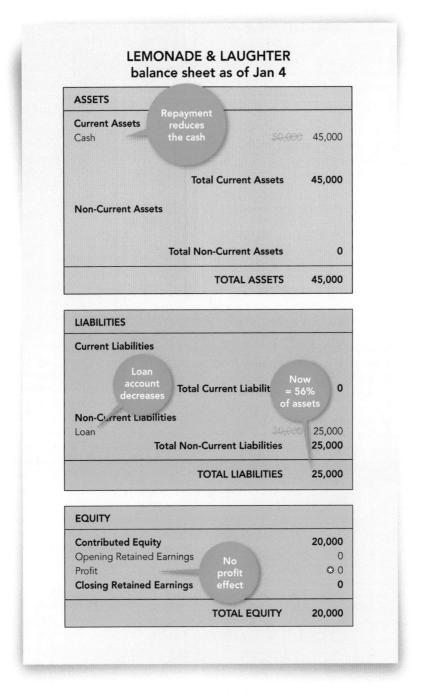

Figure 86. Balance sheet after loan repayment.

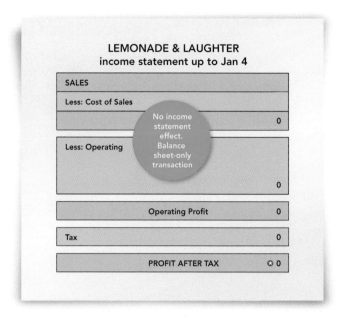

Figure 87. **Income statement after loan repayment.**

The business now has less cash, down from $50,000 to $45,000. The loan has decreased by the same amount. The obligation to the owner remains unchanged at $20,000, also known as the "net book value." From the owners' point of view, they have the same size stake (in dollar terms) in a slightly smaller (judged by asset size) business. The business has de-leveraged because the proportion of debt it is using to fund its assets has decreased. Whereas assets were previously funded 60 percent by debt, now that proportion is 56 percent. Similarly, the assets were previously funded 40 percent by equity, and now that's increased to 44 percent.

4. BUYING AN ASSET WITH CASH

Classic Transaction Four
Includes the Four Balancing Scenarios

In the fourth classic transaction, our business begins acquiring the other assets that it will need to operate. Cash is great, but most businesses need other assets to generate revenue. It now buys equipment with cash and installs it, ready for use.

Classic Transaction 4—January 5

Buy and install $6,000 of equipment. Pay immediately.

Think about where this transaction impacts the BaSIS framework. Before you look at the answer on the following pages, turn back to the previous framework in *Figure 83* and think about how to show the two impacts of the equipment purchase event. Do that now before reading any further.

OK. Assuming you did that, you may have looked at each side of that framework (the orange *sources of funds* side and the green *uses of funds* side) and asked yourself how each side is impacted. In particular, you may have been a bit puzzled about what happened on the orange sources of funds side, and that's because the answer is: nothing.

This transaction doesn't impact the Sources of Funds side of the BaSIS Framework at all. Both impacts are on the green Uses of Funds side of the framework.

Many people think (and too many books say) that you must have an entry on each side, and that's wrong. You can have two impacts on one side. You must have an entry on each side of the journal, which is to say: you have to have a green ticket and an orange ticket of equivalent value in each transaction. You can put those tickets anywhere on the framework. You don't have to put one on the orange side and one on the green side. You can put both on one side. People confuse the journal and the ledger/framework and speak imprecisely when they think you must have one on each side.

> You don't have to have a ticket on each side of the BaSIS Framework.
> You must always have both a green ticket and an orange ticket.
> You can place them anywhere on the framework and it will stay in balance.

In this transaction where we are buying an asset with cash, both impacts are going to be on assets (cash and equipment) on the green "uses of funds" side of the framework.

By buying this equipment for cash, what our business has done is to swap one asset (cash) for another asset (equipment). The assets simultaneously increase and decrease with no net change in the total amount.

No Expense

Because only assets are impacted, we can also see that no expense has been incurred. Remember, cash going out isn't what makes an expense. An expense is an activity that consumes value, and no value has been consumed here. Value has been swapped from one form to another, but not consumed. We started with six thousand of value and we ended with six thousand of value, albeit in another form. We have as much value after the transaction as we had beforehand. The total assets of the business remain at $45,000.

So, in answer to our two habitual questions: "Which elements?" and "Increasing or decreasing?," we see that the two impacts are: Assets (cash, decrease) and Assets (equipment, increase).

The two effects to reflect the impacts on the buckets are recorded in the accounting journal like this:

	Green Effect	Orange Effect
January 5	Equipment	Cash
Buy equipment with cash		
	6,000	6,000

BaSIS Framework: Buying Equipment with Cash

In *Figure 88*, see how the Equipment account increases from zero to $6,000 when we put the green ticket into the green bucket. Cash decreases from $45,000 to $39,000 when we put the orange ticket into the green bucket.

The BaSIS Framework still shows total assets of $45,000, financed by a loan and issued capital.

You'll notice that both impacted buckets are on the same side of the framework. And you should immediately ask yourself: "Does the balance sheet still balance?"

The rule of double-entry accounting is: you always need to have a green effect (ticket) and orange effect (ticket), but you can put those tickets into buckets anywhere on the framework, which will remain in balance.

The balance sheet equation (Assets = Liabilities + Equity) will remain in balance regardless of which side you post the effects to. The impacts of the effects will always cancel each other out to keep the equation in balance. This will apply to the full five-part expanded accounting equation too: Assets + Expenses = Liabilities + Opening Equity + Income/Revenue - Expenses.

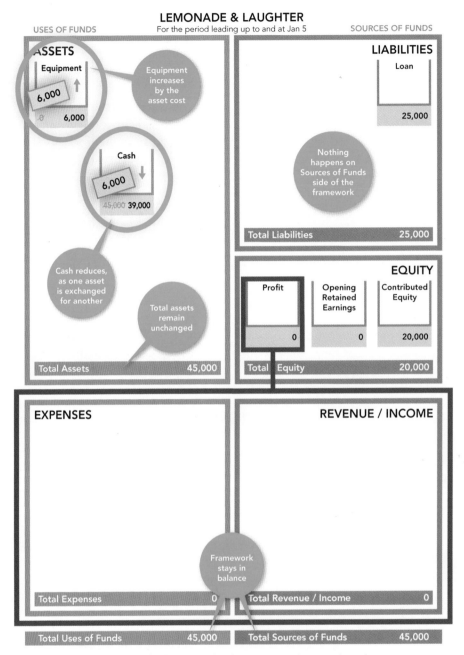

LEMONADE & LAUGHTER

For the period leading up to and at Jan 5

USES OF FUNDS

SOURCES OF FUNDS

ASSETS

Equipment

6,000

0   6,000

Equipment increases by the asset cost

Cash

6,000

45,000 39,000

Cash reduces, as one asset is exchanged for another

Total assets remain unchanged

Total Assets   45,000

LIABILITIES

Loan

25,000

Nothing happens on Sources of Funds side of the framework

Total Liabilities   25,000

EQUITY

Profit

0

Opening Retained Earnings

0

Contributed Equity

20,000

Total Equity   20,000

EXPENSES

REVENUE / INCOME

Framework stays in balance

Total Expenses   0

Total Revenue / Income   0

Total Uses of Funds   45,000

Total Sources of Funds   45,000

Figure 88. **BaSIS Framework after asset purchase with cash.**

Balancing Scenarios

There are four balancing scenarios for the balance sheet/BaSIS Framework/general ledger: both sides increase, both sides decrease, the left uses-of-funds side increases and decreases with no ultimate change, or the right sources-of-funds side decreases and increases with no ultimate change.

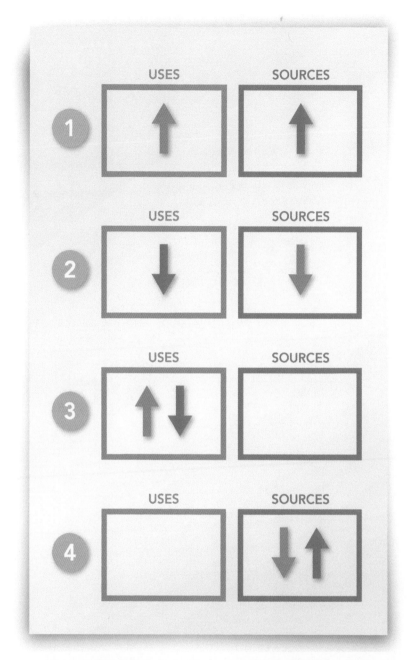

Figure 89. **The four balancing scenarios of the BaSIS Framework.**

The classic fifteen transactions cover all these four situations. So far, we've seen #1, #2, and #3. Will you spot #4?

Financial Statements after Cash Purchase Transaction 4

After the purchase of the equipment, the balance sheet and income statement of Lemonade & Laughter look like this:

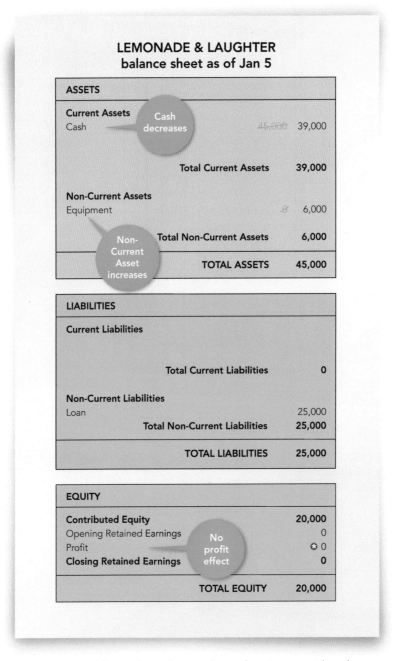

Figure 90. Balance sheet after purchase of equipment with cash.

Reminder: non-current assets are those that will remain in use for longer than twelve months.

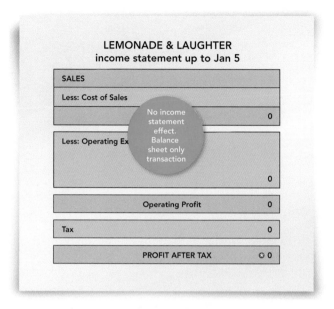

Figure 91. **Income statement after equipment purchase.**

The total assets of the business totaling $46,000 are divided into $39,000 of current assets, which are "liquid assets" expected to be used or consumed within twelve months. The remaining $6,000 assets are classified as non-current because they will last for longer than twelve months. There is no income statement impact of buying the equipment.

5. BUYING AN ASSET ON CREDIT

Classic Transaction Five

In this fifth transaction, Lemonade & Laughter buys inventory but does not pay for it immediately. It will pay cash for the goods at a later date.

Classic Transaction 5—January 21

Buy $10,000 of products to sell—put onto shelf. Supplier ZZZ gives us thirty days to pay.

Lemonade & Laughter's supplier sells the company goods and agrees to be paid up to thirty days later. ZZZ Suppliers has "provided credit" to L&L, who in turn will assume an obligation to ZZZ.

Many businesses sell their services or goods on a "credit sale" basis. This means that the customer can pay for the goods or service later, owing the company until they pay.

The important point to note is that a purchase transaction has taken place from the buyer's point of view, even though payment has not been made. And equally, from the seller's point of view—which isn't our concern here—a sale has taken place even though they haven't received payment.

So how do we account for this purchase by Lemonade & Laughter?

Habitual Questions

Let's ask ourselves our two habitual questions: Which two elements? And for each: Increasing or decreasing?

Lemonade & Laughter acquired Assets (inventory), so that will be one of the impacts. Because it didn't yet pay for the inventory, we know that L&L therefore has an obligation to pay their supplier. So, the other impact will represent that owing. L&L therefore acquired two things, each of which will be represented by a bucket on the framework: inventory and an obligation.

The inventory is an asset because it's valuable. This is important to understand. You may be tempted to think that the purchase of inventory was an expense. In this case, the temptation is not because cash has been paid out (it hasn't), but perhaps because of the sense that inventory is for giving away—unlike equipment, which is for keeping. Yes, it's true that the lifespan for the inventory will be much shorter than that of the equipment—but nevertheless, while the business has the inventory, it's considered valuable. No value was sacrificed when L&L acquired the inventory. Later, the value will be sacrificed when the inventory is handed over to a customer. We'll get to that sacrificing activity in the next classic transaction when we have a *cost of sale* event.

For the second impact, the obligation to pay later is called an account payable, trade payable, or trade creditor. The bucket represents a liability and will appear on the source-of-funds section of the BaSIS Framework.

Comparing this transaction to the loan in Transaction 1, it's as if the supplier is lending money to Lemonade & Laughter to finance L&L's assets. Of course, unlike that transaction, the supplier isn't providing cash—they're providing goods. This accounts payable account is part of what is called "working capital."

To show both buckets increasing, the two effects are recorded in the accounting journal like this:

	Green Effect	Orange Effect
January 21 Buy inventory on credit from ZZZ Suppliers	Inventory 10,000	Accounts Payable 10,000

BaSIS Framework: Buying Inventory on Credit

See how in *Figure 92*, Inventory increases from zero to $10,000 because we put the green ticket into the new green inventory bucket on the BaSIS Framework. Accounts Payable increases because we put the orange $10,000 ticket into the orange liability bucket.

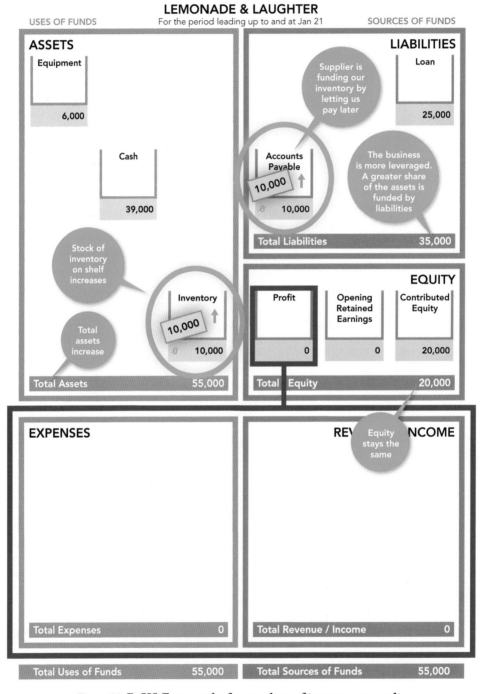

Figure 92. **BaSIS Framework after purchase of inventory on credit.**

Financial Statements after Credit Purchase Transaction 5

After the purchase of inventory on credit, the balance sheet of Lemonade & Laughter looks like this:

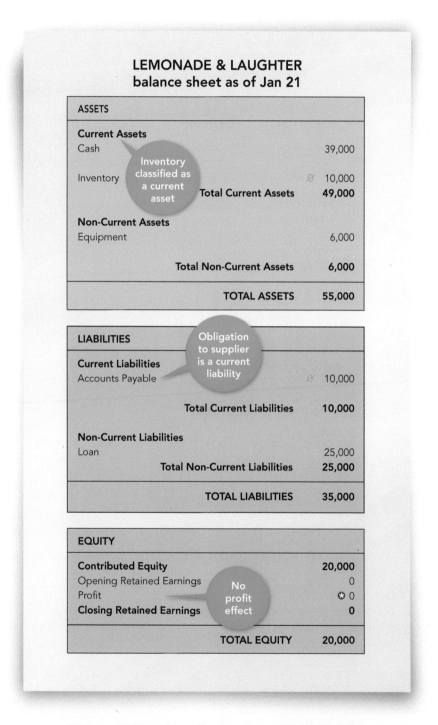

Figure 93. **Balance sheet after inventory purchase on credit.**

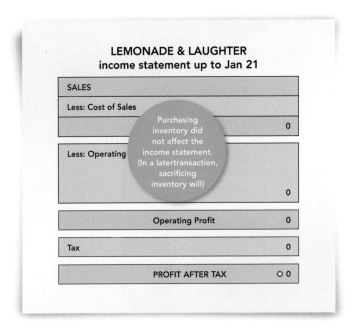

LEMONADE & LAUGHTER
income statement up to Jan 21

SALES	
Less: Cost of Sales	
	0
Less: Operating	
	0
Operating Profit	0
Tax	0
PROFIT AFTER TAX	○ 0

Purchasing inventory did not affect the income statement. (In a latertransaction, sacrificing inventory will)

Figure 94. **Income statement after inventory purchase.**

The business now has assets worth $55,000 in total. It now has three types of assets, those being cash, inventory, and equipment. The assets are funded 64 percent with debt (35,000 ÷ 55,000 × 100) and 36 percent with equity.

Discussion: Buying on Credit

Credit Terms

If you can pay for something later, why wouldn't you? Businesses hold onto their precious cash by delaying payment for as long as possible. Some vendors offer a discount for early payment, in which case it might be worth paying early to get the discount. Otherwise, it makes sense to use the credit terms offered by the supplier.

Large businesses use their clout to negotiate long credit terms so that they can hold onto their cash for as long as possible. Because a large company like Amazon or Walmart has immense buying power and vendors want to sell to it so badly, the vendors agree to allow Walmart to pay for purchases after one, two, or even three months. Then, because Walmart has such high sales volumes, it very quickly sells the inventory it has bought on credit. The company often sells goods to its customers before it has paid the supplier for those same goods. By selling fast and paying slow, Walmart generates an enormous amount of free cash.

Think about something as prosaic as toilet paper. Walmart sells a lot of it. When the company buys a delivery of paper, it likely sells it within a few days. This is called "inventory turnover." It takes Walmart about three days to receive, sell, and restock its shelves with toilet paper. It repeats this cycle 120 times a year. That is: 365 days ÷ 3 days = about 120 inventory replacement cycles.

If Walmart pays their paper supplier on ninety-day terms, then Walmart will be sitting with cash from eighty-seven days' worth of toilet paper sales before it has to pay for the first delivery. That is: ninety days less the three days it took to sell the paper. Walmart has over 5,000 stores in the US. Let's assume that each store sells about $5 worth of toilet paper to 100 customers each day. The actual figure is probably much more. That means Walmart is selling over $2.5M worth of toilet paper each day. If it hangs onto the cash from those sales for eighty-seven days, that's over $200 million of cash it gets to hold onto, interest free. Just from toilet paper!

Working capital is a term used to describe how much funding a company needs to cover its inventory and accounts receivable. It can be calculated as current assets minus current liabilities. Thinking in terms of sources of funds and uses of funds as shown on the BaSIS Framework, acquiring inventory and accounts receivable is a use of funds at Walmart. Owing suppliers in the form of accounts payable is a source of funds. Walmart has negative working capital. In recent years, its sources of funds from current liabilities have exceeded its current assets, such as inventory, by many billions of dollars. That means billions of dollars of free cash that it can invest in buildings or earn interest on by depositing the money in a bank.

The term "credit" comes from the Latin *credo*, which means "believe" or "trust." ZZZ Suppliers is trusting that Lemonade & Laughter will pay them for the inventory they've provided.

The term "invoice" comes from the Latin words *in* and *vox*, meaning "voice" or "call." Invoices call for payment. By invoicing Lemonade & Laughter, ZZZ Suppliers is announcing its call for (delayed) payment from L&L.

Not all businesses make credit sales (also known as "selling on account"). Stores like Walmart require immediate payment from the customer.

Giving credit and managing customer accounts has advantages and disadvantages. The advantages are that for some businesses, payment at the time of sale and delivery is just not practical. The person delivering the goods might not be the right person to receive payment. If a construction supplies company delivers a load of timber to a client, it probably isn't a good idea to ask the driver to collect payment for the load. And the delivery site is probably a long way from where the customer's checkbook is kept. Selling on credit allows for separation of duties between delivery, invoicing, payment receipt, etc.

Even better is getting the customer to pay *before* delivery.

Giving credit can attract extra business. Some customers will patronize a business in part because they allow delayed payment. Customers may be short of cash themselves and appreciate being able to receive goods while only having to stump up the cash later. If the goods are for resale, the customer (for example, a store) might even be able to on-sell the goods before paying the supplier (perhaps a wholesaler) for the goods, like in our Walmart example above.

But there are many disadvantages to selling on credit. It's time consuming and expensive to prepare an invoice for the client, send it to them, chase them for payment, verify and bank the payment when it's received, match the bank deposit to the correct sale, follow up on errors, and so on. Not to mention that waiting weeks or months for the money to come in starves the company of cash. While it's waiting for the payment from customers, the company has to find other sources of cash to continue to operate the business, pay for more inventory, and pay bills that won't wait, like salaries and rent, debt servicing, taxation, and more.

Further Discussion: Purchase of Inventory

Inventory

Inventory is an asset that is held with the intention of reselling it or using it in a manufacturing process for later sale. It's sometimes called "stock," and counting how much a business has on hand is called a "stocktake." Inventory is always a current asset because the expectation is that it will be sold within twelve months or within the operating cycle of the business. Certain businesses, like whisky distillers or hardwood flooring companies, keep their product for years before selling it. Even in this situation, their inventory will still be shown as a current asset on their balance sheets even though the normal operating cycle of such businesses is longer than twelve months. Inventory is a critical current asset for many businesses.

Even businesses that have little physical inventory, like a consulting firm, are likely to have an equivalent type of account called "work-in-progress," where time charged to clients by staff accumulates and is stored as an asset until it is billed. If it isn't billed quickly and accurately, it can also lose value, just like a physical asset.

Managing inventory is one of the most important tasks of any retail or manufacturing business manager. It must be stored, protected from getting too old, secured from theft and damage, insured, transported to the right location/store/warehouse, and so on. A particularly important task is making sure that the level of inventory on hand is appropriate. A supermarket manager needs to keep the shelves stocked with food and "FMCG," Fast-Moving Consumer Goods in the storekeepers' jargon. A car factory manager needs to keep their shelves stocked with parts, not for sale to customers but for use in assembling complete vehicles, which are themselves inventory.

Run out of inventory and the business grinds to a very sudden stop. Have too little inventory and you won't offer your customers enough choice. Have too much inventory and it will rot or expire or go out of style or simply tie up too much cash by sitting on the shelf too long.

Tying up too much cash in inventory is part of the conversation about working capital that we touched on in the discussion of credit above. To keep cash flowing, the idea is to have as little inventory as possible without constraining the business's rate of sales. Rather than holding 100 pots of yogurt and selling and restocking them every ten times for a total of 1,000 yogurt sales, it is better to hold twenty pots of yogurt and sell and restock them every fifty times, which also sells for a total of 1,000 pot sales. You'll have less cash tied up in the twenty pots of yogurt on the shelf than you'd have in the 100 pots on the shelf. Of course, you'll need to arrange a lot more yogurt deliveries and you'll have a higher risk of running out. But with modern electronics, automated inventory, and reordering systems, lean inventory management is more feasible. Companies use what's called "just in time" delivery to keep their shelves stocked up. Walmart has gotten just-in-time inventory management down to a fine art. At their big distribution hubs, they give suppliers "delivery windows" of just a few minutes to arrive and deliver the yogurt, toothpaste, and what have you. If their trucks are late and not ready to pull up the loading dock at the right moment, the supplier gets penalized.

A Little Bit of Fat

On the other hand, when Iceland had a volcanic eruption that grounded many aircraft across Europe for days, some car factories had to stop their production lines. Their tight "lean production" schedules didn't have a massive transport delay factored into their planning. Even a missing floor mat or door handle can hold up the delivery of cars to the sales yard and dealerships. That volcano experience led car companies to be more cautious and increase the amount of parts inventory they keep on hand.

High Risk

Inventory is a high-risk item on the balance sheet. It's high-risk for the company, which must manage it carefully. Inventory is also a high-risk area for the reader of financial statements: if the figures in a set of financial statements don't fairly reflect the true reality of the position of a company, it's often in the area of inventory where the numbers are "off," which can have significant impact on the profit result.

Balance of Power

And of course, if you are a powerful retailer, you might find it easy to convince your suppliers to:

1) Send their staff to unload the delivery truck and stock the shelves in your stores with their inventory items (saves your staff from doing it).
2) Hold their inventory on your shelves on consignment. Then you only buy it at the moment the customer buys it from you. Of course, you would still want credit terms to make the payment to the supplier—in say, forty-five to ninety days.
3) Convince your supplier to set up a mini-store/display inside your store. (1) and (2) above apply, plus the sales team are the supplier's employees, they pay for their own shop fitting and marketing and you can charge the supplier rent for their mini-store and take a commission on their sales.

Inventory is high risk because it:

- is disposed of and replaced so often,
- changes value while on-hand through spoilage or changes in fashion/demand/market price,
- can change purchase price frequently,
- can change sales price frequently, and
- is mobile and gets moved around between warehouses and stores, which means it's easy to lose track of or double-count, and it can be stolen.

6. (A) REVENUE: SALE TO CUSTOMER FOR CASH

Classic Transaction Six (a)

In this sixth transaction, the business makes its first sale. It sells some inventory to a customer and gets paid cash immediately for that sale. But notice that this transaction is numbered (a). That's because there's a part (b) coming too. It's a two-part transaction with four effects. In part (a), we won't account for the inventory—that'll happen in the next part. We first account for the sale activity and the asset generated: in this case, cash.

Classic Transaction 6(a)—January 30

Lemonade & Laughter's first sale, to Customer A, who pays cash on the spot. $1,000 cash proceeds banked.

When asking ourselves what happened in this transaction, it's tempting to think that we got cash and we gave away inventory. The business did indeed get $1,000 of cash, but it didn't give away $1,000 of inventory. If it had, it wouldn't be very good business. There'd be no profit in the transaction. There's no sense in giving away $1,000 to gain $1,000. The essence of retail is to sacrifice something of lesser value to receive in return something of greater value.

Here's what happened. A customer walked into the store, picked up some inventory, and brought it to the cash register. They ask you: "How much is this?" You reply: "That will be $1,000, thank you!" The customer says "Fine. I'll take it." Ask yourself: have we earned the right to be paid? The answer is yes—we have earned the right to be paid an asset, and, we were actually paid. An agreement has been reached that they will buy your goods and you have "closed the sale." The final step is that the customer leaves the store with what was your inventory under their arm. That will also need to be recorded (part b).

The two impacts of this transaction are an increase in cash of $1,000, and an increase in sale activity that caused the cash to come in. Recall in Chapter 9 when we discovered Value-Generating Activity, or VGA. That's what has happened here. The business did a value-generating activity—the sales activity—and this caused $1,000 of cash to flow into the business.

So, to our question: Which two impacts? The answers are Assets (Cash) and the activity that generated that cash: Revenue/Income (Sales).

To our question: "Increasing or decreasing," we know that that we have more cash, so that bucket increases. We have more value-generating activity, so the Sales bucket increases too.

Using the color logic to increase both buckets, we put a green ticket into the green Cash bucket to make it increase. And we must put an orange ticket into the orange Sales bucket to make it increase.

	Green Ticket	Orange Ticket
January 30	Cash	Sales
Cash sale to Customer A.		
	1,000	1,000

BaSIS Framework: Cash Sale

In *Figure 95* below, you can see that the Cash account increases because we put a $1,000 green ticket into that same-colored account. The Sales account increases because we put a $1,000 orange ticket into that matching-colored bucket.

Think carefully about each of the blue bubbles in *Figure 95*.

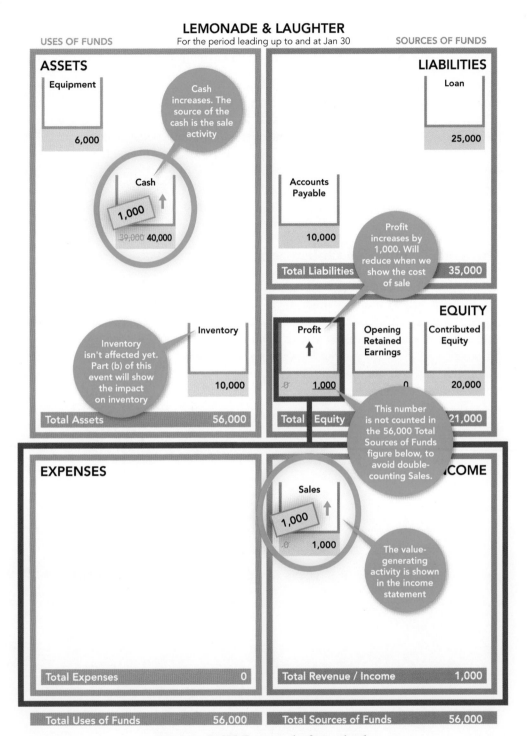

Figure 95. BaSIS Framework after cash sale.

This is the first of our classic transactions that impacts the income statement. The first five transactions only impacted the balance sheet. To be sure, this transaction also impacts the balance sheet in two places, but it does so via the income statement for the revenue component.

Notice the impacts on the BaSIS Framework: duality is maintained as the Cash account increases by $1,000, and the Sales account increases by $1,000. However, the Profit account in the Equity section of the framework increases by $1,000 too. It is important to remember that the green ticket went into the green cash bucket and the orange ticket went into the orange sales bucket. No ticket was placed into the profit bucket. The Profit account increased without a ticket because the balance of the Profit account is always equal to the total Revenue/Income less total Expenses. At this point, this equates to $1,000 less $0 = $1,000. The revenue and profit are the same because we haven't had an expense yet. We also note that the increase in revenue has increased the value of equity. So, do shareholders love revenue? Yes!

First Principles: Value and Obligation

Think about what the framework is telling us in terms of the definitions of the five elements. It's saying we have $1,000 more valuable assets. Remembering that all assets in the accounting entity are obligated to either a lender or an owner, the framework's telling us that the $1,000 of assets just acquired are obligated to the owner. That's what the profit account is telling us. Since profit is part of equity, and equity is the obligation to the owners. The profit is the incremental obligation to the owner for assets that were generated by the business through its activities (variously referred to as sales, income, revenue).

> Profit on the balance sheet is the incremental generated obligation of the company to its shareholders.

6. (B) COST OF SALE EXPENSE

Classic Transaction Six (b)

In order to generate the $1,000 in Transaction 6(a), the business had to make a sacrifice. This Part B reflects that value-sacrificing activity.

Classic Transaction 6(b)—January 30

Used up $250 worth of our product inventory in sale to Customer A.

In order to gain the $1,000 cash that the business generated in Transaction 6(a), the business had to give up some value. It literally handed over to the customer goods (inventory) worth $250 that it had acquired from ZZZ Suppliers in Transaction 5. The giving away of the inventory is a value-sacrificing activity traditionally included in Cost of Sales, or Cost of Goods Sold—often abbreviated as COS or COGS.

Cost of Sales is a category of similar expenses that vary in proportion to the sales revenue they are related to. Inventory sacrifice is a classic example of this in a retail business. The sale event triggers the cost of sale event (the inventory decreasing). Compare that with something like a shop cleaning expense, which happens irrespective of sales and is therefore not a cost of sale.

But could cleaning ever be a Cost of Sale? Yes. The determination is often situation-specific: imagine you have a new car dealership. For every new car sold, you include a free clean and polish. This cleaning expense would be a Cost of Sale.

In the physical world, Cost of Sales takes the form of a customer walking out of the shop with what used to be Lemonade & Laughter's inventory in their bag. The business has given away precious inventory, transferring its right in the goods to the customer. The business doesn't mind doing this, because it received more sought-after cash than the value of the inventory that walked out the shop.

Sometimes inventory walks out the door without anyone paying for it. In other words, part (b) happens without part (a). That's called shoplifting, shrinkage, or simply theft! In essence, shoplifting is the same as a cost of sale: value leaves the business, except that there's no associated value-gain.

Let's ask our habitual questions in order to reflect this transaction on the BaSIS Framework. The first element would be the Expenses (Cost of Sales). The second is the Assets (Inventory).

We have more Cost of Sales, so we put a green ticket into the green account to increase it.

The Inventory account reduces because some was given away, so we put an orange ticket into the green account to decrease it.

	Green Effect	Orange Effect
	COS	Inventory
January 30 Incur Cost of Sale inventory expense	250	250

BaSIS Framework: Sacrificing Inventory

The Framework in *Figure 96* shows the inventory account decreasing because inventory worth $250 is handed over to a customer. The handing-over activity is reflected in the income statement section of the framework as Cost of Sales.

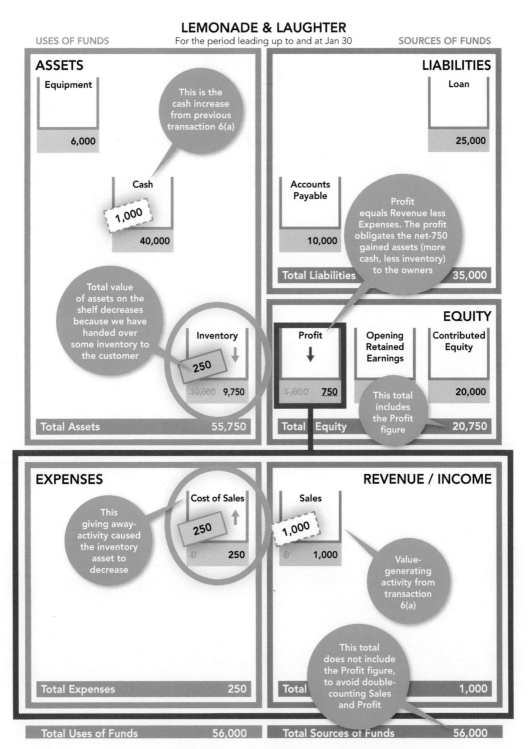

Figure 96. BaSIS Framework showing cost of sale expense.

The bottom two boxes of the BaSIS Framework (the income statement) now have two accounts feeding up to the profit account, which is currently $750.

The $750 profit represents the obligation to the owner for the net value generated by transactions (a) and (b) combined. The business generated assets (cash) worth $1,000 and sacrificed assets (inventory) worth $250, leaving a net-increase in assets of $750. The total assets are now $55,750.

The profit account represents the attribution of the $750 incremental assets to the owners in the form of the increased obligation to them.

Generalized Obligation

To be clear, no specific $750 asset, such as cash or an inventory item, is itself obligated or attributed to the owners. The obligation is a generalized duty to set aside a portion of all the assets to the funder—$750 worth of the overall assets is obligated to the owners. There's no tagging of assets for specific people. Although that can happen: assets can be secured for the benefit of a particular funder. For example, in a secured loan situation, a building purchased with a mortgage loan from a bank can be recorded as specifically obligated to the bank in the event of insolvency of the business. The bank will be able to claim the particular secured building for itself ahead of all other funders.

Financial Statements after Cash Sale and Cost of Sale Transactions 6(a) and 6(b)

The impacts of the sale and cost of sale are shown in the financial statements below. Ponder each blue commentary bubble.

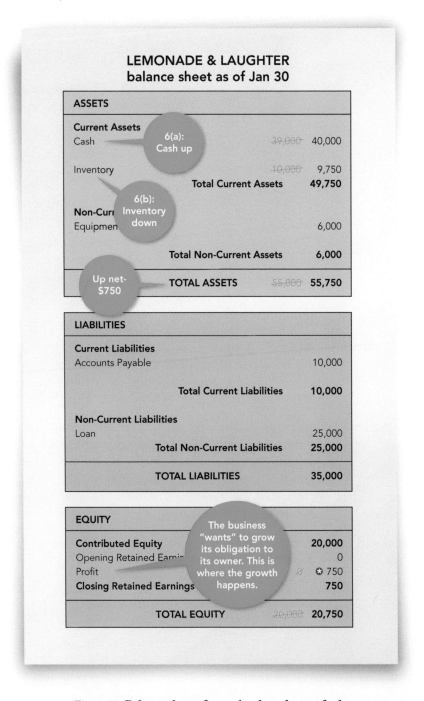

Figure 97. Balance sheet after cash sale and cost of sale.

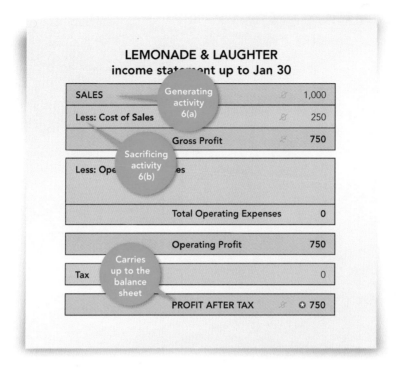

LEMONADE & LAUGHTER
income statement up to Jan 30

SALES — Generating activity 6(a)		1,000
Less: Cost of Sales		250
Gross Profit		750
Less: Ope Sacrificing activity 6(b) es		
Total Operating Expenses		0
Operating Profit		750
Tax — Carries up to the balance sheet		0
PROFIT AFTER TAX		⊙ 750

Figure 98. **Income statement after sale and cost of sale.**

Summary

The net worth of the business to the owner—which is to say, the equity—is now $20,750. $20,000 is obligated to the owners because they put that amount of assets into the business as contributed capital, and another $750 is obligated to the owners as Retained Earnings because the business generated that much in assets on their behalf.

The income statement shows that the business did activities (made the sale by consulting with a customer about their needs and persuading them to buy) that generated value to the tune of $1,000, and in order to generate that value, the business performed activities (and giving up ownership-title to inventory) that sacrificed value amounting to $250. The net result was a net gain of assets worth $750, which are attributed to the owners by the equivalent profit and Retained Earnings account in equity.

Transactions 6(a) and 6(b) are important because they describe the two fundamental financial activities that all businesses do: generating value and sacrificing value. Indeed, that's all that businesses do. We can think of it as a cycle that businesses repeat over and over.

6. (C) THE VALUE CYCLE OF BUSINESS

Accounting as a Foundation for Understanding Business Itself

We're going to pause our series of classic transactions for a moment to further reflect on the nature of business. This is an accounting book, of course. Ultimately, accounting is about business. For our purposes, the word "business" can refer to a for-profit business, a not-for-profit business, or even the business of your own personal affairs. Whatever the type of entity, hopefully it will be run in a business-like manner.

Business is about the management, preservation, use, and growth of an entity's assets. Assets are central to business. This makes sense because assets are the only things that are valuable. Nothing other than assets is valuable.

By now, you are getting familiar with the BaSIS Framework, which describes the financial parts of any business. We've seen that there are five—and only five—fundamental elements in the framework. "There are five boxes," we say, and "there's no sixth box." Assets, liabilities, equity, revenue, and expenses are all that make up a business. Of the five elements, only assets are valuable. None of the liabilities, equity, income, and expenses are ever valuable. Liabilities and equity are obligations, which are the opposite of valuable. Income and expenses are activities—nonphysical occurrences.

Asset Centricity

Because assets are the only element that is valuable, we think of them as being central to any business story. We talk about asset centricity. Extending that within the accounting framework, the other four elements can be thought of in terms of their relationship to assets. Consider what each of the other elements do to assets, referring to the four blue arrows in Figure 99 following:

- Liabilities obligate assets to creditors. It's as if they tag assets, marking them as being for the benefit of those funders. Of course, assets aren't literally tagged, and typically they aren't individually allocated to creditors... they are allocated in aggregate proportionately between creditors and shareholders. Liabilities represent the obligation of the business to hold assets for and return them to creditors.
- Equity is the obligation to hold assets for and return them to the entity's shareholders. Equity obligates assets to equity funders.
- Revenue/Income are activities that generate assets (or decrease liabilities).
- Expenses are activities that consume and deplete assets (or increase liabilities).

These four relationships to assets are shown below in *Figure 99* by the four blue arrows.

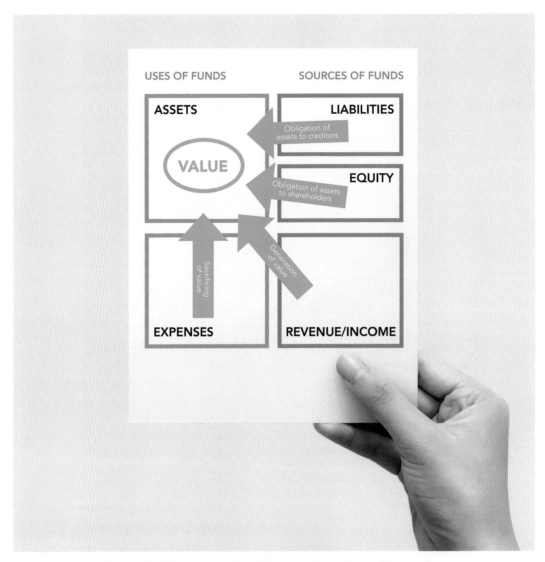

Figure 99. Obligations and activities and their relationship to value.

Accounting Literacy

Financial literacy is widely accepted as one of the underpinnings of business acumen. Business acumen, or business savvy, is the knowledge and understanding to deal with business situations.

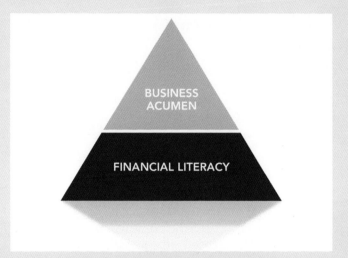

Figure 100. **Financial literacy underpins business acumen.**

Underneath financial literacy, however, is another layer of knowledge and skill that has arguably been insufficiently distinguished in society.

The ability to describe a financial situation using accounting language and concepts is an important skill in its own right. It is distinct from the myriad themes and topics covered by the term "financial literacy", which include interest rates, saving, investing, portfolio theory, tax and retirement planning, inflation, and so on.

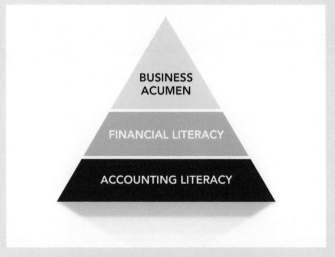

Figure 101. **Accounting literacy underpins financial literacy.**

We at Wealthvox (the publisher of the Color Accounting Learning System) think of accounting literacy as the fourth of the famous so-called "three Rs": Reading, Writing, Arithmetic—and Reckoning. Everyone should be accounting-literate!

> "You have to understand accounting and you have
> to understand the nuances of accounting.
> It's the language of business and it's an imperfect language"
> –Warren Buffett

The Value Cycle—The Very Essence of Business

When you understand the structure, language, and mechanics of the BaSIS Framework, you are accounting-literate. Your understanding of the framework gives you insight into how business in its very essence works. We call the conceptual model of how business works the "Value Cycle of Business." The cycle is the link between accounting and business. It models an answer to the question: What does a business do?

There are just two financial activities that a business undertakes to achieve its mission: it generates value, and it sacrifices value. These two activities form part of a conceptual operating cycle of the business.

Run your finger around the purple cycle in *Figure 102* as you read steps 1-6, starting in equity.

1) **Equity**
   The business sources assets by incurring an obligation to the owners in the form of equity.

2) **Liabilities**
   The business then leverages those assets by acquiring additional assets from lenders, incurring liabilities to those creditors. We lightheartedly say that the business uses "OPM from FF&F": Other people's money, from friends, family, and fools!

3) **Assets**
   The business uses its assets for the singular purpose of generating revenue. Which is to say, generating more assets. A business has assets to get more assets.

4) **Expenses**
   Unfortunately, those assets get used up and the business must sacrifice value as expenses.

5) **Income/Revenue**
   In order for the business to generate value, it must perform income/revenue activities.

6) **Profit**
   If all goes to plan in a for-profit business, more value is generated than is destroyed, which leaves a surplus. This surplus is attributed to the owners. Why? Because they took the risk of putting themselves at the bottom of the capitalization table, which ranks liabilities above equity. The profit is their reward for taking the risk

of being most responsible for losses and for being behind (subordinate to) creditors in the liquidation repayment line.

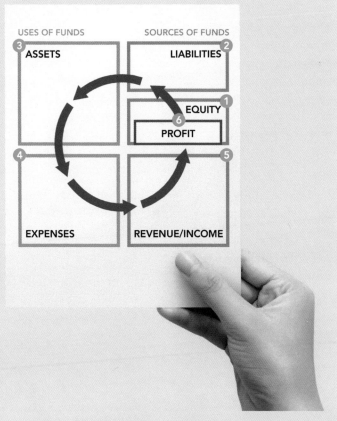

Figure 102. **Value cycle of business.**

The Value Cycle is a conceptual cycle. Of course, nothing actually moves from one box to another on the BaSIS Framework. This might be stating the obvious, but it's best to avoid a possible thinking error. People are tempted to think that, for example, you take assets and move them to liabilities when you're paying off a debt.

We have heard from business owners that thinking of their business in terms of the value cycle reframed the way they see the business and their role within it. It's galvanizing to realize that there are only two things happening in your business: value is being destroyed and value is being generated. As the manager of a business, that's what you're ultimately overseeing: value generation, and value destruction.

There are necessarily many actions—such as acquiring assets, swapping assets, incurring liabilities—that don't show up on the income statement as generation or consumption of value. Such sourcing and "arranging of the furniture" support the intended purpose of ultimately consuming value in order to generate value; that ultimate intention is what the value cycle shows us.

Not-for-Profit Value Cycle

In the US, a not-for-profit (or *nonprofit*—same thing) business that has been incorporated to build housing for the homeless might be legally formed as a 501(c)(3) corporation. This refers to a chapter of the federal tax code that allows for donations to the organization to be tax-deductible by the donors. Not-for-profit businesses exist for a different purpose than for-profit business, and there are a number of differences between the two regarding their finances. Not-for-profit businesses are usually no-shareholder businesses. Instead of shareholders, they have stakeholders who benefit from their work but who don't have the same rights over the business as shareholders have over a for-profit business. Different terminology is often used for the two types of business. For example, where we talk about the equity of a for-profit business, we refer to the net assets of a not-for-profit business. Essentially, they refer to the same thing: the obligation to non-creditors (shareholders and stakeholders.)

While their financial intent is different, not-for-profit organizations still have just the five elements that make up their finances. And they should be run in a businesslike manner, just as any other.

Run your finger around the purple cycle in Figure 103 as you read steps 1-6, starting in Donations & Contributions.

1) **Donations and contributions**
   The organization sources assets through donations or other value-generating activities.

2) **Net assets**
   The assets received are obliged to be used in service to its stakeholders.

3) **Liabilities**
   In the course of its operations, the business will incur obligations to creditors.

4) **Assets**
   The assets sourced through value-generating activities and from creditors must be retained and used in accordance with the declared mission of the organization.

5) **Expenses**
   The mission is achieved by sacrificing resources internally to serve stakeholders.

6) **Surplus or deficit**
   To the extent that the organization sacrifices more value than it generates (through donations and other value-generating activities), it generates a surplus or deficit that increases or reduces its obligation to stakeholders.

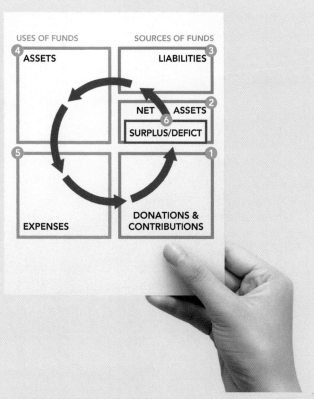

Figure 103. Not-for-profit value cycle.

Budgeting Cycle

The BaSIS Framework can also be used to reflect the budgeting process. Budgeting is when managers plan for the future by arranging for the right combination of business elements to fulfill their intended plans and goals.

The budgeting cycle may read like this:

1) **Profit**
   The business has an ambitious but realistic profit target in mind that it aims to achieve.

2) **Revenue**
   Knowing what profit margins the business is likely to have, the manager knows what level of revenue must be achieved to reach the profit goal.

3) **Expenses**
   That level of value-generating activity will result in a proportionate amount of value consumption determined by the operating margins.

4) **Assets**

That level of activity will require the use of a commensurate amount of assets in the form of inventory, cash, non-current assets, and so on.

5) **Liabilities**

The manager will aim to fund those assets with an appropriate amount of debt.

6) **Equity**

However much is not financed through borrowing must be funded by the shareholders, either in the form of retained earnings or through contributed equity capital.

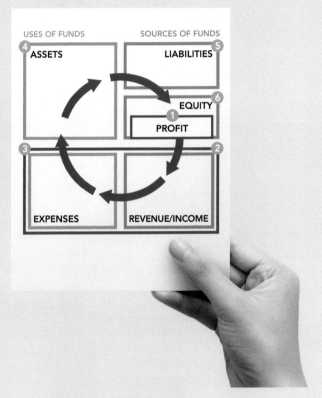

Figure 104. **Budgeting cycle.**

We find that most students get a kick out of discovering the value cycle. It's a reminder of why we have accounting in the first place. It gives greater context, meaning, and purpose to accounting.

7. EXPENSE: INCURRED AND PAID

Classic Transaction Seven

In Transaction Seven, the business incurs an expense and pays for it at the same time as the expense was incurred. There are three possible timing scenarios when it comes to the payment for an expense: you can pay for it before you incur it, when you incur it, and after you incur it.

BEFORE, SAME, AFTER

Imagine the three timing scenarios of paying for an expense in your own life.

Pay Before: Think of paying for a refundable air ticket for a flight you will take next month. You're paying now for an expense you'll incur next month when you fly.

Pay Concurrently: If you buy an ice cream cone, you pay for it at the same time as you receive and eat it. You've probably taken your first lick before you get your change back. Expenses paid for at the same time as receipt are also referred to as *cash expenses*.

Pay After: When you get home, you turn on the lights (incurring an expense by running the lights) but pay for the power later at the end of the month when the utility bill arrives.

We'll look at the accounting for each of the three timing scenarios as we go through the classic transactions.

Classic Transaction 7—February 5

Suppliers or contractors cleaned shop window and we paid them $50 in cash. Window looks great.

The cleaning company provided the business with $50 worth of window-cleaning service. For Lemonade & Laughter, it was a concurrent expense, being the consumption of services provided by the cleaning company. The expense activity causes the business to immediately lose fifty dollars' worth of cash.

Which two elements are impacted?: Expense (Cleaning), and Asset (Cash). And do they increase or decrease? The impact on Cleaning is an increase, and the impact on Cash is a decrease.

To reflect these impacts, we post a green ticket to the green Cleaning account and an orange ticket to the green Cash account.

	Green Effect	Orange Effect
	Cleaning	Cash
February 5 Pay cleaners for cleaning windows		
	50	50

Granularity

We've chosen to call the expense account "Cleaning." We could have called it "Maintenance," which would have been less specific. We also could have called it "SG&A" for "Services, General and Administrative," which is an acronym sometimes used by accountants, and which would have been even less specific. The point here is to remind you that you have choices when you set up your chart of accounts. You can have more numerous, specific, and narrow accounts, or you can have fewer, broader accounts. If there's no reason to track window cleaning separately from other cleaning and from other repairs and maintenance activities, then don't do it. The fewer accounts you must deal with, the better. Recall the discussion on grouping and categorization in Chapter 1 when we first talked about assets.

In our classrooms and workshops, we like to challenge learners at this point by asking "So a clean window is an asset to a business—should this be an asset rather than an expense?" and letting them argue their case. What would you say? The main argument for why this is wrong is that no asset has been purchased or created here. The asset is the window; the transaction is a maintenance or upkeep cost to keep the asset in good condition. We have not added any value to the window itself—but what if we used the $50 to buy laminating film to keep the sun out of the store? Then we have something valuable, even if it is of low value. The distinction between improvement and maintenance can be tricky at times.

BaSIS Framework: Cash Expense

The Framework in *Figure 105* shows cash decreasing, cleaning expense increasing, and profit decreasing. The diagram makes it clear that the expense (shown at the bottom left) is not the same as the reduction in cash (at the top left). The cleaning is the activity that caused the cash to decrease. One is the cause, the other the effect.

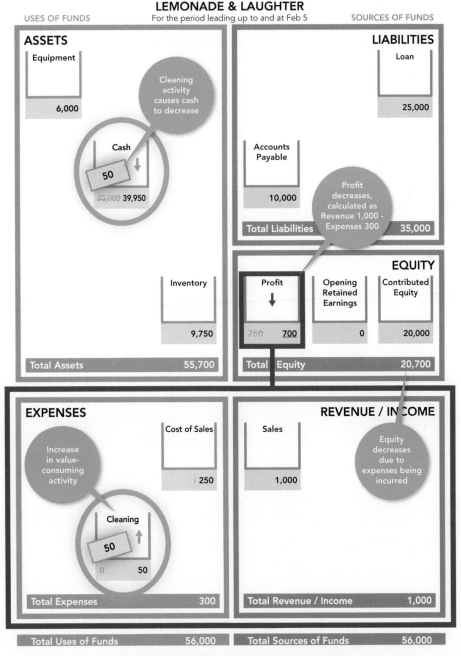

Figure 105. **BaSIS Framework after cash expense.**

Financial Statements after Cash Expense Transaction 7

After incurring the cleaning expense and paying the cleaner, the balance sheet and income statement of Lemonade & Laughter look like this:

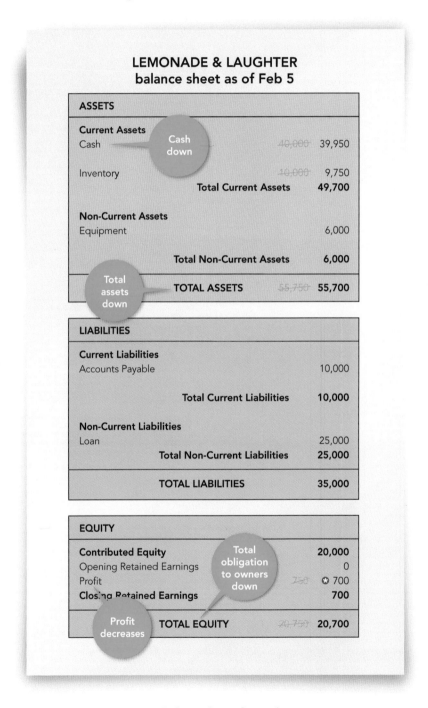

Figure 106. Balance sheet after cash expense.

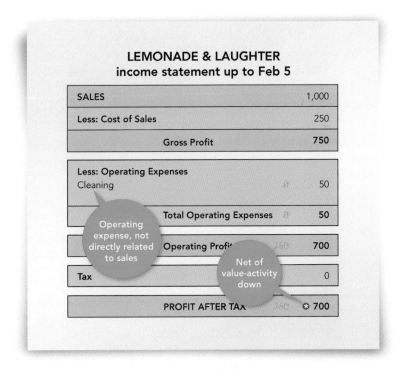

LEMONADE & LAUGHTER
income statement up to Feb 5

SALES	1,000
Less: Cost of Sales	250
Gross Profit	750
Less: Operating Expenses	
Cleaning	50
Total Operating Expenses	50
Operating Profit	700
Tax	0
PROFIT AFTER TAX	700

Figure 107. **Income statement showing changes in operating and final profit.**

The business now has less assets because it gave up $50 of cash. Keeping the accounting equation in balance, the obligation of the business to return the assets to the funders has reduced too.

Let's think about which type of funder is impacted. Is the business less obligated to the creditors or to the owners? It is the owners who must bear the pain of the business losing $50 of cash. The bank manager doesn't suffer a reduction in what they are owed. The bank's claim remains unchanged. So, it is the equity obligation that reduces by fifty dollars, and this reduction happens in the profit account within equity. The profit account decreases from $750 to $700. This reduces overall equity from $20,750 to $20,700. So, do owners love expenses? No!

The details of the reduction of profit are shown on the income statement in *Figure 107*.

Discussion: Profit Margins

Note how in Figure 107 the Gross Profit and final Profit after Tax (net profit) figures are now different. The gross profit is still $750, whereas the final bottom line profit is $700. That's because the $50 cleaning expense is classified as overhead, or an indirect expense, which isn't included in the direct cost of sales expenses.

Income statements cluster expenses into different types of expense. In this case, the expenses are divided into those that vary with each sale, and those that happen independently of sales. Note the architecture of the incomes statement shown with illustrative figures in Figure 108, take particular note of the Cost of Sales Expense of $35 and the subtotal $65 below, as well as the line with Operating Expenses of $20 and the subtotal $45.

Whenever the business makes a sale, it will likely have an associated cost of sale, which means each sale event will have a gross impact associated with that specific event. This profit or loss from the particular sales event is sometimes called a *contribution* or *contribution margin*. That contribution helps cover the expenses below, which don't vary with each sale. The indirect expenses below the gross profit line occur whether or not a sale happens. For example, indirect expenses such as rent happen each month, regardless of whether any sales are made. Indirect expenses often increase in a step manner in relation to sales over the medium and longer terms. The rent remains the same from month to month until the business grows so much that it needs another shop, at which point the rent jumps up and then stays at that new level. The indirect expenses will increase when management decides they need to incur more.

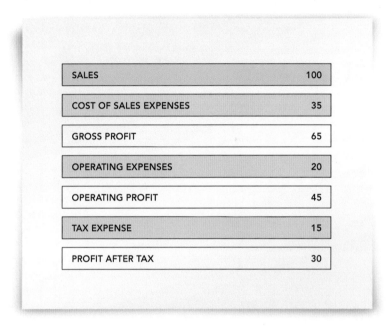

SALES	100
COST OF SALES EXPENSES	35
GROSS PROFIT	65
OPERATING EXPENSES	20
OPERATING PROFIT	45
TAX EXPENSE	15
PROFIT AFTER TAX	30

Figure 108. **Typical architecture of an income statement (illustrative totals only, unrelated to the classic transactions).**

The gross profit amount is an important number to know for a few reasons. If there isn't enough gross profit at the end of the year to cover all the overhead expenses, then the business will make an operating loss. This may not be too much of a concern if we know that the business is young and growing and all that is needed to achieve future operating-profitability is more sales volume. With more individual sales that each earn a gross profit, the sales will eventually accumulate to the point that total gross profit dollars are more than overhead expense dollars, and therefore create an operating profit.

The point at which the business makes enough cumulative gross profit on all the individual sales to cover the overheads of the business is called the "profit breakeven point," or just the breakeven point.

Gross Profit Margin

What managers also track gross is the *gross profit margin*, or GPM. This is the proportion of each sale that generates gross profit. Let's use an example.

The $1,000 sale in Transactions 6(a) and 6(b) resulted in a $750 gross profit after the cost of sale expense of $250. The gross profit margin is therefore $750 \div 1000 \times 100 = 75\%$. The gross profit margin in the illustrative income statement above in Figure 108 is 65 percent. The operating profit margin is 45 percent and the net profit margin is 30 percent.

Whether the 75 percent gross profit margin is good or bad depends upon factors such as the type of goods being sold, the industry average, what competitors achieve, and so on. A business that can maintain high gross profit margins because of its reputation or because of a monopoly profit obtained through a government-granted patent is in an enviable position.

It's challenging to improve a gross profit margin because your competitors are pushing you to lower selling prices and your suppliers are pushing you to increase your cost-of-sales buying prices. Meanwhile, you and your GPM are being squeezed in the middle.

> Gross Profit Margin is one of the most important metrics of a business. It measures how much value the business generates directly from its income/revenue activities.

8. REVENUE EARNED, CASH RECEIVED LATER: SALE & COST OF SALE

Classic Transaction Eight (a) and (b)

The business now makes another sale, but unlike the "cash sale" in Transaction 6(a), the business doesn't get paid cash immediately. It will be paid later.

Just as we talked about how there are three timing scenarios for paying cash out for an expense—before, at the same time, and after the expense activity happens—there are also three timing scenarios for receiving payment from revenue activities. The business can receive payment before the earning activity, concurrently with the earning, or after the earning has taken place.

Classic Transaction 8(a)—February 10

Another sale, to Customer B, who says an assistant will come in and pay $2,000 tomorrow.

The big question here is: has a sale taken place? You may be tempted to say that a sale has not happened because the business hasn't been paid, but recall the definition of revenue/income/sales. Revenue is value-generating activity. It's not cash-generating activity. So, the question to ask is not "Has cash been generated?" but rather "Has something of value been generated?"

And the answer is yes: a sale has taken place because something of value has been generated. The business now has generated a valuable asset that it didn't have before the sale. That asset is the present right to receive cash at an agreed future date. Note that it's a present right, not a future right. The right exists today; the cash will flow in the future.

Having a right to future cash is not quite as good as having the cash itself, but it's still very desirable and certainly a valuable asset. The right is called an account receivable, trade receivable, trade debtor, or similar.

To bring home the point that the account receivable right is valuable, consider how businesses sometimes sell those rights. If they don't want to wait the seven or thirty days or however long for the money, the business can sell the *right-to-be-paid-$2000-in-thirty-days* for, say, $1,900 cash today. The buyer of the receivable account would pay the business $1,900 now and then thirty days after, they would receive the $2,000 from the original customer. This form of financing is called *factoring* and it can be quite expensive.

A concern that people often raise at this point is: but what if the customer doesn't pay? That's a valid concern from a management point of view, but all assets have risk associated with them. A house can burn down and cash can get stolen or lost. Students learning accounting seem to get overly hung up on the risk associated with accounts receivable. Like all the risks in a business, the manager must consider, mitigate, and manage them. From an accounting point of view, if the customer owes us money, then we have generated a sale and that sale is recorded. Of course, if you knew from the get-go that the customer would not pay the debt they owe, then you wouldn't record the sale because you would know that you hadn't generated a valuable asset.

So, let's ask our habitual questions. What are the two impacts? The business has generated an Asset (Account Receivable), so that's the first impact. And the value-generating activity happened, which is an impact to Revenue/Income (Sales).

Are they increasing or decreasing? We have more Sales and more Accounts Receivable, so both increase. We show those impacts by putting a same-colored ticket into each bucket as shown in the journal:

	Green Effect	Orange Effect
February 10 Credit Sale to Customer B	Accounts Receivable 2,000	Sales 2,000

BaSIS Framework: Credit Sale

On the BaSIS Framework in *Figure 109*, the new Accounts Receivable asset bucket increases from zero to $2,000 when we put a green same-colored ticket into it. The Sales bucket increases by $2,000, from $1,000 to $3,000. This has the simultaneous impact of increasing the profit by $2,000, from $700 to $2,700.

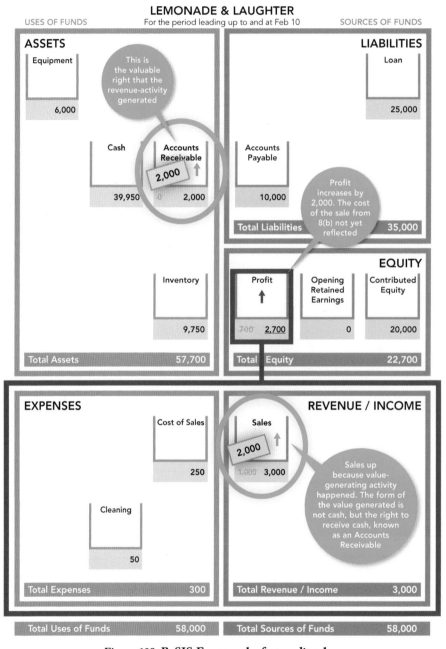

Figure 109. **BaSIS Framework after credit sale.**

Classic Transaction 8(b)—February 10

The business sacrifices $500 of inventory in sale to Customer B

In order to generate the $2,000 account receivable asset in Transaction 8(a), the business had to make a sacrifice. It gave away $500 worth of inventory in order to gain the $2,000 account receivable.

Other than the different amounts, this is the same journal entry we saw in Transaction 6(a), the cash sale.

The two accounts are Cost of Sales and Inventory. Cost of Sales increases and Inventory decreases.

To reflect those increasing and decreasing impacts, the journal below shows the green effect going to Cost of Sales and the orange effect going to Inventory.

	Green Ticket	Orange Ticket
February 10	COS	Inventory
Credit Sale to Customer B		
	500	500

BaSIS Framework: Sacrificing Inventory

The impacts of the effects are shown on the BaSIS Framework in *Figure 110*. The inventory asset account in the balance sheet section reduces from $9,750 to $9,250, and the Cost of Sales expense in the income statement section increases from $250 to $750. The profit simultaneously drops from $2,700 to $2,200.

Color Logic Applied to the Profit Bucket

Another way to think of why the profit decreases is to imagine that you put the green Cost of Sale ticket directly into the orange profit account instead of going via the income statement bucket at the bottom left. If you put the green ticket into the orange profit bucket, the usual color logic would apply: you'd be putting an opposite-colored ticket into the bucket, causing it to decrease. As you know by now, opposite-colored tickets decrease accounts and same-colored tickets increase them.

Note: the profit account is the only account in the general ledger that we do not post directly into. Changes to the profit account balance can only be affected via Revenue and Expenses.

> A green expense ticket
> posted directly into the profit bucket
> would reduce profit.

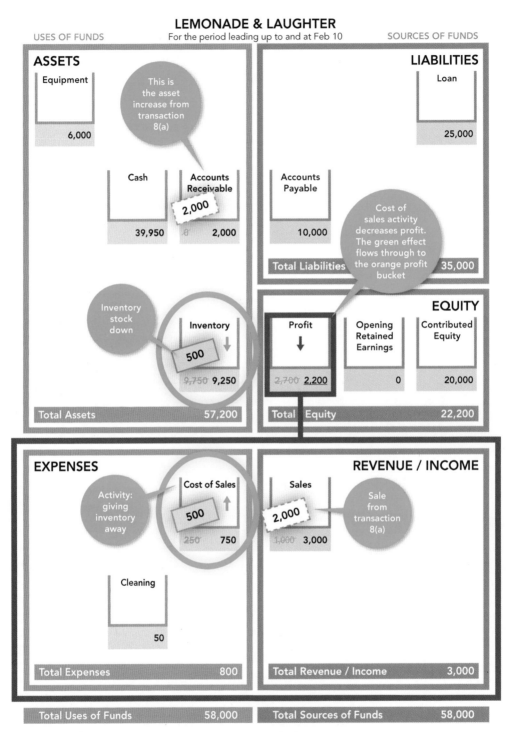

Figure 110. **Another cost of sale transaction.**

Financial Statements after Credit Sale and Cost of Sale Transactions 8(a) and 8(b)

After the credit sale and the cost of sale, the balance sheet and income statement of Lemonade & Laughter look like this:

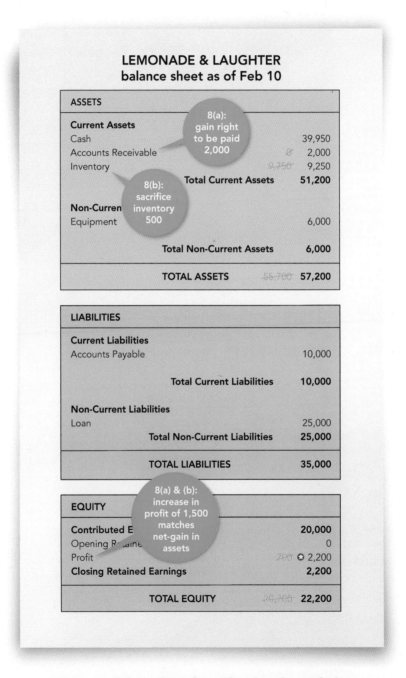

Figure 111. Balance sheet after credit sale and cost of sale.

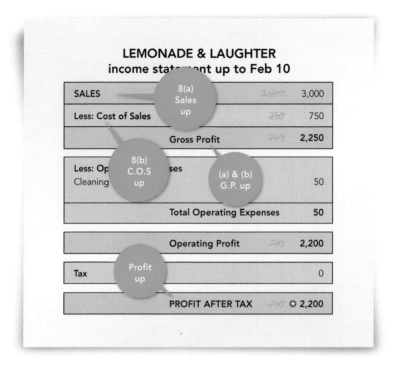

Figure 112. **Income statement after credit sale and cost of sale**

The business now has net $1,500 more assets (being $2,000 more accounts receivable and $500 less inventory). Those net generated assets are attributable to the owners, which is reflected in the increase in the profit account in the equity section of the balance sheet. The detail of how the $1,500 profit was earned is explained in the income statement, where we see that $2,000 worth of value was generated and $500 worth of value was sacrificed to arrive at the net value generated of $1,500 which is included in the total profit figure of $2,200.

Discussion: Accrual Accounting

Cash Basis vs. Accrual Basis of Accounting

There are two bases of accounting: Accrual Accounting and Cash Accounting. Accrual accounting is the kind of accounting we've been doing. It's true accounting and gives the most faithful reflection of reality.

When a business generates value in any form, accrual accounting reflects that value generation activity as revenue/income together with that asset in whatever form—similar for value sacrifices.

A challenge that accrual accounting presents, however, is that it's not always clear when the value generation activity took place (or in the case of an expense, when the value-sacrificing activity happened). In this Transaction 8, the product of the value-generating activity was an account receivable—a right created by the sales activity. It was pretty clear that the sale activity had taken place because goods were handed over.

Think about a consultant preparing a report for a client. Imagine that they are doing a month-long job, starting in mid-December of 2027 and ending mid-January 2028 with the report due at the end of the assignment. The consultant will, for argument's sake, earn a total of $20,000 for the job.

At 31 December, how much value will the consultant have generated? Have they earned $10,000 because they are halfway through the month-long engagement? In this case, the 2027 year will show earnings of $10,000 and the 2028 year will show the other half of the earnings. But what if nothing is payable unless the report is satisfactory and finished, and we're not sure if the report will be good enough and accepted? Should we instead recognize all the earnings only once the report is complete and accepted? In this case, all the earnings would fall into the 2028 year. Put another way, does the acceptance of the report by the client determine the earning or does the time passing while doing the report determine the earning?

There is no entirely clear-cut answer to these questions. Should you base the recognition of earnings on time passed, job completion, or some other agreed-upon milestones?

This is the challenge of accrual accounting. Life isn't black and white. Accounting regulators write rules and guidance for what are called "revenue recognition" and "expense recognition." Deciding how to account for the timing of earnings and expenses, and therefore when profits happen, is a key theme in accounting.

One way to avoid this uncertainty is to decide that the revenue is recognized when the client pays—that is, when the cash is received. Using the timing of cash received or paid as the basis for recognizing revenue and expenses is called Cash Accounting. The lack of ambiguity is a benefit of the cash accounting basis.

The disadvantage of using the cash basis is that it can make nonsense of income and profit figures. Imagine that you are a plumber and you do a few days of work for a customer in December 2037. You finish the job on December 29 and leave an invoice behind for $5,000. The client pays you on January 10, 2038.

Under the cash accounting system, the revenue is counted as earned in 2038. Under accrual accounting, you would recognize the revenue in 2037 and you'd have an account receivable, just as we've seen above in classic transaction 8(a) where payment has not yet happened and where the asset that was created by the activity is the right to be paid in the future.

And moreover, if you paid expenses in December to complete the job, you will have made a loss in 2037 (all expenses and no revenue) and an inflated profit in 2038 (all revenue and no expenses).

Under the cash accounting system, there is no revenue in December, and there's no account receivable. Under cash accounting, you pretend that the business isn't owed any money by the client. The revenue isn't shown in the income statement, and neither is the account receivable on the balance sheet.

In the United States, individuals submit their tax returns using the cash basis. For that reason, many people try to avoid getting paid in late December, trying to shift the receipt of the payment to early January instead. They wait a couple of weeks before invoicing the client or before depositing the received payment so that the revenue falls into the next tax year. The IRS assesses income based on when the payment for it was received, not when earning activity happened. For a delayed January cash receipt, the income tax payable is assessed a year later. And who minds delaying their tax bill by a year!

Most modern small business accounting systems like QuickBooks or Xero have a switch that you can use to toggle between showing the accounts on a cash basis and an accrual basis. They record all transactions on an accrual basis, but they will show you the income statement and balance sheet on a cash basis if you want a cash accounting view. They show the cash basis view by ignoring the accounts receivable resulting from unpaid value-generation activities.

For the rest of *The Joy of Accounting*, we'll continue to focus on the fullest and most true-to-life accounting system, which is the accrual accounting system.

When using Cash-based Accounting...

• income/revenue can be thought of as Cash-Generating Activity rather than the broader Value-Generating Activity.

• expense can be thought of as Cash-Sacrificing Activity rather than the broader Value-Sacrificing Activity.

---

9. CASH RECEIVED BEFORE REVENUE EARNED: DEFERRED REVENUE

Classic Transaction Nine

So far in the classic transactions, we've seen revenue that generated cash at the same time as the earning activity (Transaction 6), and we've seen income that hasn't been paid for yet (Transaction 8). Now we get to see what happens when a client pays Lemonade & Laughter before the company does the income activity for the client.

Classic Transaction 9—February 15

Charlie drops in and pays cash for a gift voucher as a present for a friend, Dale. Cash banked, $150.

This is the most misunderstood classic transaction. We are so used to thinking of revenue as being the receipt of cash that we want to think this transaction describes a revenue situation. We talk about "selling" a gift voucher, so it even sounds as if a revenue-sale has happened. The handing over of the gift voucher to the customer tempts us to think that we've provided something, so we must have earned income.

But we haven't. No revenue has taken place here. It's more akin to a loan than a sale.

What's happened is that a customer has paid Lemonade & Laughter $150 cash in return for a gift voucher, which is like an *IOU* (I Owe You) to the customer, who will return with the voucher later to redeem it, or give it to a friend to do so. Until they've redeemed the voucher to get their toaster or haircut or book or coffee or massage or whatever, Lemonade & Laughter owes them. We have an obligation to them. Even if the gift voucher is not refundable, the business nevertheless has a $150 obligation to the holder of the voucher. It has an obligation to provide the customer with $150 worth of goods or services, albeit not cash.

The main difference between this sale of a gift voucher and a loan situation like Transaction 1 (borrowed $30,000 from a lender) is that we won't be repaying cash to settle the obligation—we'll be providing goods or services. Now, we're ready to ask our questions.

What are the two impacts? The business receives cash, so the Assets (Cash) account will be impacted. And we've established that the business has an obligation to fulfill, so we'll need to create a liability account.

But what should we call the new liability? We won't use the existing Loan account because we're reserving it for that specific loan. And we won't call it Accounts Payable, because that describes an obligation to our suppliers—this is a customer. Rather, we create a new Liability account called Deferred Revenue.

Increasing or decreasing? Both accounts are increasing, so we put both tickets into the same-colored buckets: green into Cash and orange into Deferred Revenue.

	Green Ticket	Orange Ticket
February 15	Cash	Deferred Revenue
Charlie drops in and pays $150 for a gift voucher as a present for her friend Dale. Cash banked.	150	150

BaSIS Framework: Deferred Revenue

The Framework in Figure 113 shows the receipt of cash in assets. And the total liabilities have increased by 150 because of the new Deferred Revenue obligation.

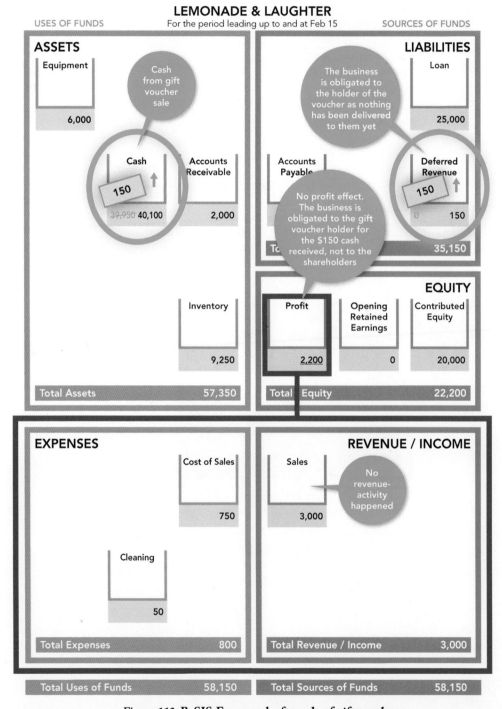

Figure 113. **BaSIS Framework after sale of gift voucher.**

On the BaSIS Framework, the Cash account increases from 30,950 to 40,100. The new bucket called "Deferred Revenue" appears as a source of funds in the liabilities section.

There is no impact in either of the bottom two income statement boxes of the framework, and therefore no change to the profit bucket in equity. Nothing has been earned, so there's no profit impact.

Name of Account

One of the learning themes we hope you're picking up on in *The Joy of Accounting* is how there are many different possible names for accounts in the BaSIS Framework. Different countries, businesses, and people use different names by habit or tradition. What's much more important than knowing the actual name of an account is knowing the element in question—in other words, in which of the five boxes of the framework each impact lands. In this case, those are assets and liabilities.

The Deferred Revenue bucket we've just created is interesting for having a particularly wide range of synonyms. Other names used to describe deferred revenue include:

- Deferred Income
- Deferred Sales
- Prepaid Revenue
- Unearned Income
- Unearned Sales

- Unearned Revenue
- Income In Advance (even though it's the cash that's in advance, not the income)
- Deposits
- Gift Vouchers

The term *deferred revenue* derives from the Latin *de* (from) and *ferre*, which means "to carry." Other English words with the same etymology include "ferry" and "ferrous" (describing metals that contain oxygen-carrying iron). Deferred revenue is revenue that is carried or pushed into the future. In that distant land, we'll see how it turns into actual revenue. What matters is that in the here and now, deferred revenue is not revenue. It is a liability.

> Deferred revenue is not revenue. It's a liability.

We talk about the language paradox of deferred revenue not being revenue—just as deferred expenses, as we will shortly see, are not expenses.

Financial Statements after Deferred Revenue Transaction 9

After Transaction 9, the balance sheet and income statement of Lemonade & Laughter look like this:

Figure 114. **Balance sheet after sale of gift voucher.**

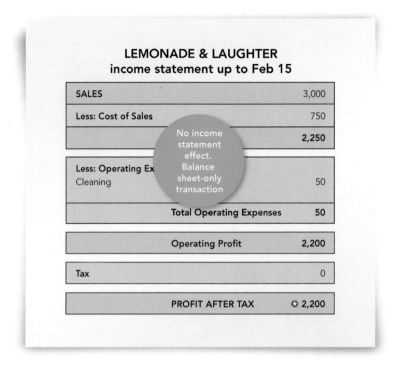

Figure 115. **Income statement showing no impact from sale of gift voucher.**

The business now has more cash and more debt. As such, this gift voucher transaction slightly increased the leverage of the business. A greater proportion of the assets of the business are now funded through debt rather than equity.

Discussion: Receiving Cash in Advance of a Sale

Interest-Free Cash

Deferred revenue is a very significant matter for some businesses. Those enterprises that get paid for their goods or services before providing them to customers are fortunate because they can find themselves with a lot of client-sourced cash that rarely attracts interest. In that sense, they get free money. They get to use their customers' cash to run their businesses and pay for the inventory they will sell. Having the customers' interest-free cash means that the businesses can avoid borrowing cash from a bank, which would carry a rate of interest.

The business, of course, takes on a significant responsibility in accepting customers' cash in advance. In particular, the business must make sure that they keep enough cash on hand to fulfill the obligation. If the business, for example, must pay a contractor to deliver the service that's been promised, then they better have the money to pay the contractor when the time comes to deliver on that obligation.

Certain industries are associated with high levels of advance payment. These include:

- Subscription publications
  Subscribers pay for months and years of magazines and periodicals in advance.

- Insurance
  Insurance contracts are typically paid in advance; insurance companies have little trouble collecting the advance premiums because the insured customers are concerned that their insurance won't be valid if they don't pay up.

- Airlines
  Most people pay for their air tickets weeks or months in advance. Until they fly, the airlines hold a deferred revenue obligation to the future passenger.

- Retail
  Many stores offer gift vouchers, which bring cash into the business in advance—it's easy to see why.

Gift Vouchers

Many retailers offer gift vouchers and have numerous motives for doing so. The vouchers accelerate the receipt of cash into the business, they allow customers to buy something even when they don't know what present their friend will want, and other stores can sell the retailer's gift cards (for a cut of the action), expanding the footprint of the retailer and bringing more customers through the door.

Perhaps the best reason to sell gift vouchers is that a lot of them get lost. Some say up to 10 percent or more of cards are never presented for redemption. When that happens, it's like the retailer has made a sale with no associated cost of sale. That results in revenue with 100 percent gross profit margin. We'll see how this works in Transaction 12 when our gift voucher gets redeemed.

Before we do that, have a guess at how much cash Starbucks reported sitting on from unredeemed gift cards in December of a recent year. It's probably a lot, right? Twenty-dollar coffee cards are a very nice little thank-you gift to give a colleague who's done you a good turn. If you look at Starbucks' balance sheet, you'll see deferred revenue from coffee cards of over a billion dollars. Wow! That's an awful lot of coffee waiting to be drunk and cards sitting in people's wallets (or lost). The amount of money deposited in this way with Starbucks is more than most US banks have from their customer savings accounts.

Here is a recent list of the deferred revenue of some well-known retailers:

- Amazon $2.8B
- Walmart $1.9B
- Starbucks $1.6B
- Target $727M

10. ACCOUNT RECEIVABLE SETTLED

Classic Transaction Ten
Includes "Debit" and "Credit" Terminology,
Sub-Ledgers, and Special Journals

Back in classic transaction 8(a), Lemonade & Laughter earned revenue by selling goods to Customer B. We didn't gain cash from that sale, however. Instead, the business gained another form of asset, that being an account receivable. Now it's time to turn that right-to-receive-cash into actual cash—or at least part of it.

Classic Transaction 10—February 20

Customer B's assistant comes in and pays part of what they owe—cash banked, $800.

The eagle-eyed will notice that Customer B did not keep their word. On February 10, they promised to send their assistant to pay the next day, and now it's ten days later. Not only that, but they aren't paying the full amount. Alas, such is life. But the scenario reminds us of an important business risk, which is managing cash flow by ensuring that payments come in on time, and the risk of not getting paid at all. Perhaps we should have stipulated a penalty for late payment, which some businesses do.

Anyhow, we're happy that the customer is paying us something.

The key learning point is this: When we receive this $800 of cash, we don't recognize any revenue. We've already done so. There's no earning happening now. The earning happened back on February 10. All that happened now is that Lemonade & Laughter swapped one asset (the right to receive money) for another asset (actual money). The transaction is a switch of value-form, not a generation of value.

Both impacts of the transaction happen inside the assets box of the BaSIS Framework. So, let's ask:

Which two accounts? Cash is impacted, and Accounts Receivable (Trade Debtors) is impacted

Are they increasing or decreasing? We've got more cash, so that account increases. And the customer owes us less, so the receivable account decreases.

Using the journal below, to make the green Cash account increase, we add a green ticket. To make the Accounts Receivable account decrease, we add an orange ticket.

	Green Ticket	Orange Ticket
February 20 Customer B part-pays their account	Cash	Accounts Receivable
	800	800

BaSIS Framework: Settlement of Account Receivable

Both effects from the customer's payment impact the green "uses of funds" side of the BaSIS Framework in *Figure 116*. The Cash account increases because we put a same-colored green ticket into the green cash account. The Accounts Receivable bucket decreases because we put an opposite-colored orange ticket into the green receivables account.

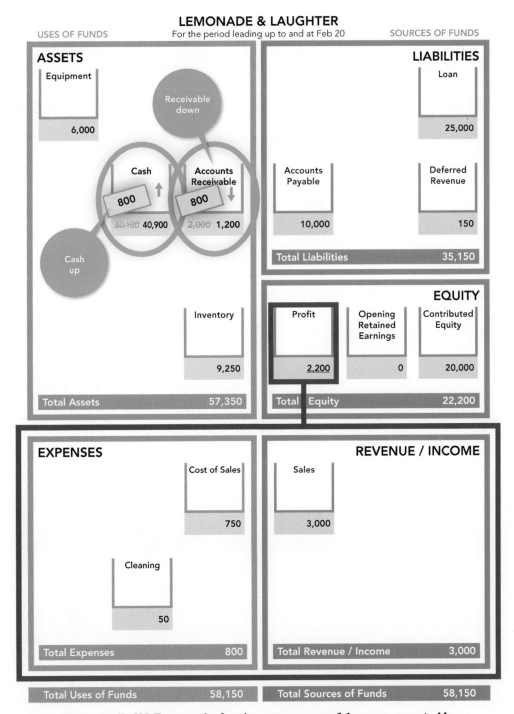

Figure 116. **BaSIS Framework after the part-payment of the account receivable.**

Figure 116 shows how Cash increases to $40,900 and the Accounts Receivable account reduces to $1,200 from $2,000.

Debits and Credits

Perhaps the most infamous terms in accounting are *debit* and *credit*. They are rather strange words, often misunderstood and confused, with a centuries-old heritage and a provenance in Italy.

 The Italian "grandparents" of the terms are *debito* and *credito*. In turn, those Italian words derive from the Latin words *credo* and *debito*. *Credo* means "belief" or "trust." Hence the English word "creed," to describe a set of beliefs. *Debito* comes from the concept of debt.

Introducing the idea of trust and debt doesn't really help us understand the meaning of the terms debit and credit any better, though, because we still don't know who is owing whom. Is it a debt-to or debt-from? Am I trusting you or are you trusting me?

People are confused about debit and credit for a number of reasons. For starters, the terms mean less than people think—people often want to attribute more meaning to them than they actually hold. Secondly, each term is used in two ways—but it's all quite simple, really, and easy to fix.

For starters, let's just get clear on what debit and credit do *not* mean. The terms don't mean good/bad, up/down, increase/decrease, in/out, plus/minus, or positive/negative. If you have these connotations in your mind, you must unlearn them.

Here's the silly secret: Debit means green. And Credit means orange.

DEBIT means GREEN
CREDIT means ORANGE

Figure 117. **Debit and credit: there's less to it than we often think.**

These are the colors we chose when we the Color Accounting Learning System. The beauty of using colors to explain debits and credits is that colors don't have those misleading connotations. Nobody instinctively thinks that green must mean up and orange down in the way that they do with debit and credit. Green and orange are seen for what they are: simply colors. So how do we use the colors?

The colors and the terms "debit" and "credit" are used in two ways: to describe buckets and to describe tickets. In traditional accounting language, they are describing accounts and journal entries.

1) Buckets: debit-type and credit-type accounts.

Debit and credit describe the types of accounts in the general ledger—it's an either-or situation. The words are used as adjectives to describe the nature of accounts: green accounts and orange accounts.

Asset accounts and expense accounts are green, use-of-funds, debit-type accounts.

Liability, equity, and income/revenue accounts are orange, source-of-funds, credit-type accounts.

The Color Accounting BaSIS Framework is divided into the green debit side and the orange credit side.

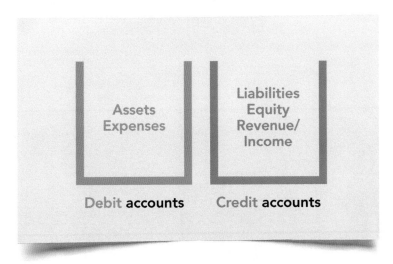

Figure 118. **The two types of account**

2) Tickets: debiting and crediting effects—journal entries

The terms "debiting" and "crediting" describe journal effects. In this sense, the words are used as verbs to describe an action you do to an account—increasing or decreasing.

In Color Accounting, we represent the journal entries as tickets.

Debiting is represented as a green ticket. Crediting is represented as an orange ticket.

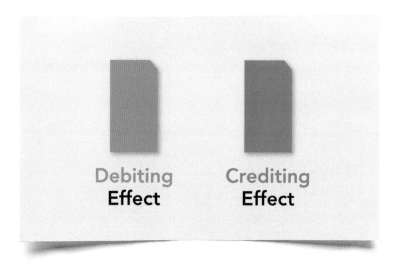

Figure 119. There are two types of action.

The two types of account combined with the two types of effect give only four possible combinations.

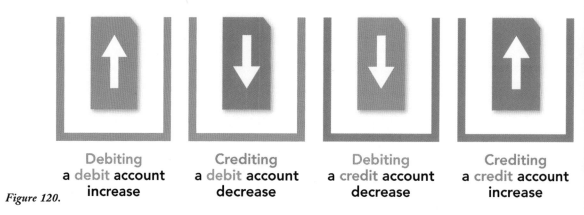

Figure 120.

Figure 121. Two possible actions on two possible types of account give four results.

1. **Debiting** a **debit** account increases it
2. **Crediting** a **debit** account decreases it
3. **Debiting** a **credit** account decreases it
4. **Crediting** a **credit** account increases it

Re-Languaging our Accounting Journal

Let's now revisit the same account receivable settlement transaction, but express it using traditional accounting language of "debiting" and "crediting."

February 20	Debiting Effect	Crediting Effect
	Cash	Accounts
Customer B pays down account receivable		Receivable
	800	800

In this transaction, we are debiting Cash and crediting Accounts Receivable. Because Cash is a debit-account, debiting it increases it. Because Accounts Receivable is a debit-account, crediting it decreases it.

Financial Statements After Receivable Settled Transaction 10

After the receipt of cash in Transaction 10, the balance sheet and income statement of Lemonade & Laughter look like this:

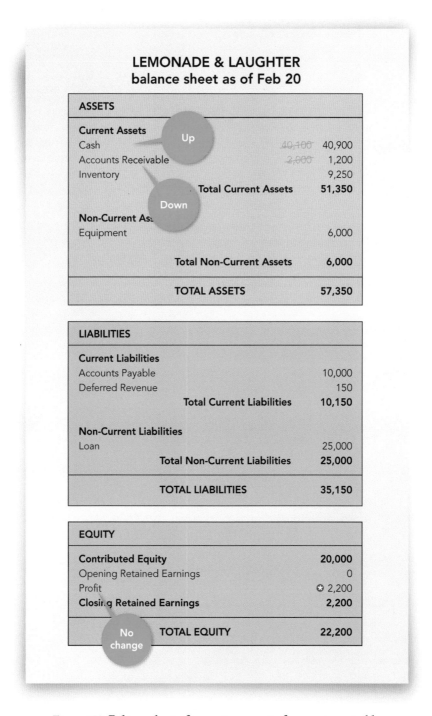

Figure 122. Balance sheet after part payment of account receivable.

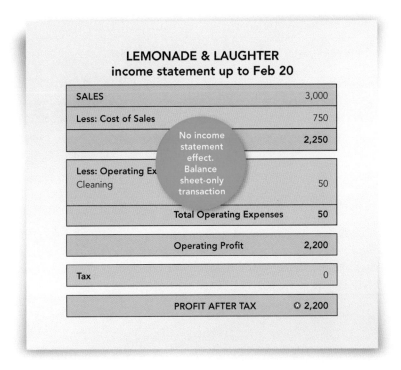

Figure 123. **Income statement showing no impact after part payment of account receivable.**

The business has the same amount of assets, liabilities, and equity. The only change is within assets where cash has increased and accounts receivable have decreased. The income statement shows no change to revenue or expenses, and consequently there is no change to the profit account in equity.

Remembering that profit represents the generated obligation to the owner to return assets to them, this statement makes sense. The assets haven't changed in total, and the same proportion of those total assets are obligated to the lenders and owners respectively.

Discussion: Selling on Credit

Sub-Ledgers, Special Journals, and Growing Pains

Being paid later by selling on credit can be a necessary evil in business. In many businesses, it is simply impractical to collect cash at the time and place of delivering the good or service provided. If you are a supplier to Lemonade & Laughter, it would make no sense for you to exchange cash at the store or depot where you delivered your goods. The payment is done electronically from bank account to bank account. No physical cash is involved. It's much safer this way, too.

On your side as a vendor selling to L&L, you have an accounts receivable or debtors clerk whose job is to invoice L&L. The clerk already has a purchase order or confirmation from L&L and now receives delivery notes from truck drivers, signed by L&L warehouse personnel, as proof that delivery of the physical goods took place. With this confirmation, the clerk raises an invoice against L&L's account in your general ledger system. On L&L's side, those invoices are received and reviewed by an accounts payable or creditors clerk, whose job is to make sure that L&L is only getting billed for goods it ordered and which were all received in good condition.

Where adjustments need to be made, Lemonade & Laughter might report a short delivery or that some items were damaged. L&L therefore requests a credit to their account. The vendor then issues a credit note, which reflects that in the vendor's accounting system, the L&L account receivable is credited, thereby reducing it (because it's a debit-type asset account in the vendor's ledger).

Sub-Ledgers, Special Journals

On the BaSIS Framework above in *Figure 116*, we're showing an account titled Accounts Receivable. It currently has a balance of $1,200, reflecting the debt that Customer B owes us (as before, informally talking about "we" and "us" where we mean the separate entity Lemonade & Laughter).

We may make further credit sales to customer B, and we will of course have many other customers over the life of the business, each with their own balance owed to us. Mixing up the debts owed to us by different customers would be bad. For that reason, we need a sub-account for each credit customer. Because a business might have dozens or hundreds or even millions of customers, it doesn't make sense to have an account on the BaSIS Framework—like we've shown above—for each customer. Or in traditional terminology, it doesn't make sense to have an account for each customer at the top level of the General Ledger.

Instead, we have, in Color Accounting-speak, "sub-buckets," or in traditional language, the accounting system has sub-accounts recorded in a sub-ledger. Each sub-account will use a unique reference code in the accounting system to identify each customer.

Figure 124. **Accounts Receivable control account (showing arbitrary numbers).**

The top-level account that aggregates the sub-accounts is known as a Control Account. Instead of posting entries into the top-level account (the Control Account) using the General Journal (GJ) that we've been using, we would post the debiting and crediting entries into the sub-accounts using (depending upon the type of transaction) a Sales Journal (SJ) or a Cash Receipts Journal (CRJ).

The Sales Journal is used in relation to a sale involving accounts receivable. The Cash Receipts Journal records all cash received by type, including customers paying their accounts. For purchases, the entries are made with a Purchases Journal (PJ) into the Creditors Sub-Ledger, also known as the Accounts Payable Sub-Ledger. The Cash Payments Journal (CPJ) records all payments by type, including payments to suppliers.

A Purchases Journal is used to affect the Accounts Payable sub-accounts.

- The Purchases Journal posts to the Accounts Payable Sub-Ledger, which feeds into the Accounts Payable Control account in the General Ledger.
- The Sales Journal posts to the Accounts Receivable Sub-Ledger, which feeds into the Accounts Receivable Control account in the General Ledger.

> 1. Purchases Journal posts to the Accounts Payable Sub-Ledger
> 2. Sales Journal posts to the Accounts Receivable Sub-Ledger

Similarly, the cash account may also have a specialized journal, called the Cash Book, Cash Journal, Cash Receipts Journal, or Cash Payments Journal.

These special journals are a form of control because they capture additional information, like a sequential invoice number, customer name, customer account number, purchase order number, check (*cheque* in Britain) number, due date, and so on. Furthermore, one of the effects on the journal can be fixed so that, for example, the cash receipts journal can only be used to make cash deposits but not cash withdrawals. That can be useful if you want some members of staff to be authorized only to receive payments but not make cash or other payments.

Example Sales Journal

Description	Date	Order #	Customer Name	Account #	Debit Accounts Receivable	Credit
Credit sale to Brownlee Barry	Feb 21	123987	Brownlee Barry	00567	Brownlee Barry $900	Sales $900

Figure 125. **Example sales journal showing additional details compared with general journal.**

Growing Pains and Working Capital

Selling on credit is great because it's selling, but selling on credit can also cause cash shortages.

To have a right to be paid by a client is to have a valuable asset. But you can't use an account receivable to pay bills or make payroll with. Having insufficient cash with which to pay bills and employees is a problem, even while having plenty of accounts receivable.

Most for-profit businesses try hard to grow their revenue, and rapid sales growth is something to celebrate. Growth is great. However, rapid sales growth can make even a profitable business run out of cash.

Think about any credit sale (like Transaction 8 where the business earned $2,000 and incurred a cost of sale of $500), and then the subsequent receipt of $800 cash (Transaction 10, in this chapter).

When the sale is made, inventory that was previously purchased is handed over. In our scenario, Lemonade & Laughter purchased $10,000 of inventory in Transaction 5. We debited Inventory and credited Accounts Payable. Let's assume that L&L needs to settle that account payable soon, or we could even imagine a scenario where L&L paid cash for the inventory immediately. The point is that Lemonade & Laughter will pay for the inventory, possibly long before it receives cash, by selling the inventory to a customer on credit.

When that inventory is sold, it will have to be replenished, or possibly more than replenished to increase the level of inventory to match the increased rate of sales. Because inventory is bought and paid for first and cash received later from selling it, each sale causes negative cash flow for a short while. In other words, in the short term, more cash goes out than comes in from each new sale. Profit on a sale is immediate, but net cash inflow from the sale can take a while to happen.

The more the rate of sales increases, the more cash goes out. Extra funding is needed to grow the increasing amount of accounts receivable and inventory and cash on hand. As previously mentioned, businesses call this funding to finance sales "working capital." It's the sourced funding (debt or equity) needed to finance the accounts receivable and the inventory and cash on hand. Accounts payable is a source of funding, reducing the total amount of other funding needed to finance those three current assets. The amount of funding needed is therefore equivalent to the amount of inventory, accounts receivable, and cash, less the amount of accounts payable.

> The amount of working capital is calculated as the amounts of
> accounts receivable + inventory + cash
> minus
> accounts payable.

Depending upon the type of business, inventory might sit for a very long time before it is sold. This means that a lot of cash is "tied up" in the inventory. The retail industry and Walmart in particular are unusual in that inventory turns over quite rapidly, but in many businesses it doesn't. Think of a car parts business where rarely requested parts need to be on hand, or a wine cellar where wine is sitting for a long time, aging to that gorgeous oaky bouquet. Producing all those barrels and bottles of wine can tie up a lot of money. The barrels have all long since been paid for by the business by the time the wine is sold and cash is received. The staff who plucked the vines and crushed the grapes have also been paid by the business before any cash flows into the business from the fruits of their labor. So as the business grows, more cash is needed to finance the inventory.

Inventory Turnover

The number of times that inventory is sold and then replenished each year is referred to as "inventory turn." If a business sells an item once every three months, then the annual inventory turnover is four times. Generally speaking, the higher the inventory turn, the better. With double the inventory turn, the same amount of sales can be achieved with half the inventory. Half the inventory means less cash is tied up in that inventory. Less cash tied up means less interest expenses and more cash available for other projects or for returning to the owners.

Some powerful businesses insist that their suppliers provide their inventory "on consignment." This means that even though the inventory is sitting on the business's shelf ready to be sold to a customer, the business only buys it from the supplier at the same moment that the customer buys it from the business. This means in effect that the business is not holding inventory and therefore does not need to finance it.

If the business can still negotiate delayed payment terms, they have the customer's money and don't have to pay their supplier until later.

> *Inventory turn* per year
> = 12 ÷ months taken to sell the inventory

11. PREPAY FOR AN EXPENSE

Classic Transaction Eleven

We have already paid for services that help us run the business, like the cleaning services we used in Transaction 7. And we're going to do that again. Except this time we notice that while Lemonade & Laughter pays for the service now, it doesn't actually consume the service right away. And that makes a big difference to how we account for the event.

Classic Transaction 11—February 25

Paid for advertising campaign that will run March through May. Used a bank (wire) transfer for $240.

The biggest mistake people make when interpreting this transaction is jumping to the conclusion that an expense has happened—no doubt because money is being spent. It's an easy mistake to make. We're in the habit of connecting cash going out with expenses. Vague use of terminology like "expenditure" encourages the bad habit. The word sounds like expense, but means spending—that is, cash going out.

> Expenditure and expense are not the same thing

In this scenario of paying for future advertising, the cash out and the expense have not both happened. Money has gone out, but no value consumption activity has taken place. This means there's no expense. Remember, that's what an expense is: value-sacrificing activity.

The payment for the advertising happens on February 25, but the campaign only starts running on March 1. So, at the time of this transaction, no advertising has happened because it's all only been promised.

The question we want to ask here is: What did Lemonade & Laughter get in exchange for paying out the cash? The business must have exchanged something of perceived equivalent value, otherwise we wouldn't have handed over the money.

What we got was a right. Specifically, a right to an advertising slot. That's an asset because it's valuable. The business enjoys having an advertising slot that it will use. It might be exchangeable for cash. That is, we might get be able to get a refund from the supplier, or we could sell the future advertising slot to someone else.

Imagine winning a 30-second slot to broadcast a Super Bowl advertisement of your choice. Those slots are famously expensive, costing millions of dollars. If you had a slot, you can be sure that someone would pay you money to use it.

Unfortunately, this type of asset where cash is paid in anticipation of a future expense happening is often called a prepaid expense. This makes for another language paradox. A prepaid expense sounds like it's some type of expense, but it's not. It's an asset.

Prepaid expenses are also referred to by names such as *deferred expense*, *deposits paid*, or *prepayments*.

LANGUAGE PARADOX

Prepaid expenses mirror deferred revenue. Where the deferred revenue we saw in the gift voucher transaction was a liability, a prepaid expense is an asset. In both cases the anticipated activity is located in the future.

What the business has done is convert one asset (cash) into another asset (advertising receivable). With that clear, we can now answer our two questions.

What are the two impacts? Assets (Cash) and Assets (Prepaid Expense).

Are they increasing or decreasing? Cash decreases and Prepaid Expense increases.

So, using traditional terminology now, we are debiting Prepaid Expense and crediting Cash.

	Debiting Effect	Crediting Effect
February 25 Paid for advertising campaign that will run March through May. Used a bank (wire) transfer.	Prepaid Expense 240	Cash 240

BaSIS Framework: Prepay for an Expense

Figure 126 below shows the debiting of a Prepaid Expense debit-type account, causing an increase impact on the account.

Crediting the Cash account decreases that debit-type account.

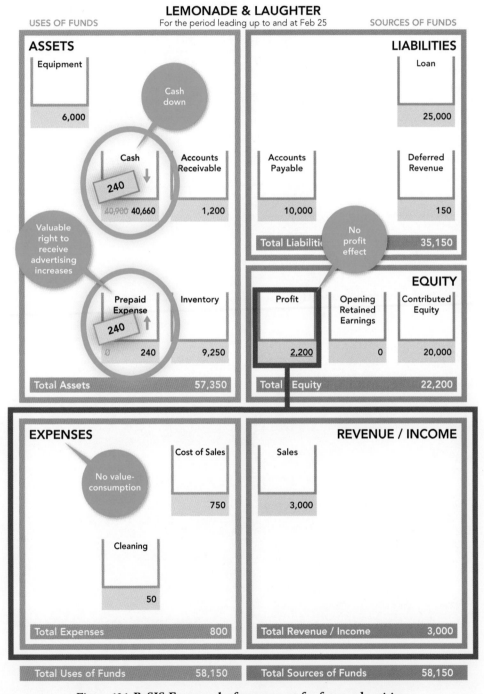

LEMONADE & LAUGHTER
For the period leading up to and at Feb 25

USES OF FUNDS   SOURCES OF FUNDS

ASSETS

Equipment
6,000

Cash down

Cash
240
~~40,900~~ 40,660

Accounts Receivable
1,200

Valuable right to receive advertising increases

Prepaid Expense
240
~~0~~ 240

Inventory
9,250

Total Assets 57,350

LIABILITIES

Loan
25,000

Accounts Payable
10,000

Deferred Revenue
150

Total Liabilities 35,150

No profit effect

EQUITY

Profit
2,200

Opening Retained Earnings
0

Contributed Equity
20,000

Total Equity 22,200

EXPENSES

No value-consumption

Cost of Sales
750

Cleaning
50

Total Expenses 800

REVENUE / INCOME

Sales
3,000

Total Revenue / Income 3,000

Total Uses of Funds 58,150   Total Sources of Funds 58,150

Figure 126. **BaSIS Framework after payment for future advertising.**

Financial Statements after Prepaid Advertising Transaction 11

After buying future advertising, the balance sheet and income statement of Lemonade & Laughter look like this:

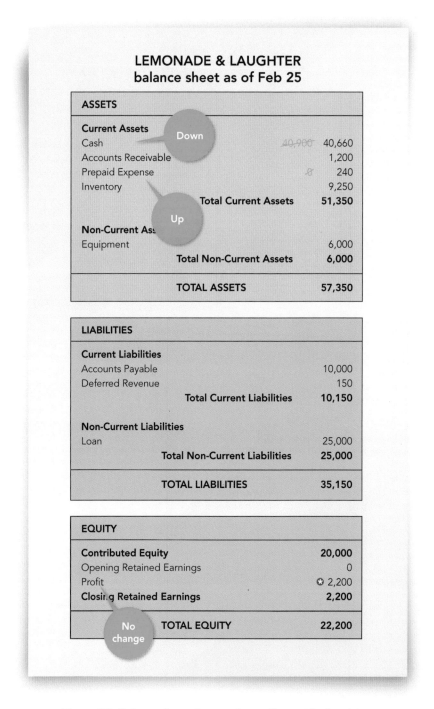

Figure 127. Balance sheet after purchase of prepaid advertising.

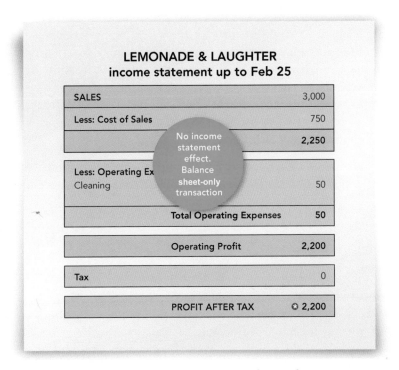

Figure 128. **Income statement showing no impact of prepaid expense transaction.**

The business now has $240 less Cash and $240 more Prepaid Expenses. Both are current assets, so the current ratio of the business has remained the same. The current ratio is an imprecise indicator of the liquidity of the business, comparing the ratio of Total Current Assets to Total Current Liabilities. The ratio is 51,350/10,150, or about 5:1. That seems high because it suggests there are plenty (maybe too many?) of current assets available to use to settle the current liabilities when they fall due. The ratio is unchanged by this transaction because both totals stayed the same.

There's no impact on the income statement, and therefore there is no change to the Equity section of the balance sheet.

The Current Ratio

The current ratio is a metric widely used by analysts, but we should be wary of treating it as anything more than it is. It assumes that all current assets are as liquid as cash and they are all available to pay the current liabilities when they fall due. This assumption means the current ratio may not reveal some serious issues with cash flow.

Consider the following. Imagine that there were twice as many current assets as current liabilities, and those current assets were almost wholly accounts receivable due in 90 days. Imagine also that the current liabilities consist of debts due immediately. So the business could be insolvent, with a whole lot of debts due immediately but no cash to settle them with, and yet the current ratio would appear to be a healthy 2:1

Another aspect to consider is: what is a satisfactory current ratio, anyway? It's common for texts to promote a 2:1 ratio as ideal. You may also find commentary that anything approaching or less than 1:1 indicates financial instability or even insolvency. Modern retailers could have a normal ratio of 0.8:1 or even lower: they have a laser focus on minimizing working capital financing, have very few receivables (cash sales), minimal inventory (just-in-time ordering or even holding the inventory on consignment), and significant accounts payable (paying their suppliers on extended terms of 45 to 90 days). All of these things mean they have few current assets and relatively more current liabilities.

In summary: the current ratio is commonly used, and as one of a number of indicators, provides general information. Sudden unfavorable and unexplained changes would be noteworthy.

Discussion: Prepayments

Show Me the Money, Honey

Many businesses demand prepayment as a normal course of business. Airlines will almost always want payment before they fly you where you want to go. If you're getting a new carpet installed, the carpet installer may ask for part payment before the job starts. She might want to make sure that she's at least covered the upfront costs that she's going to incur, so that if she doesn't get paid at the end, at least she won't be out of pocket and worse off than when she started.

These examples are different, of course, from the scenario we discussed in Chapter 9 on page 179 ("Discussion: Receiving Cash in Advance of a Sale"). In that transaction, Lemonade & Laughter was receiving cash. In this chapter, L&L has been the one paying the cash for the future advertising. In the airline scenario and the carpet installer examples above, the prepayment is in the accounts of the airline passenger and the homeowner buying the carpet. The accounts of the airline and the carpet installer would show deposits as liabilities on their balance sheets.

The risk consideration where we are paying the money is whether the supplier will fulfill their obligation to us. Will they still be around to provide the advertising we've paid for? And what if we change our mind or don't like the job they are doing? Can we cancel and get a refund or partial refund? The risk is as if we've lent somebody money, leaving us with the credit risk of not getting it back or not getting full value.

From the vendor's point of view, there are several reasons that would influence whether they would choose to require upfront prepayment for goods or services. In a low margin business, the risk of not getting paid might be so high that the business does not want to risk it. If a business makes just 10 percent gross profit on the sale of an item such as a camera and it doesn't get paid for a sale as a result, it must sell nine more cameras to cover the cost of that first camera it lost and didn't get paid for.

Businesses also consider how difficult and expensive it is to collect payment after providing a service. Allowing customers to run accounts requires a lot of administration and staff to manage the process. Think about all those returned bills that didn't make it to the right address, queried bills, and the cost of the staff to handle it all. The prepaid phone business was pioneered in developing economies where offering credit (that is, allowing customers to pay later) to millions of people who don't have credit cards or bank accounts to automatically charge is uneconomic. So instead, the phone companies pioneered a way to sell prepaid airtime. Pay cash now, make the call later. Again, the prepayment is from the point of view of the consumer. The phone company shows a deferred revenue liability matching all the cash received from the sale of prepaid airtime.

Especially in very high turnover businesses, collecting payment after the sale would be a logistical nightmare. Next time you're in a McDonalds or Burger King, think about what the business would have to do if they let you eat the burger and milkshake first, and then pay later. Next time you're at a Michelin-starred restaurant, you might equally wonder how often the waiter has to run out the door to chase a diner who hasn't paid.

We'll discuss one particular form of prepayment—gift vouchers—in the next chapter.

12. CASH RECEIVED BEFORE REVENUE EARNED: EARNING & COST OF SALE

Classic Transaction Twelve

Includes Profit Margin vs. Markup and

Comprehensive Definition of Revenue

In Transaction 9, we saw the "sale" of a gift voucher, even though no revenue was recognized on the income statement in the Sales account. Instead, we recognized that the business is obligated to the holder of the voucher. It was as if the customer had lent the business $150, except that this "loan" is going to be settled with goods, not cash.

And now that time to settle has come. Dale (the friend who was given the gift voucher by Charlie finally comes in and uses the gift voucher to buy goods.

Classic Transaction 12—March 15

Dale buys some products and presents the gift voucher as payment. $100

So far in the classic transactions, we've seen two other sales transactions:

- Transaction 6 was a cash sale—the sale event and the cash receipt occurred at the same time.
- Transaction 8 was a credit sale for which the payment of $2,000 happened later, in Transaction 11.

This sale represents the final of the three possible timings for cash receipt from a sale: yesterday, today, and tomorrow. Or more commonly: before the sale, at the same time as the sale, and after the sale. This sale of $100 is the "before" scenario.

YESTERDAY, TODAY, AND TOMORROW

In this sale, receipt of the cash has already taken place (in Transaction 9) before the sale event happens.

As with all sales involving inventory, we'll again have a two-part transaction with the revenue recognized in Part A of the Transaction and the inventory expense recognized in Part B.

Recognizing the Revenue—12(a)

The act of serving the customer and fulfilling the obligation to them means that the sale has now happened. Because the customer has now received goods from us (recorded in 12[b] following), we no longer have the obligation to provide the goods or service. The act of serving the customer eliminates the obligation and is our value-generating activity, or revenue. The retail price of the goods that Dale chose was $100, which means that the gift voucher was only partly redeemed with $50 of obligation remaining after this sale.

Which two buckets? Deferred Revenue and Sales.

Increasing or decreasing? The liability account decreases, and the revenue/income account increases.

	Debiting Effect	Crediting Effect
March 15 Recognize revenue from gift voucher sale	Deferred Revenue 100	Sales 100

BaSIS Framework: Redemption of Gift Voucher

The BaSIS Framework below shows the gift voucher obligation being partly redeemed, along with the associated income/revenue.

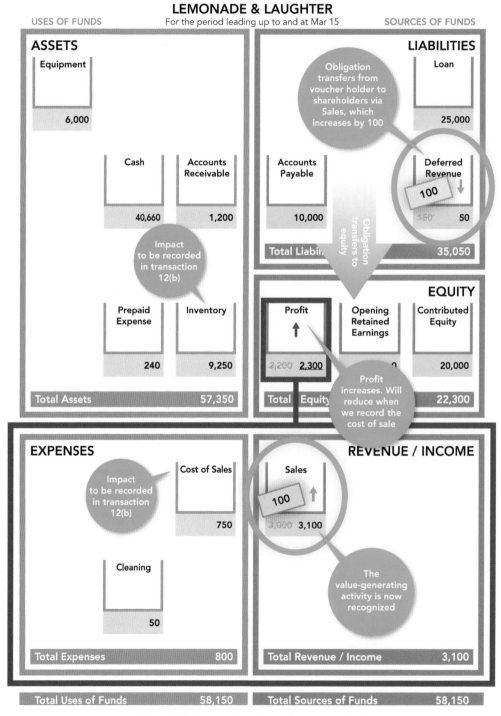

Figure 129. **BaSIS Framework after redemption of gift voucher.**

Revenue is now recognized because the sale (Value-Generating Activity) has taken place, marked by the delivery of goods. This will be recorded in Transaction 12(b).

Note the elegant point being made by the large shaded blue arrow in *Figure 129* that points from liabilities to equity. It's showing how the obligation of the $100 worth of cash received from the gift voucher purchaser has shifted from the gift voucher holder to the shareholders of the business. Where $100 of assets was previously obligated to a creditor (the customer), it is now obligated to the shareholders. Because the company fulfilled its part of the economic transaction by delivering goods to the customer, the company is entitled to obligate $100 of its assets to its shareholders instead of to its customer. So, it cancels $100 of obligation to its creditors and increases $100 of obligation to its shareholders. The blue arrow is representing this "move" or "transfer" of obligation from one funder of the business to the other.

Recognizing Cost of Sale—12(b)

The business sacrifices $20 of inventory in sale to Dale.

To fulfill the sale to the customer, the business handed over inventory, just as it did in the previous two sale events: 6(b) in Chapter 6 where the cost of sale was $250, and 8(b) in Chapter 8 where the cost of sale was $500.

As always, we ask, what are the two impacts? Assets (Inventory) and Expenses (Cost of Sales).

Are they increasing or decreasing? Inventory decreases and COS increases. So, we debit the expense account and credit the asset account.

	Debiting Effect	Crediting Effect
March 15 Used some of our inventory in sale to Dale. 20.	COS	Inventory
	20	20

BaSIS Framework: Cost of Sale

The four impacts of the sale and cost of sale can be seen on the BaSIS Framework in *Figure 130* following.

- Inventory is credited, decreasing by $20.
- Cost of Sales is debited, increasing by $20 and automatically reducing the Profit account by the same amount.
- Shown from part 12(a), Deferred Revenue is debited, decreasing by $100, and
- Sales is credited, increasing by $100 and automatically increasing Profit.
- The combined profit impact is an increase of $80.

Stand back for a second and see what's happened overall on the Framework as a result of the sale and subsequent part-redemption of the gift voucher in Transactions 9 & 12.

Assets are up by a net $130 (cash increase of $150 from the gift voucher sale, less inventory given away of $20). These $130 of assets (Uses of Funds) are being funded (Sources of

Funds) partly by creditor Dale, who holds the remaining $50 balance on the gift card, and the remainder by shareholders as profit in the amount of $80.

STUFF CIVILIZATIONS ARE BUILT ON

Isn't that just so clever? This is the brilliance of accounting on display. Keeping track of what value the entity has and to whom it is obligated for the value, and how it was sourced by funders and through the value activities of the business. This is the stuff that civilizations are built on! It's why this book is called *The Joy of Accounting*. Gotta love it!

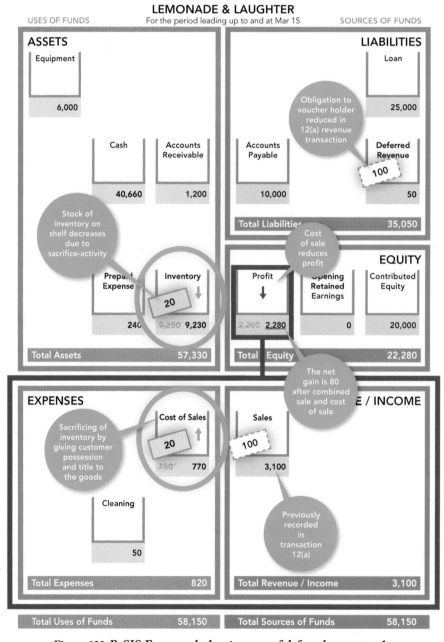

Figure 130. **BaSIS Framework showing cost of deferred revenue sale.**

Financial Statements after Gift Voucher Partial Redemption and Inventory Expense 12(a) & 12(b)

After Transaction 12, the balance sheet and income statement of Lemonade & Laughter look like this:

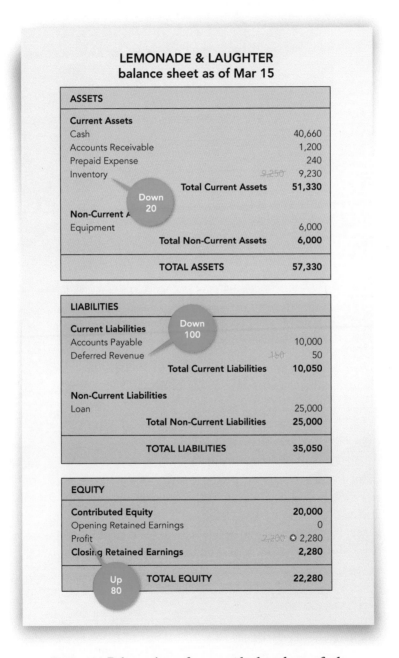

Figure 131. Balance sheet after prepaid sale and cost of sale.

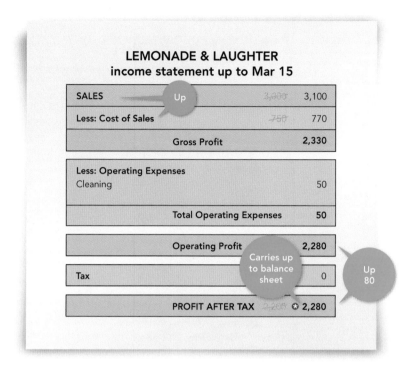

Figure 132. **Income statement after prepaid sale and cost of sale.**

Reflecting on where the combined Transactions 9 and Transaction 12 left Lemonade & Laughter to this point, we will see:

- The business has $130 more assets as uses of funds. The sources of those funds are $80 worth of funding by shareholders as profit, and $50 funded by Dale as a creditor holding a gift voucher.
- Assets: the $130 of extra assets is from the $150 of extra cash less the $20 inventory given away.
- Liabilities: the $80 profit arises from the $100 value-generating activity revenue recognized, and the $20 value-sacrificing activity of inventory consumption.
- Equity: the $50 creditor funding is the balance on the gift voucher and the $150 original amount less the $100 redeemed.
- How the $80 of profit was generated is explained in the income statement. Value of $100 was generated and value of $20 was sacrificed, resulting in the net value generation of $80.

Discussion: Gift Vouchers

Use 'Em or Lose 'Em

Gift cards are big business.

They solve the problem of not knowing what toy to buy your friend's child. You just buy the gift card and let the kid choose the toy they want in the toy department.

The toy shop secures a customer that it may not have captured otherwise, locking in the future revenue by receiving the cash up front. The store knows that revenue will at some point eventuate because gift cards usually declare in the fine print that they are non-refundable for cash. The store only wants to settle its gift card obligation by selling you some inventory, not by giving back cash.

There are other benefits for the retailer too. For example, you may have noticed racks in a pharmacy of other retailers' gift cards in addition to the pharmacy's own. It's a win-win for both retailers because the pharmacy sells a gift card for, say, $50 that it will pay the toy shop (or Apple, if it's an iTunes gift card), say, $45 for. The pharmacy has just made a $5 profit. Apple will receive $45 from its sale and make a profit on that, albeit at a lower profit margin than if it had collected the full $50 by selling its gift card directly.

There is, of course, another matter that you've probably already thought of: so many gift cards get lost. And clearly retailers like it when that happens. They never have to hand over any goods to fulfill the obligation—but what happens to that obligation that shows in their accounts?

These days, most retailers put an expiry date on any gift card they sell. When the card expires, the obligation is cancelled on the balance sheet and revenue is recognized in the way it was in Transaction 12(a) above, although you might use a separate "sales-type" account in revenue to track this information. The big difference, however, is that there's no Transaction 12(b). That is, there's no cost of sale. So, the transaction represents pure profit. The amount of revenue recognized is the same as the amount of profit recognized.

There are laws in many countries that protect consumers who hold gift cards. The laws specify a minimum duration before which the card may expire. In the United States, the federal law was changed in the mid-2000s to allow retailers to charge an annual 25 percent holding fee after a year. So, after four years, the gift voucher would be worth nothing to the consumer, and there would be no obligation from the retailer's point of view. States in the US may impose more stringent burdens on retailers, perhaps requiring a five-year duration before expiry or no expiry at all. In such circumstances, the business can still conservatively predict that a percentage of gift card obligations incurred in a reporting period will never be redeemed (say 10 percent, for example). It will therefore recognize that amount as revenue in that reporting period.

Thinking about how Deferred Revenue appears on a balance sheet, here's something else to consider. When you pick up the balance sheet of your company, would you rather see a Deferred Revenue obligation of $150 or an Account Payable obligation of $150?

The answer lies in what it will take to make the respective obligations disappear. To eliminate the Account Payable obligation, the company will have to pay $150 of cash to the creditor. To eliminate the Deferred Revenue obligation, the company will have to hand over some inventory, but not $150 worth of inventory. In the example above, giving away $20 worth of inventory eliminated $100 worth of gift voucher-obligation. In other words, there's a profit margin element built into the Deferred Revenue number, but the profit is only realized or "released" when the sale is made or the voucher is cancelled.

A final thought on the nature and benefits of gift cards to retailers relates to the $50 left over on the card in our scenario. The customer didn't manage to find something worth exactly $150 to buy today. So they'll either come back and probably find something more expensive, meaning additional sales for the store, or they'll forget about the remaining balance on the card and the store will eventually recognize it as revenue and pure profit when the card expires.

Nice business, gift cards!

MARGIN VS. MARKUP

Margin versus Markup

There are two important terms to describe the rate at which a company generates profit: profit margin and markup.

Describing them as a "rate" means that we're comparing two measures. As miles per hour describes how much distance you would cover in an hour, Profit Margin describes how much profit you will make on a dollar of sale. Markup describes how much profit you will make on a dollar of inventory.

In Transaction 12, our company Lemonade & Laughter made a $100 sale with a cost of sale of $20 and profit of $80.

Profit Margin

The rate at which the company made profit was $80 on $100 of sales. Expressed as a percentage, this is an 80 percent profit margin.

In this case, the profit is a Gross Profit. The term Net Profit will be used further down the income statement after other expenses that indirectly supported the sale are taken into account, like the cleaning. It would be a naïve exclamation for a customer to simply declare "wow, the business made $80 profit off of me." That would be to forget that the company must incur additional sacrifices like rent, salaries, transport, administration, stock theft, and more on the way to getting the client the item that cost the business $20. The only difference between the $20 inventory value sacrifice and the other sacrifices like rent, etc., is that the inventory was directly linked to this sale, whereas the other expenses are not directly attributable to the particular sale but are apportioned over all the company's sales.

Markup

Retailers are in the habit of thinking about the goods they acquired as a starting point for their calculations. Starting with the cost they paid for the goods that they bought wholesale, they then calculate the higher price for which they will on-sell the goods. They decide how much markup they will add. That is, they start with the Cost of Goods price, and then work out the retail price at which they will sell the goods.

In Transaction 12, the $20 base cost of goods was marked up four times, or 400 percent, to get to the $100 sale price. Starting with $20, it was then marked up →40→60→80→100.

1) Adding $20 once to the base cost of goods would make the sale price $40, reflecting a 100 percent markup.
2) Adding $20 twice to the base cost of goods would make the price $60, reflecting a 200 percent markup.
3) Adding $20 thrice to the base cost of goods would make the price $60, reflecting a 300 percent markup.
4) Adding $20 four times to the base cost of goods would make the price $100, reflecting a 400 percent markup.

An 80 percent Gross Profit Margin is equivalent to a 400 percent Markup.

Sale Price	Start with $100	100%
Cost of Sale	less $20 cost	20%
Gross Profit	gives $80 profit	80%

Gross Profit Margin percentage is calculated as Gross Profit ÷ Sale Price × 100 = 80 ÷ 100 × 100 = 80%

Purchase price	Starting with $20 cost, and	100%
Markup profit	adding $80 markup	400%
Retail price	gives $100 sales price	500%

Markup percentage is calculated as Profit ÷ Cost of Goods × 100 = 80 ÷ 20 × 100 = 400%

REVENUE

Comprehensive Definition of Revenue

We've been defining revenue as value-generating activity. We saw in Transaction 6(a) how the sale generated valuable cash worth $1,000. Similarly, in Transaction 8(a) we saw revenue generating an asset in the form of an account receivable worth $2,000.

Now in Transaction 12(a), we've seen revenue doing something different. In this chapter, revenue caused a reduction in liabilities rather than an increase in assets.

In all three Transactions, the revenue caused an increase in Profit and Equity, which represents a benefit to the owners. When equity increases, that means more assets are obligated to the owners, regardless of whether there are more or less total assets.

To embrace both scenarios where assets increase and also where liabilities decrease, we expand the definition of revenue to be: any activity that increases assets or decreases liabilities to the benefit of the shareholders.

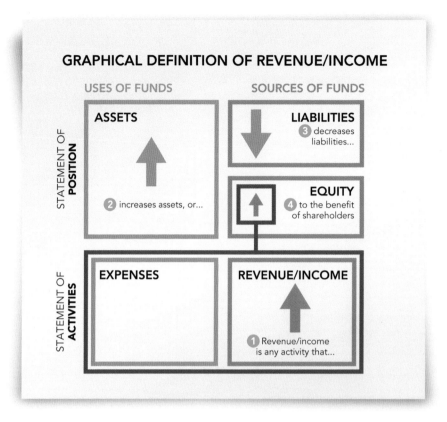

Figure 133. **Graphical definition of revenue.**

Read the text within the BaSIS Framework, in the sequence of the blue numbers. Think about the color logic as you do so. That is, there is both a green arrow and an orange arrow, as there must be in double entry accounting. When the arrow is the same color as the side, it's an up arrow. When the arrow is the opposite color from the side, it's a down arrow.

> The expanded definition of revenue is:
>
> any activity that increases assets or decreases liabilities
> to the benefit of the shareholders

Net Assets

To capture how revenue generates assets or diminishes liabilities, we can also express revenue as any activity that generates net assets to the benefit of the shareholders.

Comprehensive Definition of Expense

We'll see in the discussion after Transaction 13 in the next chapter how *expense* is defined comprehensively in a similar way, in *Figure 137*. Feel free to skip ahead and have a look at that graphical definition of expense now. But make sure to come back here, as we continue our journey through the classic transactions. Three more to go!

13. ACCRUED EXPENSE INCURRED

Classic Transaction Thirteen

Includes Comprehensive Definition of Expense

Lemonade & Laughter now incurs another expense, much like the previous expenses. This time, it doesn't pay for the expense immediately. In fact, it is not even completely sure of the final amount that it will have to pay.

Classic Transaction 13—March 31

Ace Co. cleaned the shop during March. We estimate the bill will be $170.

The business has consumed cleaning services. It's incurred an expense, but we have no invoice yet. As we've just discussed, under the accrual accounting system, we will record the expense activity even though no cash has been paid to the supplier for the expense.

We remind ourselves that there are three timing scenarios when paying for an expense. We can pay before, at the same time, or after the expense happens. In this case, we are paying for the expense afterwards. The agreement with the supplier is that we can pay up to fourteen days later.

Accrued Expenses

The term "accrual accounting" refers to the accounting basis used to prepare a set of accounts, as discussed in Part 2, Chapter 8. It contrasts with the cash accounting basis or simply "cash accounting". The term "accrual accounting" sounds similar to making an accrual, but it is used differently.

The terms accrual, expense accrual, revenue accrual, or to make an accrual are used to describe the recognition of an expense or revenue, specifically when no invoicing has taken place (yet).

When a business has done a value-consuming activity—in other words, has incurred an expense—but has not yet received an invoice for that expense, we talk about recognizing the expense on the income statement (and affecting profit) by making an accrual and showing it as an accrued expense.

Accruals like this are often recognized—that is, journaled—at a period end so that the reported profit figure at the period-end date is correct on the income statement and balance sheet. If, at period end, you know an expense has been incurred but the supplier hasn't yet sent you the invoice for it, you would recognize the expense by making an accrual.

So, let's ask our habitual questions for this scenario.

What are the two impacts? We know there has been an expense, and we can use the same account as before, so we'll use Cleaning. The fact that we haven't paid for the cleaning makes no difference to the expense account. The second account will be a liability account. We won't use the account payable account, because the cleaners don't legally have to be paid until we receive an invoice from them. Remember how in the chapter about buying on credit, we said that the word "invoice" comes from the Latin *in* + *vox* because an invoice calls in what's due? Well, Ace Cleaners haven't called in our debt yet, but we know that we are nevertheless indebted. So, we will create another short-term liability account, which we'll call Accrued Expenses. Yes, this is another language paradox. The word "expense" appears in the title of the account but it's not an expense account.

Are they increasing or decreasing? Both accounts are increasing.

To reflect the increase-impacts, we use the journal to debit the debit-type expense account and credit the credit-type liability account.

	Debiting	Crediting
March 31 Recognize un-invoiced cleaning done by Ace Cleaners during March.	Cleaning 170	Accrued Expenses 170

BaSIS Framework: Accrued Expense

The Framework in *Figure 134* below shows the Cleaning expense account debited and the Accrued Expenses liability account credited in order to recognize the cleaning activity that has been consumed but not yet invoiced.

Cleaning expenses have now increased to $220 from $50, and the Accrued Expense liability has appeared, going from zero to $170. The profit account has decreased by $170 from $2,280 to $2,110.

Changing Obligations

The business now has the same total assets of $57,330 as it had just before the cleaning expense happened. No change there. The existing assets are now just obligated differently.

The two balance sheet impacts are both on the "sources of funds" side of the framework.

Total liabilities increased by $170 and total equity decreased by $170 (via an increase in expenses). The equity reduction happened in the profit account.

In other words, the business has the same amount of assets, but the mix of obligations to the funders has changed. From the funders' point of view, the creditors are claiming a greater share of the business's assets and the owners are claiming a lesser share.

Timing

Sometimes, students of accounting will say something pragmatic like "Why not just wait until the invoice comes in and record it as an expense in the next period? At least we won't have to guess at the invoice amount!"

Yes, the amount will be accurate, but the profit earned for the current period will be overstated, and for the next period it will be understated. The expense was incurred in the March period and should therefore impact the March result. And while an expense of this amount is likely to be immaterial to the results, if we don't have a process in place to catch such events, then a much larger impact could be missed.

The accrual entry is put through as a "balance-date adjustment" (general journal) on the last day of the reporting period. On the first day of the next reporting period (i.e., the following day), this journal is reversed so that when the invoice is received and recorded as per usual, we won't be double counting this expense.

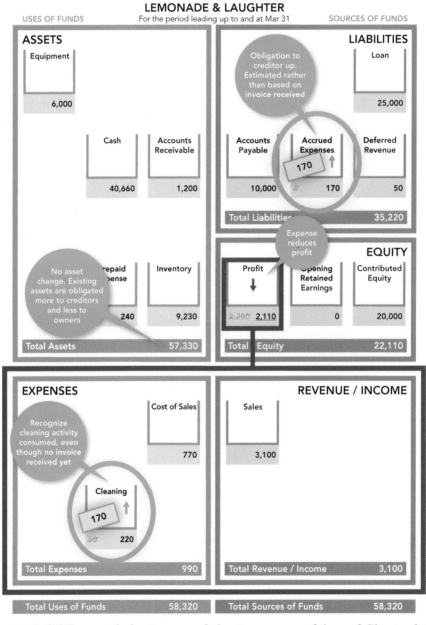

Figure 134. **BaSIS Framework showing accrued cleaning expense and Accrued Cleaning liability.**

Payroll Expense and Reversing Journal

Payroll is an expense that commonly gives rise to an accrual because employees don't invoice their employers. Contractually, employees can expect their employers to automatically pay their salary and wages per the agreed schedule, be it weekly, fortnightly, monthly, etc.

On a balance day (end of reporting period), if a business hasn't paid its employees for work they've done, then the business recognizes that expense and resultant liability as an accrual when preparing its accounts.

This is how it works: assume that a business pays its employees every other Friday, and let's say this means that Friday January 2 was a payday. In 2015, for example, January 2 fell on a Friday, which means the work done by the employees from December 19, 2014 through January 1, 2015 was paid on January 2, 2015.

So, for a company preparing their balance sheet on December 31, 2014, there were nine days in December 2014 for which the employees had not yet been paid. Without an accrual, the payroll expense shown in the accounts for December 2014 would be too low and January 2015's would be too high. The solution is to accrue nine days' worth of payroll expense on December 31.

When accruing the payroll expense on 31 December 2014, the accountants would put through a reversing journal entry dated 1 January 2015. On that first day of the new accounting period, they would debit (reduce) the accrued liability and credit (reduce) the payroll expense account. This means that when ten days of work was paid for and recorded on January 2, 2015, the payroll expense wasn't double-counted. After the reversing entry is posted, on January 1 there would be a negative expense for nine days of work. On January 2, an entry for ten days of work would be posted, meaning that a net one day of that payroll period impacts the 2015 year. This is how it should be. Even though that day, January 1, was a public holiday, salaried employees earn on public holidays too!

Financial Statements after Accrued Expense Transaction 13

After recognizing the accrued expense, the balance sheet and income statement of Lemonade & Laughter looks like this:

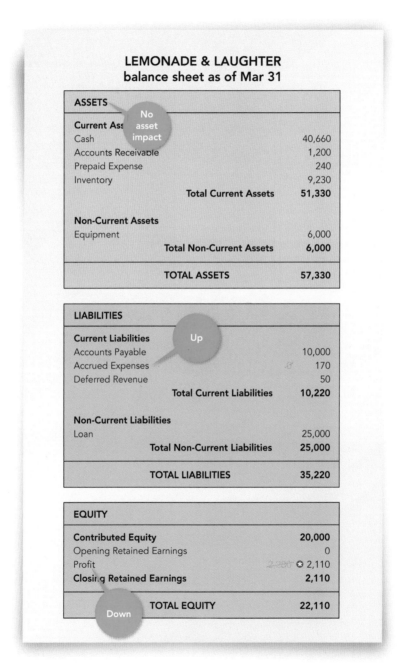

Figure 135. Balance sheet after accrued expense incurred.

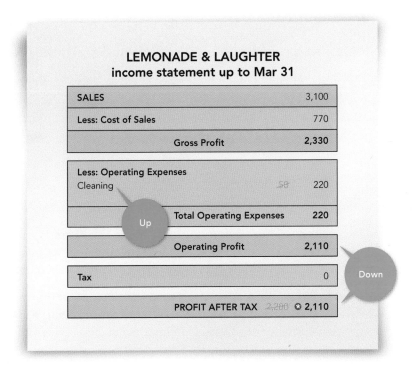

Figure 136. **Income statement after accrued expense incurred.**

The business has total assets of $57,330, funded by $35,220 of debt obligation and $22,110 of equity obligation.

The equity obligation comprises $20,000 contributed equity and $2,110 generated equity. The generated equity came about from $3,100 of value-generating activity and $990 of value-sacrificing activity, giving a net value generation of $2,110 during the period. The net value generation links to the balance sheet where the generated obligation to the shareholders is shown.

The $990 of value-sacrificing activity comprises $770 of sacrifices directly associated with the revenue generation and $220 of sacrifices indirectly linked to revenue generation, often referred to as *overhead*.

Discussion: More About Expenses

Comprehensive Definition of Expense: Net Value-Sacrificing Activity

Until now, we've defined an expense as an activity that consumes assets. We've seen a couple of examples of such activities. In Transactions 6(b) and 8(b), the activity involved handing over ownership of our valuable inventory to customers who walked off with what were formerly our possessions. We called that activity Cost of Sales, or Cost of Goods Sold.

In Transaction 7, the activity was window cleaning, which resulted in $50 of our precious cash being given to the window cleaners.

However, in Transaction 9, no asset was reduced. Instead, a liability increased.

In both cases, whether an asset was reduced or a liability increased, the profit account in equity was reduced to the detriment of the shareholders. The result was detrimental to the owners because their claim on the business reduced, mirroring the decrease in total equity.

Seeing the two different manifestations of an expense (asset decrease or expense increase) has us define what an expense is more comprehensively. Rather than thinking of an expense only as an activity that reduces assets, we now define an expense as any activity that decreases an asset or increases a liability to the detriment of the owners.

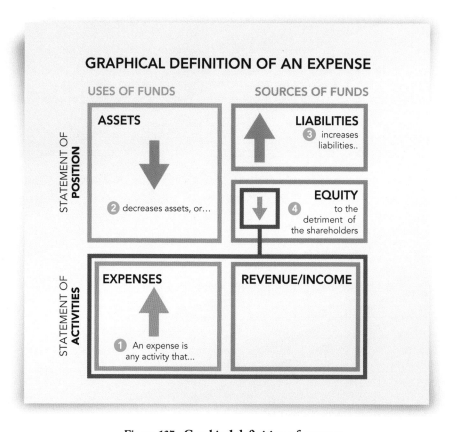

Figure 137. **Graphical definition of expense.**

Read the text within the Framework in *Figure 137* following the sequence marked by the blue numbers.

Be sure to think about the double entry color logic as you do.

The large green arrow represents an expense happening. The matching orange effect decreases assets or increases liabilities. Because the green expense arrow falls within the purple income statement section of the BaSIS Framework, the expense links to profit and automatically reduces profit and equity.

Net Assets

To capture how expenses either diminish assets or increase liabilities, we can also express an expense as any activity that sacrifices net assets to the detriment of shareholders.

Assets Reduced, but Not Expense

Now ask yourself, why do we need to say "to the detriment of the owners"?

 Recall how in Classic Transaction 3, the business repaid a loan. The result was that assets (cash) decreased by $5,000, and so did liabilities (loan account) by $5,000. You could quibble and say that the repayment activity decreased assets and was therefore an expense—but it isn't, because the reduction in cash wasn't to the detriment of the owners. Profit didn't decrease and the business's obligation to the owners didn't decrease. The balancing offset wasn't to equity, but to liabilities. It was the lenders' claim on the business that decreased, not the owners' claim. We make this clear by saying that expense activities are to the detriment of the owners.

We haven't seen it in the classic transactions, but in the same way you can repay a loan, you can also repay equity. You can do this, for example, by buying back shares from the owner. When you do this, Cash reduces and Equity reduces. It's the opposite of what happened in Classic Transaction 2. This share buyback scenario doesn't involve an expense either because a buyback isn't to the detriment of the owner. In the owners' accounts, they have less claim on the business, but they gain cash. They are no worse off.

> The expanded definition of expense is:
>
> any activity that decreases assets or increases liabilities
> to the detriment of the shareholders

Discussion: Current Liabilities

The Most Dangerous Thing on a Balance Sheet

Being able to buy goods and services on credit is a great funding resource for a business. Particularly if the business can negotiate longish payment terms with its trade creditors, it means that the business can get on with its business of generating profit and cash flow without immediately having to fork out cash. Trade creditors can be a significant source of funds for a business. On Global's balance sheet, you will see that its Payables creditors are funding $182,475 of Global's assets.

How long a supplier will give you to pay them depends on their terms, which may be part of a negotiated arrangement between you and them. When one business is powerful and buys a lot from a supplier, they can often demand very generous payment terms, like thirty, sixty, or even ninety days.

A huge company like Walmart pays its suppliers slowly because it can. Walmart also sells its inventory very quickly. The company's stock turn, or inventory turnover, is extremely high, and that velocity is part of their formula for success. The general idea in business, especially retail, is to keep as little inventory as you can and then to replenish the shelves as quickly as you can so that you don't run out and lose sales. Nobody wants to go to a chicken shop that's run out of chicken.

NOT TOO MUCH, NOT TOO LITTLE

Insolvency

Having said that accounts payable is an important source of funding for many businesses, it is also often the most dangerous line on a balance sheet.

The fatal danger to any business is that it can't pay its debts as and when they fall due. If it can't, then it's judged to be insolvent. Any creditor who is owed payment by a company can ask a judge to force the company to pay up. If the judge decides that the debt is valid and the company can't pay, the judge can declare the company bankrupt. The word comes from the mid-sixteenth century Italian *banca rotta*, meaning "broken bench." In years gone by, creditors would smash the workbenches of their debtors when they didn't pay up. Those debtors were also thrown into what were called debtors' prisons. Both practices, of course, were not very enlightened because it's harder to pay off your debts when you've got no workbench or when you're shackled in a dungeon.

BANCA ROTTA AND SHACKLES

Modern legal jurisdictions now have a more enlightened approach to bankruptcy. Companies in the US can, for instance, be put into Chapter 11. This is the title of a chapter of the US Bankruptcy Code. The provisions of the Chapter allow the debtor or creditor to petition a bankruptcy court to approve a reorganization arrangement. This reorganization gives the company the right and ability to break certain agreements and cancel contracts, and to obtain new loans that rank above prior obligations. The intention is that the reorganized company can trade its way out of insolvency, and overall people will be better off.

Liquidation

Sometimes there's no light on the horizon and the courts will decide to liquidate the business. This means it will stop operating and its frozen assets will be sold off to pay its creditors. They are paid in their order of entitlement, from secured creditors down through unsecured and subordinated creditors. Many will expect to get less than the full value of their debt. Shareholders are at the back of the queue, and often lose their total investment. Recall the discussion about Debt vs. Equity, particularly the discussion about priority.

One of the biggest instances of bankruptcy and liquidation was Lehman Brothers, Inc., a US bank that had assets of about $700 billion with which to settle its obligations. The authors of this book were owed money for teaching at that bank. In the end, we got 43 cents on the dollar, as they say, or 43 percent of what we were owed.

Tomorrow's Deadline

The reason, of course, that accounts payable are dangerous is that they are short-term debts. Chief Financial Officers don't lay awake at night worried about whether they will be able to pay off a twenty-year bond. What keeps them up at night is concern about next week's payroll, and those suppliers who are due to be paid tomorrow. In the case of key suppliers, such as a manufacturer supplying white goods to an appliance store, not only will they demand payment for their debts owed, but they may also stop supplying further inventory to the store, which further worsens the store's plight. Having found that they are at risk of not getting paid for goods already delivered, they will think twice before delivering any more goods for which they might also not get paid. The supplier might find themselves in the uncomfortable position of cutting off a foot (contributing to the demise of the business and not getting paid fully) to save the leg (staunching even further losses).

Do they keep supplying the retailer to help it continue to operate and hopefully repay all that's due but in the process risk getting in deeper and possibly losing even more? Or does the supplier cut their losses and stop supplying any further goods, accepting—and perhaps crystalizing—some non-repayment, bad-debt loss?

We met the Current Ratio and talked about how it measures the amount of current assets available to pay for the current liabilities of the business. As mentioned earlier, the current ratio is a crude indicator that management and creditors keep an eye on as they manage the risk of default.

14. DEPRECIATION

Classic Transaction Fourteen—Dust to Dust

For dust thou art, and unto dust shalt thou return.

The book of Genesis in the Bible, reminds us we don't last forever. Neither do the assets that a business has. They get used up and lose their value gradually, which gradual loss of value must, of course, be accounted for.

Classic Transaction 14—March 31

Account for three month's loss of value of equipment, which will last for five years with no resale value at the end.

When a business pays for and consumes a service like window cleaning, we show the expense immediately to reflect the value consumption that has taken place. This is typically measured precisely with an invoice and a cash payment.

When the business buys inventory, we show the inventory as an asset, as we did in Transaction 5. Then, as soon as we give away that inventory in a sale event, we reflect the loss of that value as a Cost of Sale expense, as we did in Transactions 6(b), 8(b), and 12(b).

Equipment also loses its value. It wears out and devalues over its useful life. That value loss must be accounted for as an expense activity, like any other.

The main difference between a cost of sale expense or a cleaning expense and equipment wearing out is timing. Whereas our cleaning expense was immediate, and whereas the cost of sales expenses we've seen were triggered by an event (the handing over of inventory), the loss of value of the equipment is typically time-based and progressive. The key difference between equipment losing value and the other scenarios is that this loss of value happens gradually over several accounting periods.

At the end of an accounting period (in this Classic Transaction, the period is the three-month quarter January through March), the value of the equipment will be less than it was at the start of the period. But how much less? What is the value of the equipment to the business?

DUST TO DUST

In Part 1, Chapter 2, we discussed how we value assets. We saw that it is possible to value them in a number of ways, such as: what you paid for them, what a reasonable person would say they're worth, what you could sell them for, and so on (see Methods of Valuing Assets on page 21).

In this case, Lemonade & Laughter's equipment is currently recorded on the balance sheet at the cost value we used when we acquired it in Transaction 4. In that transaction at the beginning of January, we put the equipment onto the balance sheet at the purchase price of $6,000.

So how much value should we record the equipment as having lost in the period from the start of January until March 31? We can't know as an absolute truth, so we make an estimate based upon some assumptions. We'll come up with a value that will be called Cost Less Depreciation, or Written Down Value (WDV).

Assumptions

The key assumptions we make are:

- the equipment will last five years (sixty months), and
- the equipment will lose the same amount of value in each of those months, and
- it will be worth zero at the end of its useful life.

This approach of assuming that the equipment loses the same value each month is called the "straight-line deprecation method." An alternative method would, for example, assume that the equipment loses more value in the earlier periods than it loses in the later periods. Such an approach is called the "reducing balance depreciation method" and might better match the loss in value over time of something like a new motor vehicle, which drops value as soon as it leaves the lot and then more steadily from there in subsequent years.

There are also methods that use "time in use" measures such as "machine hours" for a crane or a bulldozer, for example. This method is considered to better match the pattern of value loss for this type of depreciable asset.

We also assume that the equipment will have no resale or scrap value at the end of its estimated useful life. If it did have such value, we would reduce the depreciable amount accordingly so we don't over-depreciate this asset.

Using the straight-line method, we work out that the loss of value during the three months or first quarter of the year is $300, calculated as being 1/60 of $6 000, or $100 per month, for three months. We've assumed the purchase happened at the very start of January, ignoring that it was actually January 5.

In each of the sixty months of the equipment's life, we estimate that it will lose $100 worth of value, so that at the end of its useful life it will have lost 60 × $100, or $6,000 of value, which is to say all of it.

To record the impact of the depreciation on the balance sheet and income statement, we must answer the following:

What are the two impacts? Assets (Equipment) and Expenses (Depreciation).

Are they increasing or decreasing? We increase Depreciation Expense by debiting it, and we decrease Equipment by crediting it using the journal as shown here:

	Debiting	Crediting
March 31	Depreciation	Equipment
Deprecation of equipment for the	Expense	
three months January-March.	300	300

BaSIS Framework: Depreciation of Equipment

The depreciation journal entry impacts the BaSIS Framework as shown in *Figure 138*. The Equipment asset (WDV) decreases to $5,700, the Depreciation Expense increases from zero to $300, and profit reduces to $1,810.

We're not done with this transaction yet, but go ahead and examine the BaSIS Framework in *Figure 138*, and then we'll look at another issue that influences how we account for the event.

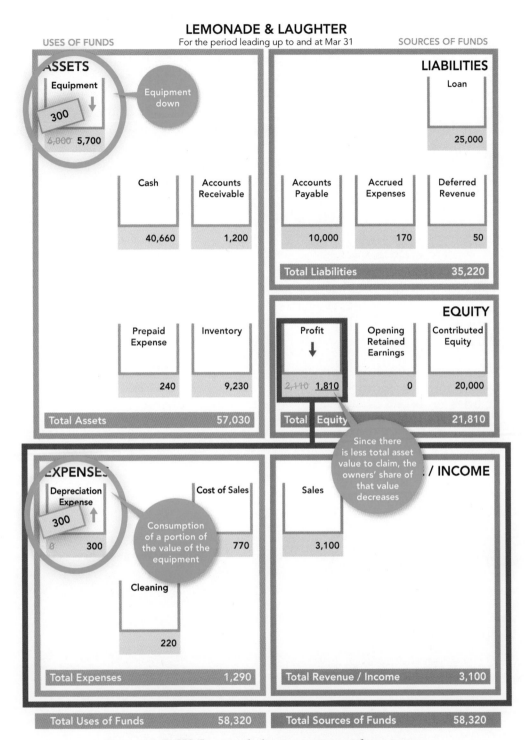

Figure 138. BaSIS Framework showing equipment depreciation
with no accumulated depreciation account.

Slight Problem

Even though the total value of all the assets is correctly stated, as is the total expenses and the profit, we have a small issue. Thinking ahead to next month or quarter, during which the equipment will lose more of its value, we will again need to work out how much value has been lost. We've assumed that each month, the asset is losing 1/60 of the original value. But what is that original value? Right now, the value of the asset is shown as $5,700. The loss of value isn't 1/60 of $5,700. It's 1/60 of $6,000, but that amount isn't shown anywhere anymore. We changed the balance of the equipment account when we posted the journal entry, and now we need to know the original amount.

WHERE DID WE START?

So, what we need to do is keep the original cost value of the asset intact. In a related asset account, we'll capture the reduction impacts of $100 per month or $300 per quarter. We'll change the name of the Equipment account to Equipment at Cost. The adjacent related account is what's called a contra account, because it offsets the account it's paired with. The word *contra* derives from Latin and means "against" or "opposite." We'll call this contra account "Accumulated Depreciation" because the balance in it accumulates.

Take note of the two depreciation accounts we have now: Accumulated Depreciation lives on the balance sheet, next to its related asset account. The Depreciation account is an expense account, living in the income statement.

Redoing the journal entry to keep the cost of the asset intact, we now go ahead and ask our habitual questions again.

What are the two impacts? Expenses (Depreciation) and Assets (Accumulated Depreciation). Note, we've also changed the name of the Equipment account on the balance sheet to "Equipment at Cost" and it is untouched in the revised journal entry.

Are they increasing or decreasing? Debit Depreciation Expense to increase it, and credit Accumulated Depreciation to decrease it. Since the Accumulated Depreciation account started at zero, and we're reducing it by putting an orange ticket into the green account, it will now have a negative value. It's gone from zero to negative 300.

In color terms, it's a green account with an orange balance.

	Debiting	Crediting
March 31	Depreciation	Accumulated
Deprecation of equipment for the three	Expense	Depreciation
months to the end of March.	300	300

On the BaSIS Framework in *Figure 139* following, we now see that Equipment at Cost is $6,000 and Accumulated Depreciation has a negative (credit) balance of -$300. The written-down value of the combined buckets, shown with the dotted green rectangle around them, is $5,700.

The income statement still shows the Depreciation expense as $300. Profit is still showing as having reduced to $1,810.

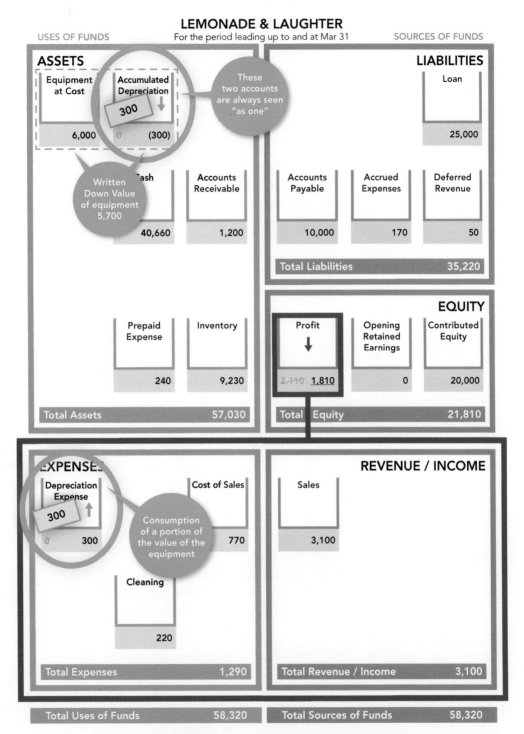

Figure 139. BaSIS Framework showing depreciation expense
and accumulated depreciation contra-account.

Financial Statements after Depreciation Transaction 14

After Depreciation Transaction 14, the balance sheet and income statement of Lemonade & Laughter look like this:

Figure 140. **Balance sheet after depreciation expense showing accumulated depreciation.**

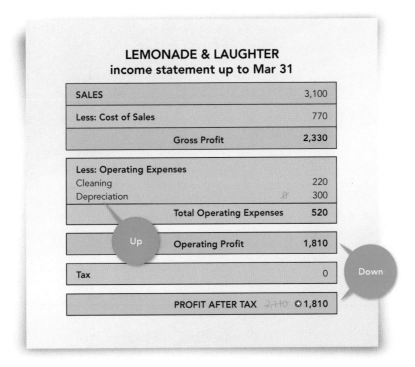

Figure 141. **Income statement showing depreciation expense and reduced operating profit.**

The business now has a net worth on the books of $21,810. The Total Assets have declined to $57,030. Those assets are being funded $35,220 by creditors and $21,810 by the owners. When the assets lost value due to depreciation, the obligation to the creditors was not affected, but the obligation to the owners was reduced (via the Profit account) because the business has less assets that it can obligate to those owners.

Remember, the accounting equation tells us that the business can only obligate to its funders what assets it has. The amount of the total assets is equivalent to the total amount of funding from creditors and shareholders.

The income statement shows a reduction in the profit of $300, and the Depreciation line has gone from zero to $300. The depreciation is an overhead expense, appearing below the Gross Profit total as an Operating Expense.

Discussion: Depreciation

Non-Cash Expense and Cash Flow

Depreciation is probably the most famous so-called "non-cash expense." Any business with non-current assets on their balance sheet will have a depreciation expense in their income statement.

Depreciation is a very real expense. Equipment loses value and eventually it needs to be replaced, then creating a very real cash impact. Depreciation reduces profits just like any other expense. Nevertheless, investors looking at a company's financials are very interested in the depreciation expense. Here's why:

Analysts of a company's prospects know that in the long run, generating a profit is the most important thing the company can do. Doing so is the reason the company exists. So, the analyst carefully looks at profitability.

In the short and medium term, the analyst is often more interested in how much cash will flow into and from the business than in how much profit will be generated. In other words, analysts are sometimes more interested in cash flow than profit.

Analysts are conscious to compare profit and cash flow. When comparing the two, they often start with a profit figure, and from that, work out what the cash flow is. Depreciation is one of the main factors that account for the difference between cash flow and profit.

By now you know that a company's profit is not the same as the amount of the net cash flow into the business. Businesses can make a profit and have more cash from operations going out than coming in. This might be because the accounts receivable has increased. When accounts receivable increase, there were sales for which customers haven't yet paid. The sales made a profit, but they didn't (yet) bring in cash.

Another reason why profit might be higher than cash flow is that the business has used its operating cash to pay down accounts payable, which causes an outflow of cash. So, cash flowed out of the business but didn't decrease profit.

PROFIT VS. CASH FLOW

Inventory follows a similar path. Operating cash might have been used to increase the amount of inventory on hand, which reduction of cash didn't reduce profits. Remember that consuming inventory reduces profit but acquiring inventory does not.

Other than movements in accounts payable, accounts receivable, and inventory, a big difference between the amounts of profit and cash flow is caused by the depreciation expense. In a simple business, if accounts payable, accounts receivable, and inventory stay the same from beginning to end of the accounting period, then cash flow from operations is equal to the profit plus the amount of depreciation.

If you add depreciation back to the profit figure, you arrive at the opening cash flow figure. That is to say, the amount of cash generated by the business's operations.

With all other things staying the same:

Operating profit	$70
Add back depreciation	$30
Operating profit without depreciation	$100 <Equates to cash flow from operations

We're specifying operating cash flow here because there are other types of cash flow that would affect the total cash flow in or out of the business. There are three types of cash flow:

1) Operating cash flow
2) Investing cash flow
3) Financing cash flow.

Getting a long-term loan for the business causes financing cash inflow. Repaying that loan would be a financing cash outflow.

Paying for a piece of equipment causes an investing cash outflow. Selling one of the company's warehouses for cash (that is, divesting the business of the asset) causes an investing cash inflow.

Depreciation is an important part of the gap between the amount of operating cash flow a company generates and the amount of profit it generates.

Equipment's impact on the cash flow and profit

The timeline in *Figure 142* below shows the cash impact and profit impact of buying and using a piece of equipment. It cost $6,000 and lasts five years, with no residual value. It is depreciated on a straight-line basis.

On acquisition, the equipment is paid for and reduces cash by the cost of the equipment. There's no profit impact on acquisition because it's a balance sheet-only transaction. One asset (equipment) is swapped for another asset (cash).

For each of the next five years, there's no further loss of cash, but the profit is decreased by 1/5 of the cost of the equipment.

Ultimately, the accumulated profit impact is the same as the cash impact. The disparity between the cash and profit impacts is what we call a timing difference.

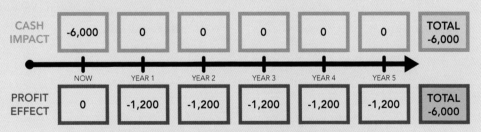

Figure 142. **Timeline showing timing difference between cash and profit impacts of buying equipment.**

Depreciation Rates

In the example above, the depreciation rate is 20 percent per year. Why? What rate of depreciation should a company use? Why not 10 percent or 25 percent or some other rate?

The key question we must ask when choosing a depreciation rate is: How long will the asset last? As with all matters-future, it must be an estimate. It's a calculated guess. Accountants refer to the useful economic life of an asset. Depreciation then spreads the expensing of the asset over that useful life.

A depreciation rate of 20 percent per year implies a useful life of five years, a depreciation rate of 10 percent per year implies a useful life of ten years, and a depreciation rate of 25 percent implies a useful life of four years.

All these examples assume that the depreciation of the asset is the same in each year of its life.

If a piece of equipment is depreciated at 20 percent per year but it turns out that after the fifth year it is still working fine and the business keeps on using it, then it is simply kept on the books of the company fully depreciated. This doesn't mean that it's worth nothing or that it's not useful. The market value of the equipment might be significant, but on the books of the company it is shown as being worth zero on a written down value or cost less depreciation basis.

If the equipment that has been shown as having zero value is then sold, the sale is recorded as revenue called *Profit on Sale or Disposal*. Profit increases by the full value of the sale as there's no cost of sale, because no value was lost from assets since the equipment had no value recorded on the balance sheet.

USEFUL LIFE

If, on the other hand, equipment has been depreciated at 25 percent per year but stops being useful at, say, the start of the third year and is disposed of for nothing, then at that point an expense will be recorded equal to the remaining value of the equipment, i.e., 50 percent of the original value. An expense called Loss on Equipment Disposal or similar will be recorded.

Example

A machine cost $250,000, is expected to be useful for twenty years, and you expect to dispose of it as scrap metal for $10,000 at the end of its useful life. What would the yearly depreciation charge be?

The depreciation charge would be the loss of value over its life, divided by the number of years it would be useful for. The loss of value would be $240,000, calculated as $250,000 less the disposal value of $10,000. The useful life is twenty years. So, $240,000 divided by 20 gives the answer, which is a deprecation per year of $12,000.

Tax and Depreciation

Companies pay tax on their profits, for example at a rate of 20 percent of profits. Expenses reduce profits, and therefore reduce your taxes. The tax authorities typically allow depreciation as an expense that reduces your taxes, also known as a deductible expense.

Because the tax authorities, like the Internal Revenue Service in the US, have an interest in collecting as much tax as they can from companies, they limit how much—or at least how quickly—businesses can incur depreciation expenses. They do this by saying that assets are longer-lived rather than shorter-lived. They specify a minimum depreciable lifespan for various categories of assets.

If they say that a $40,000 truck will last for ten years, then your taxable profit is reduced by $4000 each year. At a 20 percent tax rate, the depreciation expense saves you $800 tax.

If the IRS allowed you to depreciate the truck over four years instead of ten, then your depreciation rate would be $10,000 per year. At the 20 percent tax rate, the expense would save you $2,000 tax.

Longer depreciation periods mean lower depreciation rates. Lower depreciation rates mean higher profits. Higher profits mean more tax.

Shareholder versus Tax Reporting

In preparing their accounts, companies often choose to simply use the depreciation rates that the tax authorities specify for the various types of assets such as Plant & Equipment, Computers, Motor Vehicles, etc.

But companies are also in a bind. If they believe an asset will last longer than the tax authorities do, should they use the shorter or the longer useful life in their accounting? A company wants to report as much profit as it can to its shareholders, but it wants to report as little profit as it can on its tax return. For tax reporting, the company wants short lifespans with high deprecation rates. For shareholder reporting, the company wants long lifespans with low depreciation rates.

Public companies get around this bind by legally preparing two sets of financial reports. They report and pay their taxes to the tax authorities using the tax-specified rates. They report to their shareholders based upon a shareholder set of accounts that use management-determined depreciation rates.

TWO SETS OF REPORTS

This dual reporting can result in an asset or a liability on their shareholder accounts called a Deferred Tax Asset or a Deferred Tax Liability. These come about when the company pays more or less cash to the tax authorities than the amount of the tax expense shown in the shareholder accounts. The asset or liability in the shareholder accounts reconciles the cash-basis tax expense (determined by the actual payments made to the tax authorities) with the accrual-basis tax expense (determined by applying the tax rate to the business's profit as reported to shareholders).

A deferred tax asset represents the right to pay less tax in the future (than the profit in the income statement would otherwise suggest is payable). A deferred tax liability represents the duty to pay more tax in the future (than the income statement implies is due).

Amortization

Amortization is to intangible assets what depreciation is to tangible assets. It's the same principle of spreading the loss of value of an asset over its life. We talk about depreciating tables and chairs, but we talk about amortizing patents and insurance policy assets.

15. PREPAID EXPENSE: CONSUMED GRADUALLY

Classic Transaction Fifteen
Includes Accrual Accounting Summary

In Transaction 11, the business swapped cash for the right to receive advertising. We referred to the right as Prepaid Advertising, Prepaid Expense, or Deferred Expense. Although these accounts might sound like an expense, they represent an asset. The business now consumes part of the asset.

Classic Transaction 15—March 31

Account for advertising used up in the month.

As you know, the dates in this book are not trying to be fully true to life. They are simplified for our learning purposes. We're now at the end of March and want to recognize that we've used up some of the Prepaid Expense that we purchased the previous month.

We're not told how much we used up, but we can work it out. We were told that the campaign will last from March through May, which is three months. We're therefore one third of the way through the campaign. Since it was a $240 campaign, we'll show the consumption of 1/3 of $240 = $80 worth of expense.

To record this in the financial statements…

What are the two impacts? Expenses (Advertising) and Assets (Prepaid Expense).

Are they increasing or decreasing? Debit the advertising expense to increase it and credit the prepaid expense asset to decrease it.

	Debiting	Crediting
March 31 Use of advertising campaign.	Advertising 80	Prepaid Expense 80

BaSIS Framework: Prepaid Expense Consumed

On the BaSIS Framework in *Figure 143*, we see that the Advertising expense account has appeared in the income statement section with a balance of $80. This value-consuming activity had the impact of reducing the Prepaid Expense asset in the balance sheet from $240 to $160.

The $80 expense has reduced profit from $1,810 to $1,730.

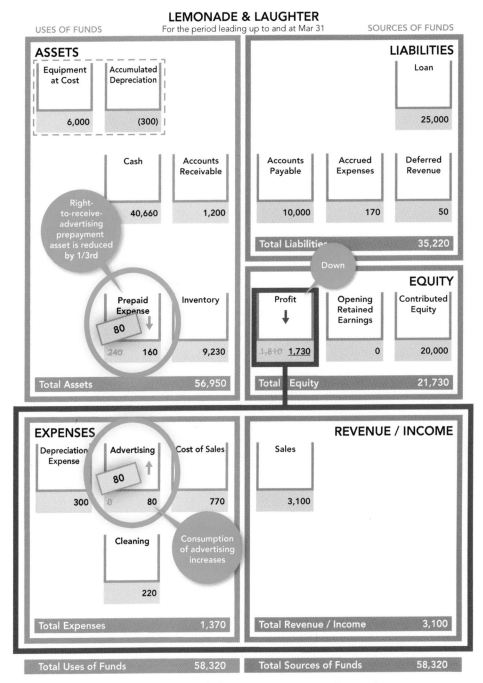

Figure 143. BaSIS Framework showing consumption of prepaid expense.

Note on Layout of the BaSIS Framework Accounts

We're using a few patterns on the BaSIS Framework to create additional order.

In the Assets box, we've put the longer-term non-current accounts in the top row and the current assets in the lower rows. Non-current assets are expected to last more than twelve months, current assets for fewer. We've done this to align with traditional reporting.

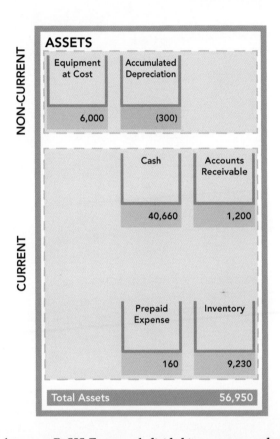

Figure 144. **Assets on BaSIS Framework divided into current and non-current.**

Outside of the US, on a balance sheet that's compliant with IFRS (International Financial Reporting Standards) rules, you'll usually find the non-current assets listed first, above current assets. On a US balance sheet compliant with US GAAP (Generally Accepted Accounting Principles), non-current assets appear below current assets.

In the Liabilities box on the Framework, we've similarly put the non-current Loan liability above the current liabilities.

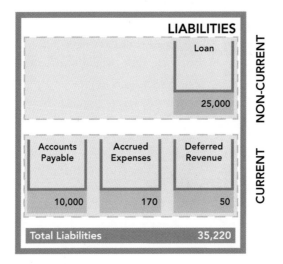

Figure 145. **Liabilities on the BaSIS Framework divided into current and non-current.**

We've also aimed to align pairs of accounts in the balance sheet and income statement.

- Cost of Sales is immediately underneath inventory because those two accounts work together.
- Advertising is underneath Prepaid Expense because the advertising expense impacted that account.
- Depreciation lines up Equipment at Cost and Accumulated Depreciation because they work together.

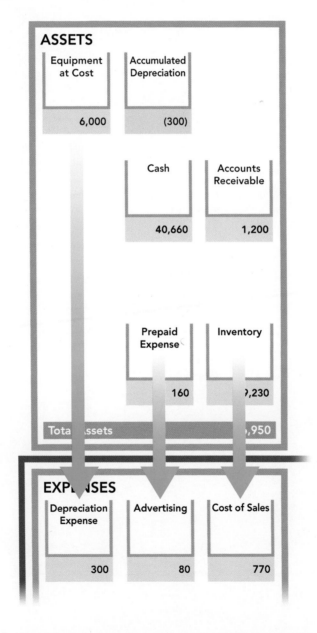

Figure 146. **Extract of the BaSIS Framework showing alignment of expenses under corresponding asset accounts.**

In the income statement section of the BaSIS Framework, Sales and Cost of Sales are next to each other. The difference between those two accounts is calculated as a subtotal and reported as Gross Profit. Have a look for this on any of the income statements.

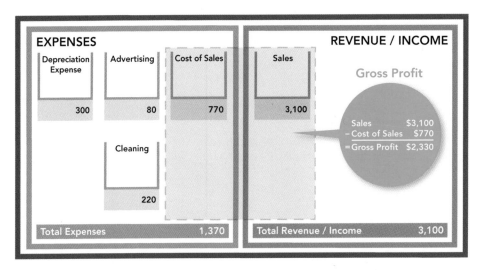

Figure 147. **Income statement section of BaSIS Framework showing Sales aligned with the only direct expense.**

The indirect expenses are then shown below the direct expenses on traditional income statements, and on the BaSIS Framework to the left, further away from the Sales and Cost of Sales. In our scenario there are three: Cleaning, Depreciation, and Advertising.

The gross profit minus the indirect expenses, gives the net profit.

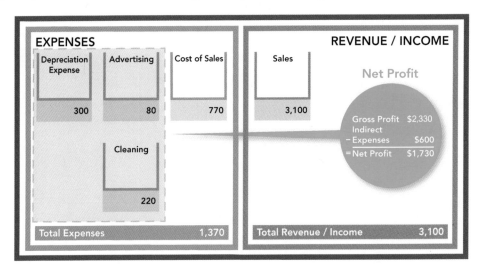

Figure 148. **Income statement section of BaSIS Framework showing three indirect expenses.**

Financial Statements after Prepaid Expense Amortization Transaction 15

After the amortization of the prepaid expense, the balance sheet and income statement of Lemonade & Laughter look like this:

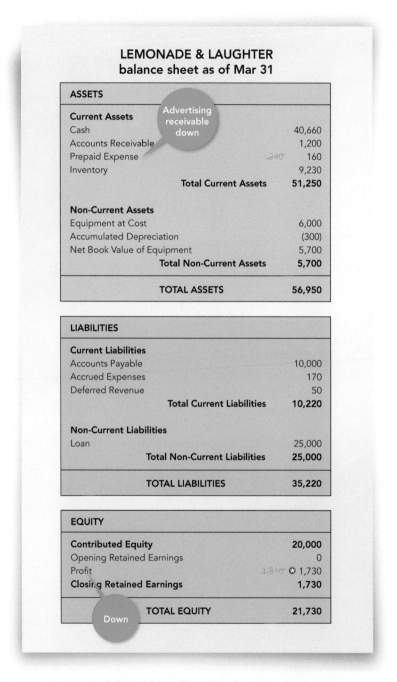

LEMONADE & LAUGHTER
balance sheet as of Mar 31

ASSETS		
Current Assets		
Cash		40,660
Accounts Receivable		1,200
Prepaid Expense	240	160
Inventory		9,230
Total Current Assets		**51,250**
Non-Current Assets		
Equipment at Cost		6,000
Accumulated Depreciation		(300)
Net Book Value of Equipment		5,700
Total Non-Current Assets		**5,700**
TOTAL ASSETS		**56,950**

LIABILITIES		
Current Liabilities		
Accounts Payable		10,000
Accrued Expenses		170
Deferred Revenue		50
Total Current Liabilities		**10,220**
Non-Current Liabilities		
Loan		25,000
Total Non-Current Liabilities		**25,000**
TOTAL LIABILITIES		**35,220**

EQUITY		
Contributed Equity		20,000
Opening Retained Earnings		0
Profit	1,810	1,730
Closing Retained Earnings		1,730
TOTAL EQUITY		**21,730**

Advertising receivable down

Down

Figure 149. **Balance sheet after prepaid expense amortization.**

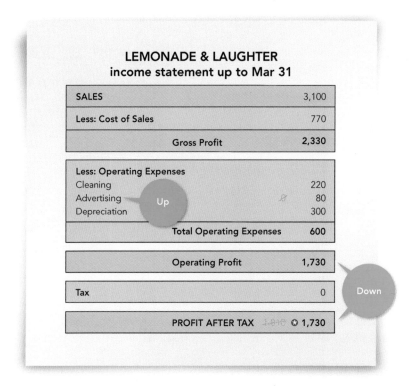

Figure 150. **Income statement after advertising expense.**

The business now has $56,950 of total assets, $80 down from $57,030. In the Sources of Funds side of the balance sheet, the obligation of those assets has also been reduced. The reduction in obligations happened via the reduced profit balance with the Profit account reduced to $1,730. The income statement explains that the profit was generated by $3,100 of value-generating activities and $1,370 of value-sacrificing activities. The layout of the income statement shows that of the $1,370 of expense activities, $770 were direct costs of sale and $600 were indirect expenses of running the business.

The $1,730 on the income statement matches with the same $1,730 profit within the Closing Retained Earnings of the balance sheet.

Discussion: Advertising

Half My Advertising Works!

The famous adage about advertising is that half of it works. The only problem is that you don't know which half.

The advertising we've just seen here hopefully contributes to an increase in sales.

To the extent that the advertising has created market awareness and generated future customers, it has created an asset for the business. So perhaps we should have debited an asset account called Future Sales rather than the expense account called Advertising.

WHICH HALF?

But the reason we don't do that is because of the asset recognition criteria we explored in Chapter 2. To be recognized on a balance sheet, an asset must be both owned/controlled and must be measurable. This Future Sales asset would pass neither of those tests. We don't own the customers and can't claim them as ours, nor do we know how much in sales will result from the advertising campaign. We'd just be guessing.

For this reason, we spread the consumption of the advertising campaign over its life, similar to the depreciation of the equipment. But where we *depreciated* the equipment, we have *amortized* the prepaid advertising asset.

Accrual Accounting Summary

You've now completed the fifteen classic transactions that we said would capture the essence of almost every financial scenario that happens in a business. Six of those possible business scenarios relate to the payment for revenue and expenses. Specifically, they relate to the timing of those payments.

An expense that a business incurs can be paid for (settled):

1) before the expense activity happens,
2) at the time the expense activity happens, or
3) after the expense activity happens.

In our classic transactions, for example:

1) The advertising was prepaid, and subsequently the advertising expense was incurred (Transaction 15).
2) The window cleaning expense of $50 (Transaction 7) was incurred and paid for at the same time.
3) The $170 shop cleaning (Transaction 13) was accrued and the supplier was to be paid afterwards.

These three possible expense payment timing scenarios are shown in the figure below.

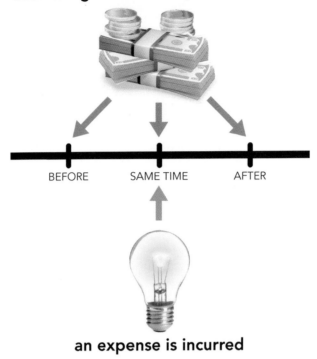

Figure 151. **Timing of payments made for an expense.**

Similarly, revenue has the same three timing possibilities. Cash can be received:

1) before,
2) at the same time as, or
3) after the revenue activity happens.

In our classic transactions, for example:

1) The cash was received (when we sold the $150 gift voucher in Transaction 9) before the related revenue of $100 was earned in transaction 12(a).
2) Concurrent revenue was earned in Transaction 6(a), when we made a $1,000 cash sale to Customer A.
3) We made a $2,000 sale on credit to Customer B in transaction 8(a) and recognized an account receivable asset on our balance sheet; then later in Transaction 12, the cash was received.

The three possible revenue payment timing scenarios are shown in Figure 152 below.

Cash can come in before, when or after...

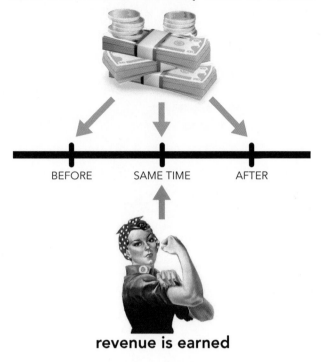

BEFORE   SAME TIME   AFTER

revenue is earned

Figure 152. **Three timing possibilities for payment for revenue.**

Classic Transactions—Conclusion

The transaction in this chapter—the amortization of prepaid advertising—is the final transaction in the series of Classic Transactions.

We've called this collection of journal entries "classic" because they capture the essence of what happens in every business. The particulars will be different in different businesses, but the concepts are the same. The transactions capture the sourcing of funds, the repayment of funds, and the swapping of assets. They describe the generation and sacrifice of value with examples of prepayment, concurrent payment, and post-payment for both of those types of activity.

By exploring the double entry effects of all the classic transactions, you have entrenched your understanding of the principles of accounting that we discovered in Part 1 of this book. You've gained clarity on the three aspects of accounting that are the pillars of accounting literacy: Structure, Language, and Mechanics.

You have seen how the Structure of accounting works, such as the two-sidedness of the balance sheet (rights and obligations) and the two sides of the BaSIS Framework (sources of funds and uses of funds). You've seen how the income statement activities impact the profit in the equity section of the balance sheet. These are structural aspects of how accounting works.

You've seen the importance of the meaning and clear definition of the words that describe the five accounting elements, represented by the five boxes of the BaSIS Framework. We sometimes nickname them RELAX, for **R**evenue/Income that are value-generating activities, **E**quity, **L**iabilities, **A**ssets, and e**X**penses that are value-sacrificing activities.

Other Scenarios

Of course, there are some business transactions that we haven't covered in the fifteen classics. For example, the payment of a dividend, the conversion of debt to issued equity, the issuing of new shares to an employee as part of a remuneration package or ESOP (Employee Share Ownership Plan), or the capitalization of an expense.

What we do know is that you now have all the tools to readily understand and describe any scenario no matter how obscure with your new accounting literacy. All you need is your BaSIS Framework and a finger to point to where the impacts will land. Download a BaSIS Framework to print out as a handy letter-sized reference sheet or a poster-sized reference chart for your meeting room or classroom wall.

Before we leave journal entries entirely, we will look at one last one, which closes the books so that we can start a new accounting period.

PART 3

FINANCIAL REPORTING

ACCOUNTING CYCLE

Distribution of Earnings and the Trial Balance

At the end of each new accounting period, the income statement accounts are set to zero in readiness for the start of the next period, when no revenue, no expenses, and no profit will appear. The balance sheet, on the other hand, starts each new period the same as it ends the previous one. In this chapter, we'll look at how we reset the income statement to zero at the end of each period.

The timeframes of the balance sheet and income statement are different. The balance sheet always describes a particular moment in time. Its heading reads, for example, "Balance Sheet as of March 31, 2028." The analogy with photography is that the balance sheet is a snapshot of the assets and obligations of a business. It thus makes sense that another title for the balance sheet is the Statement of Position.

The income statement, on the other hand, is analogous to a video recording. It captures activities that necessarily occur over a period of time. The title of an income statement reads, for example, "Income Statement for the Period Ending March 31, 2028." Similarly, it thus makes sense that an alternative title for the income statement is the Statement of Activities.

The reporting period of an income statement can be any length of time. A day, a week, a month, a quarter, six months, or a year.

Because the BaSIS Framework captures both the balance sheet and the income statement, the framework is dated: "For the period up to and at …"

The BaSIS Framework in Figure 153 below (which is as we saw it after Transaction 15) covers the period 1 January to and at 31 March. That is, it covers one quarter of a year.

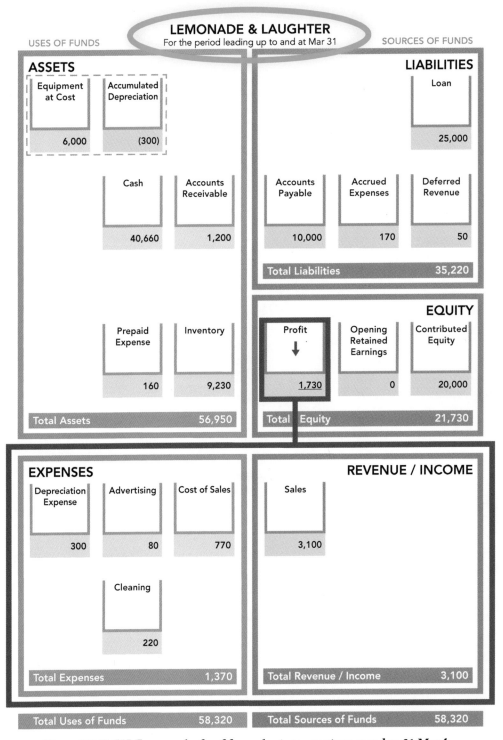

Figure 153. **BaSIS Framework after fifteen classic transactions at and to 31 March.**

In our fifteen classic transaction events, we recorded entries January through March 31, representing the first quarter of the year. Now we want to begin a new income statement for the second quarter. We need to zero out all the revenue and expense accounts.

Until now, there have been no actual tickets (entries) shown in the profit account that lives in the equity section of the Framework. What we're going to do is effectively move the tickets—or at least the balances—from the income statement accounts up to the profit account. But because we have a rule of not taking tickets out of buckets, we're going to make a closing journal entry that cancels out the balance of each revenue and expense account.

To do that, we reduce each of the accounts by the amount of its balance. For each expense account with a debit balance, we credit the account for the same amount. For the Sales account, which has a credit balance, we debit it by the same amount.

We can do this with a single composite journal entry, as follows:

	Debit	Credit
		Cost of Sales
March 31		770
Closing the income statement accounts.		**Cleaning**
		220
		Advertising
		80
		Depreciation
		300
	Sales	**Profit**
	3,100	1,730

This is what's called a composite journal entry with multiple tickets/entries impacting more than two accounts. The rule for journal entries is not that there has to be the same number of tickets, but just that the total value of the green ticket(s) must equal the total value of the orange ticket(s), which is the case here. The green tickets total 3,100 and so do the orange tickets. The debits equal the credits.

This is shown on the BaSIS Framework in Figure 154 following.

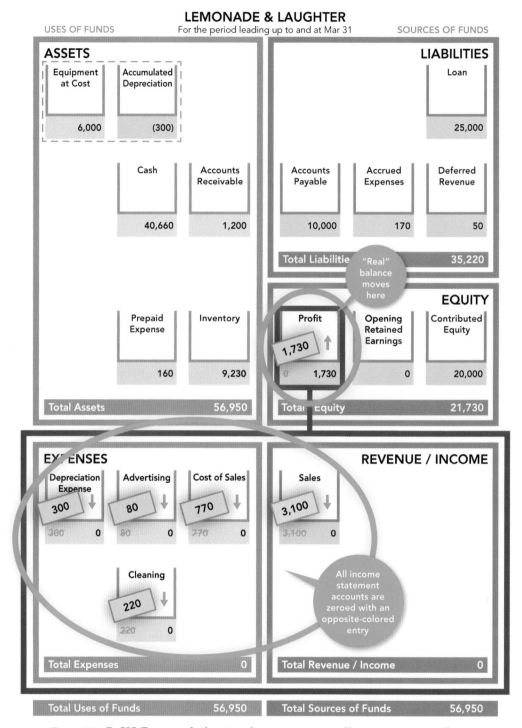

LEMONADE & LAUGHTER
For the period leading up to and at Mar 31

USES OF FUNDS | SOURCES OF FUNDS

ASSETS

Equipment at Cost	Accumulated Depreciation
6,000	(300)

Cash	Accounts Receivable
40,660	1,200

Prepaid Expense	Inventory
160	9,230

Total Assets 56,950

LIABILITIES

Loan
25,000

Accounts Payable	Accrued Expenses	Deferred Revenue
10,000	170	50

Total Liabilitie "Real" balance moves here 35,220

EQUITY

Profit	Opening Retained Earnings	Contributed Equity
1,730		
0 1,730	0	20,000

Total Equity 21,730

EXPENSES

Depreciation Expense	Advertising	Cost of Sales
300	80	770
300 0	80 0	770 0

Cleaning
220
220   0

Total Expenses 0

REVENUE / INCOME

Sales
3,100
3,100   0

All income statement accounts are zeroed with an opposite-colored entry

Total Revenue / Income 0

Total Uses of Funds 56,950 | Total Sources of Funds 56,950

Figure 154. BaSIS Framework showing closing entries to roll over to next period.

Zeroing Out Profit

We're not quite done with our closing process yet. The profit account now has an actual balance in it of $1,730. (Note how it's no longer underlined because it is no longer excluded from the Total Sources of Funds balance at the bottom of the Framework.) But at April 1 it should be $0. So, we will move that balance out of the Profit account and into a Retained Earnings account.

Retained earnings are all the profits that have been earned from all the periods, less any reduction in retained earnings due to the distribution of earnings in the form of drawings or dividends

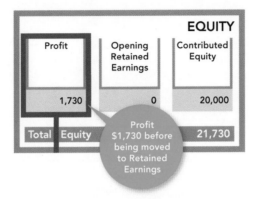

Figure 155. **Equity section of balance sheet before period-end rollover.**

The journal entry to move the balance from the Profit Account to the Retained Earnings account:

	Debit	Credit
March 31 Moving profit to retained earnings.	Profit 1,730	Opening Retained Earnings 1,730

Now the equity section of the BaSIS Framework looks like this:

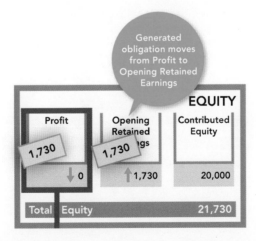

Figure 156. **Equity section of balance sheet showing movement of obligation from Profit to Opening Retained Earnings.**

The full BaSIS Framework of Lemonade & Laughter at 1 April, the start of the next quarter, is shown in Figure 157 following.

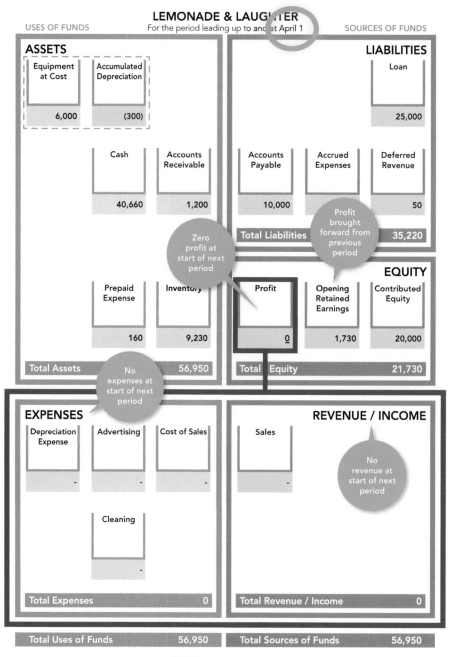

Figure 157. **BaSIS Framework at start of period.**

Note on Language Used to Describe Earnings

We remind ourselves that while earnings and retained earnings are a good and desirable thing, they are not assets. Retained earnings, being part of equity, must be an obligation because all equity is an obligation. Retained earnings are a desirable obligation because the very purpose of the business is to obligate itself to its shareholders.

In casual conversation, we often talk about "distributing earnings" to describe the paying of a dividend. This doesn't, strictly speaking, make sense because you can't distribute an obligation. What we mean, of course, is "distribute assets that were sourced from earnings." It's an example of "collapsing the duality," where we mean one side of the accounting duality but refer to the other.

Paying a Dividend

Dividends are one way that the company distributes assets to its shareholders. Dividends are to shareholders as interest payments are to lenders. They reward them for their funding of the business. It is up to the board of directors to decide whether the company will pay a dividend. Generally, company law requires that a dividend can only be paid out of earnings, which in the case of our example, Lemonade & Laughter, means that the maximum dividend that could be paid is $1,730. If the company paid more than that as a dividend, it would require decreasing the Contributed Equity account, which is not allowed because it would prejudice the creditors who know that the $20,000 capital account stands behind what they are owed and makes their loans safer.

At a public company, it is usually a two-step process to declare a dividend. First, the dividends are declared and become payable, and then the cash is distributed to settle that payable account.

The journal entry to pay a dividend would be as follows.

When the dividend is declared by the board of directors:

	Debit	Credit
On date of declaration of dividend Dividend declared	Retained Earnings $99	Dividend Payable $99

The Dividend Payable is a current liability account on the balance sheet.

When the divided is subsequently paid:

	Debit	Credit
On date of dividend payment Dividend paid	Dividend Payable $99	Cash $99

Reinvesting Earnings

People often say that companies "reinvest their earnings." What they mean is that the company keeps its assets to use in the business to generate further profits. The expression could suggest that the business had to put the money back into the business, which isn't the case. The money never left the business. By "reinvesting profit," we really mean "not paying a dividend." The money was in the business all along, funded by the retained earnings obligation.

Trial Balance

A Trial Balance is a report that accountants sometimes use to present the totals of all the accounts in the general ledger. That is, all the debit accounts and all the credit accounts from the balance sheet and the income statement. All the balance sheet and income statement accounts are listed together to give two somewhat meaningless totals. The point of the report is to check that the total of all the debit accounts is the same as the total of all the credit accounts.

Trial balances were critically important in the days before computers. Back then, the risk of arithmetic errors was much greater, and the purpose of the trial balance was to guard against those. Our trial balance that reflects the results of the fifteen classic transactions is shown below. You will notice that the current period profit of $1,730 is not included separately, as that would be double counting (it's already included via the revenue and expense account totals).

LEMONADE & LAUGHTER
trial balance as of Mar 31

ACCOUNT	DEBIT BALANCE	CREDIT BALANCE
Cash	40,660	
Accounts Receivable	1,200	
Equipment at Cost	6,000	
Accumulated Depreciation		300
Inventory	9,230	
Prepaid Expense	160	
Cost of Sales	770	
Cleaning	220	
Depreciation	300	
Advertising	80	
Loan		25,000
Accrued Expenses		170
Accounts Payable		10,000
Deferred Revenue		50
Retained Earnings		0
Contributed Equity		20,000
Sales		3,100
Total	**58,620**	**58,620**

Figure 158. **Trial balance at period end**

THE BUSINESS NARRATIVE

PUTTING WORDS TO THE VALUE CYCLE

Human beings do stories. For millennia, we've sat around fires telling each other meaningful stories. Stories make sense of our world, aggregating facts into useful, connected, threaded, and logical sequences that help us understand and manage our lives. They give us context for our decision-making. Beginning, middle, end. Intention, outcome, conclusion.

From a learning point of view, being able to take a balance sheet and an income statement and create a cogent narrative from the data they provide is a significant milestone and accomplishment. Doing so is confirmation that we've achieved accounting literacy.

HUMANS DO STORIES

With the Value Cycle that we discovered in Chapter 6(c) in mind, let's create just such a narrative that takes the data from the two main accounting reports—the balance sheet and income statement—and makes a meaningful story from it.

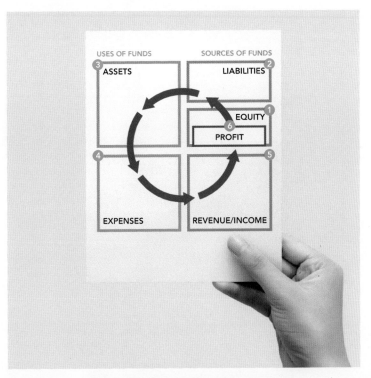

Figure 159. **Value Cycle of business.**

LEMONADE & LAUGHTER
balance sheet as of Mar 31

ASSETS	
Current Assets	
Cash	40,660
Accounts Receivable	1,200
Prepaid Expense	160
Inventory	9,230
Total Current Assets	**51,250**
Non-Current Assets	
Equipment at Cost	6,000
Accumulated Depreciation	(300)
Net Book Value of Equipment	**5,700**
Total Non-Current Assets	**5,700**
TOTAL ASSETS	**56,950**

LIABILITIES	
Current Liabilities	
Accounts Payable	10,000
Accrued Expenses	170
Deferred Revenue	50
Total Current Liabilities	**10,220**
Non-Current Liabilities	
Loan	25,000
Total Non-Current Liabilities	**25,000**
TOTAL LIABILITIES	**35,220**

EQUITY	
Contributed Equity	**20,000**
Opening Retained Earnings	0
Profit	⊙ 1,730
Closing Retained Earnings	**1,730**
TOTAL EQUITY	**21,730**

Figure 160. **End of period balance sheet**

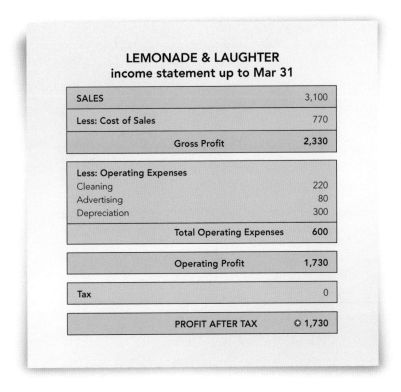

Figure 161. End of period income statement.

Figure 162. Lemonade & Laughter element totals.

The Story of Lemonade & Laughter

This is the story that the above balance sheet and income statement are telling.

---

1. EQUITY

On March 31 Lemonade & Laughter was using funding from shareholders in the amount of $21,730 to finance 38% of its assets.

2. LIABILITIES

The business was using funding from lenders and creditors in the amount of $35,220 to finance the remaining 62% of its assets, leveraging the size of the business.

3. ASSETS

Using these two sources of funds Lemonade & Laughter had total assets totaling $56,950 in use for the purpose of generating a return for the shareholders of the company.

4. EXPENSES

During the period leading up to March 31 the company had to sacrifice value of $1,370 as expenses, in order to…

5. REVENUE/INCOME

generate value of $3,100 as revenue.

6. PROFIT

The net value generated of $1,730 was attributed to the shareholders as profit for the period and is recorded on the balance sheet as the end of period retained earnings (because there were no opening retained earnings and no dividend was declared).

And there it is. You can kick back and relax. We took the jargon-filled terms that describe the life of a business and turned it into a simple, compelling, and powerful story that we can act upon.

CONGRATULATIONS!

That is the cogent business story of the accounts you created, step by step, doing a series of journal entries. If it makes sense to you, you are accounting literate. You understand where a business is and how it got there.

Part 4 of *The Joy of Accounting* presents a few themes that people use accounting information for. We can't know exactly how you will use what you've learned in this book. Some readers will be passing exams, some will be using it to partake in budget discussions in a corporate environment. Some will use the knowledge to read published financial reports to inform their investment decisions. Overall, we hope you will use the knowledge, concepts, distinctions, and tools (such as the BaSIS Framework) to be more financially conscious and clear-thinking in your personal and day-to-day lives.

Part 4 presents a few examples of applied accounting literacy that can inspire you to continue learning and developing your financial consciousness.

CASE STUDIES

Up to this point in *The Joy of Accounting* you have discovered and worked with the principles of accounting. When you read the business narrative, based on the information presented by a balance sheet and income statement you showed yourself to be accounting literate.

So now, what to do with your newfound accounting literacy skills? As with any language, you can use it for endless purposes.

This final part of the book is to give you the opportunity to follow along in a sample of financial discussions. They are interesting and reflect a range of topics. The most important thing is, they will show you that you are quite capable of following along in a sophisticated financial conversation. The discussion will make sense when you recall the principles that you've learned, and you will see that you have indeed come a long way in your learning.

CASE STUDY 1: SPOTTING ISSUES - TED BAKER

By Toby York

Ted Baker is a United Kingdom-based retailer and wholesaler of clothing and accessories. There is no Ted—it was founded by Ray Kelvin who started out selling shirts in the late 1980s from a single store in Scotland.

Growth was meteoric and in 2018, revenues were approaching $750m and pre-tax profits just shy of $88m, which is nearly 12% of the sales. In the cut-throat rag trade that's an impressive profit margin. In early 2018 the shares were trading at $38 (£30) making Ray's personal fortune almost $625m and the value of the company's shares $1.6billion.

But the 2019/20 year saw cataclysmic changes.

In March 2019 Ray left the business under a bit of a cloud following allegations of misconduct and in January 2020 the company reported that its inventories had been overstated by $72m.

By April 2020 the shares were trading at $1.25 (£1)—they lost 97% of their value, and Ray's fortune had shrunk to $19m.

Could this have been predicted? We do not make any claim that analysis of historical financial statements can predict the future, but with the benefit of hindsight, we can see some warning signs.

Let's have a look at some of the published financial information. Here is an extract of he income statements for the previous 5 years:

To end of January	53 weeks 2015	52 weeks 2016	52 weeks 2017	52 weeks 2018	52 weeks 2019
Revenue	$485m	$570m	$664m	$740m	$772m
Cost of sales	$191m	$229m	$259m	$289m	$322m
Gross profit	$294m	$341m	$405m	$451m	$450m
Gross margin	60.7%	59.9%	61.0%	61.0%	58.3%
Operating profit	$63m	$74m	$78m	$88m	$68m
Inventories	$139m	$157m	$198m	$234m	$283m

As shown in by the blue numbers gross margin took a bit of a hit in 2019. It dropped by nearly 2.7%. It's only about 3% points, but that's a significant drop in a retail business. Look how in the previous 4 years the gross margin hovers within a band of 1% points. A 2.7% decline is meaningful.

Think of it this way. Revenues for 2019 were $772m. If the gross margin had been 61.0%, the same as that reported in 2017 and 2018, operating profits would have been 30% greater at more than $88m instead of the actual $68m. That's $20m extra.

That's right, a decrease in the gross margin of 2.7% translates into a reduction in operating profit margin of more than 30%.

But that's not all. Let's look at inventory values. At the end of January 2019, Ted Baker's inventory was $283m. The question we can now ask is, "how long would it take the business to use up all that inventory?"

For that we look at the cost of sales figure. That's where we see inventory being sacrificed. The cost of sales for the year ended 31 January 2019 was $322m. That's 87% of the inventory on hand at the end of the year. Expressed as a duration, 87% of the year is 46 weeks. That's an awfully long time to be sitting with inventory.

Other retailers in the same sector have comparatively much less stock. H&M would sell theirs in 18 weeks and Next in just 11 weeks. So, 46 weeks starts to look much too long.

It could be justifiable if sales growth is explosive, but sales increased just 4% in 2019. Note too, like many retailers, Ted Baker reports at the end of January – when holdings should be at a seasonal low – just after the Christmas sales and before the Spring/Summer arrivals.

You don't need to be a certified accountant to spot this. A simple question that should have been asked in the Ted Baker boardroom was "why are we holding inventory equivalent in value to almost a whole year of sales?"

The formula for inventory turnover

Inventory/Cost of sales x 365

281/323 x 365 = 320 days (or 46 weeks)

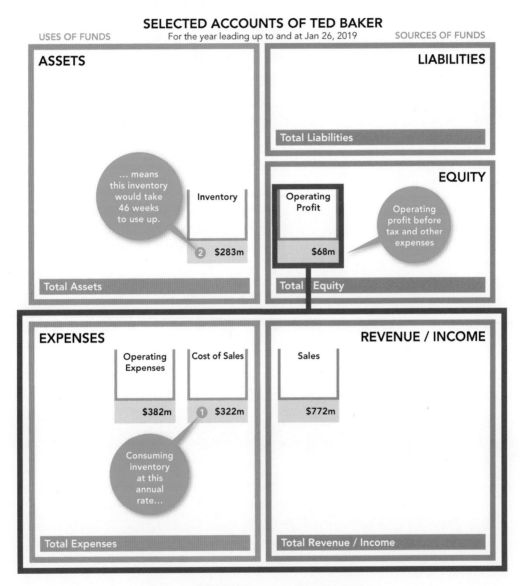

Figure 163. Ted Baker inventory consumption

CASE STUDY 2: CASH FLOW

Revenue and cash flow are very different things. Revenue is activity that benefits shareholders by generating assets or eliminating liabilities. Cash flow is the flow of cash into and out of the business, for any of a number of reasons. Because cash flow is critical to a business, investors monitor it with great interest.

Revenue is reported on the income statement. Cash flow is reported on the third major financial report after the balance sheet and income statement: the cash flow statement.

We think of the income statement as an unpacked profit account. We used the analogy of double-clicking the balance sheet profit account to reveal the income statement. That report explained how the profit was arrived at through value-generation and value-sacrifice activities.

We can use the same unpacking and double-click analogy to explain the cash flow statement. Instead of opening up the profit account to reveal value-activities, we double-click the cash account to reveal the movement of cash into and out of that cash account. That movement is categorized into three types: operational causes of cash flow, investing causes, and financing causes of cash flow.

Operational cash flows are the inward and outward flow of cash due to day-to-day operational changes in the business. The increase in the profit account (due to revenue and expenses), causes cash to flow into the business, as does a decrease in accounts receivable, a decrease in inventory, or an increase in accounts payable. Think about how that works... if everything else stayed the same on the balance sheet expect, for example, inventory and cash... if inventory increased cash would have to have decreased to make the balance sheet balance.

Investing cash flows are caused by the acquisition or disposal of non-current assets like plant and equipment. If everything stayed the same and equipment decreased, then cash must have increased.

Financing cash flow is caused by changes in long-term loans and issued capital. If the company buys its own shares in a share-buyback scheme, then if everything else stays the same, we know it must have used cash to do so.

Let's look at two famous companies – **Apple** and **Tesla** – and see how their cash flows differ.

In Figure 164 we see how Apple corporation started its financial year to September 2019 with nearly $26 billion cash and ended that year with over $50 billion of cash.

The increase of over $24 billion of cash was due to

- $69 billion cash flowing in from day to day operations and sales, and
- $46 billion cash flowing into the business due to selling non-current investments, and

- $91 billion cash flowing out of the business because of financing activities involving repaying long-term debt, paying dividends, and buying back shares from Apple shareholders. Nearly $67 billion went to buying back common stock.

Share buybacks is a way to return cash to shareholders, similar to dividends. Buying shares back from shareholders means there are less shares outstanding. The remaining shareholders each own a greater percentage of the company, albeit one with less cash. Share buybacks tend to prop up the company's share price because they create demand for the shares in the market.

Apple Inc.
Consolidated Statement of Cash Flows
Period Ending September 28, 2019 (US$ millions)

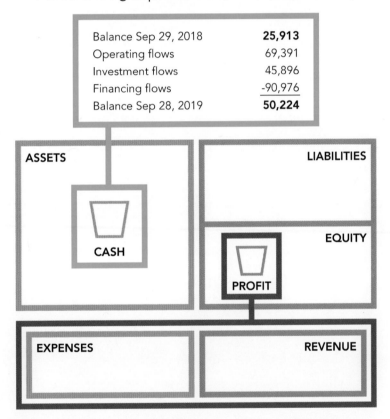

Balance Sep 29, 2018	**25,913**
Operating flows	69,391
Investment flows	45,896
Financing flows	-90,976
Balance Sep 28, 2019	**50,224**

Figure 164. **Cash account "exploded" to reveal the cash flow statement.**

As you can see, Apple is a cash generation machine! It started the 2019 year with $25.913 billion of cash and ended with $50.224 billion. And that was after returning nearly $91billion to funders as financing cash outflow.

CASH FLOW COMPARISON
$ millions

	APPLE		TESLA	
	28-Sep-19	29-Sep-18	30-Dec-19	30-Dec-18
Starting Cash	25,913	20,289	4,277	3,965
Operating Cash Flow	69,391	77,434	2,405	2,098
Investing Cash Flow	45,896	16,066	(1,436)	(2,337)
Financing Cash Flow	(90,976)	(87,876)	1,537	511
Movement	**24,311**	**5,624**	**2,506**	**312**
Ending Cash	50,224	25,913	6,783	4,277

Figure 165. **Comparison between Apple and Tesla cash flows.**

Tesla is a smaller company than Apple. It generated $2.405 billion of cash from its sales operations. Unlike Apple, it didn't gain cash from its investing activities. Rather it used $1.436 billion cash, mostly to buy plant and equipment. Tesla was building factories in China and Germany, so this investing cash outflow shouldn't be a surprise.

Also unlike Apple, Tesla gained cash from financing activities to the tune of over $1.5 billion, mostly from the sale of common stock. So, whereas Apple was distributing cash by buying back shares from its shareholders, Tesla diluted its shareholders and gained cash by selling more shares to existing and new stockholders. Overall Tesla's cash grew by over $2.5 billion in 2019.

CASE STUDY 3: THE ULTIMATE MEASURE OF SUCCESS - ROE

What is the ultimate measure of success for a business? From an investor's point of view, the question she or he is asking is "what value did you generate for me using the value I have given you?" In other words, "what return did you generate for me relative to the assets I invested into the company?" Or, "how much—proportionately—did you grow the assets I entrusted to you?"

From the company's point of view this is to ask, "what profit did the company generate relative to the equity the company used to do so?"

Expressed as a comparison this is: PROFIT/EQUITY. The name for this ratio is return on equity.

Return on Equity

Let's look at giant retailer Amazon.com. In the year ending December 31, 2019 Amazon earned a profit of $11.64 billion and had equity of $62.1. As a ratio, the profit is 11.64/62.1x100 = 18.7%

Amazon took $100 of money from a shareholder and generated $18.50 for that shareholder.

That is a healthy return, and beats putting money in the bank and getting low single digit returns as interest.

Improving Return on Equity

It is worth asking ourselves, how can a company improve its return on equity?

Working Smarter

If every time the company made a sale, it managed to earn a greater profit on the sale, then that would increase the overall profitability of the company, with no extra equity needed. Return increases, equity stays the same, giving greater return on equity.

The metric for profitability measure is PROFIT/REVENUE. So, the idea is to work smarter by lowering expenses or increasing prices charged to customers to increase profit margins.

Amazon made profits in the 2019 year of $11.6 billion and its revenue was $281 billion. The company's profit margin was therefore 11.6/281 x 100 = 4.12%. For each dollar earned from a customer the company had about 96 cents of expenses and 4 cents of profit.

Getting Bigger

Another way to improve returns to shareholders is to simply increase the size of the company by getting more assets with which to do more business. But, of course it wouldn't help to use more equity as the source of funding to get those assets. That would only serve to increase both returns and equity. We want to increase returns while holding equity the same. So, how do you get more assets without using more equity? You use the other source of funding: debt.

By increasing assets and liabilities while keeping equity the same, the company will have more assets with which to earn profits, with no increase in the denominator of the profit/equity calculation. Using more debt is what we've talked about earlier in *The Joy of Accounting* as "leverage".

In this case we'll measure leverage as ASSETS/EQUITY.

Increasing a company's leverage increases its return on equity. Amazon has assets of $228 billion at the end of 2019 and equity of $62 billion. The leverage multiple was therefore 3.67 times. For each dollar of equity the company had, it had assets of $3.67.

Working Faster

What if the company used the same amount of assets and debt, and maintained its profit margins, but it made sales more frequently. In other words, it increased its inventory turnover by selling the goods on its shelves and them restocking them every, say, week instead of month. This is called the velocity of business.

Comparing the sales with the assets the company used gives us the velocity measure. , calculated as SALES/ASSETS

Amazon's velocity metri for 2019 was $281 billion/$225 billion = 1.24

Smarter, Bigger, Faster

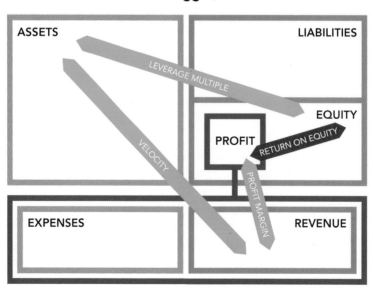

Figure 166. **Three ways to increase profitability**

Smarter Bigger Faster

And there you have it... three ways to increase the return on equity of a company to give shareholders a greater return on their investment. Work smarter to be more profitable, expand to get bigger, and work faster.

But wait, why not aim to use all three of these strategies to maximize the return to stock-holders?! That would give us a multiplier effect.

Multiplying velocity by leverage by profitability gives us the return on equity we started with. Let's look at that a bit closer...

$$\text{Smarter} \quad \text{x} \quad \text{Bigger} \quad \text{x} \quad \text{Faster}$$

$$\frac{\text{Profit}}{\text{Sales}} \quad \text{x} \quad \frac{\text{Assets}}{\text{Equity}} \quad \text{x} \quad \frac{\text{Sales}}{\text{Assets}}$$

Multiplying the ratios together, we see that the assets cancel out and the sales cancel out, to give Profit/Equity, which is return on equity. How neat is that! Let's test it for Amazon, whose ROE ration we calculated above was 18.7%

And yes, multiplying Amazon's Smarter, Bigger and Faster measures (and taking rounding error into account) does turn out to be just that.

$$4.12\% \quad \text{x} \quad 3.67 \quad \text{x} \quad 1.24 \quad = \quad 18.7\%$$

All the numbers used in this case study came from Amazon.com's annual filing to the U.S. Securities & Exchange Commission, called a "10-K" report. You can download that report at Amazon's investor relations website.

CASE STUDY 4: PATISSERIE VALERIE

By Toby York

Patisserie Valerie is a premium continental patisserie operating from 152 stores predominantly in London and across England. It prides itself on handmade, freshly baked premium cakes and pastries, high quality teas, coffees, and continental breakfasts.

In 2018 it was reported that the company had been subject to an accounting fraud which included alleged falsification of the financial statements. Drawing conclusions based on false information is difficult but we can, with the benefit of hindsight of course, look for the tell-tale signs.

This is an extract of the income statements for the 5 years to 30 September 2017, the last year before its troubles were uncovered:

Patisserie Valerie

PATISSERIE VALERIE

	2013	2014	2015	2016	2017
Revenue	£60.1m	£76.6m	£91.9m	£104.1m	£114.2m
Operating profit	£9.6m	£11.3m	£14.6m	£17.2m	£20.1m
Operating margin	15.9%	14.7%	15.9%	16.5%	17.6%

Figure 167. **Patisserie Valie operating profit margins**

You'll notice a smooth upward trend in turnover, gross profits and operating profits. The operating profit margin is a healthy 17.6% in 2017. It looks very much like a well-managed growing business. What's more, it was run by a hugely successful serial entrepreneur, Luke Johnson, who has been responsible for multiple high street success stories in the restaurant sector.

Let's check these results against another UK coffee chain, Costa Coffee, part of the larger listed group Whitbread PLC (and recently acquired by Coca-Cola Inc for an eye-watering £3.9bn).

Costa Coffee

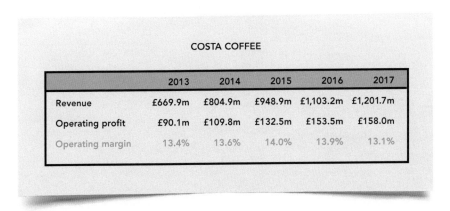

COSTA COFFEE

	2013	2014	2015	2016	2017
Revenue	£669.9m	£804.9m	£948.9m	£1,103.2m	£1,201.7m
Operating profit	£90.1m	£109.8m	£132.5m	£153.5m	£158.0m
Operating margin	13.4%	13.6%	14.0%	13.9%	13.1%

Figure 168. **Cost Coffee operating profit margins**

Admittedly, in 2017 it had 2,200 coffee shops and about ten times the turnover of Patisserie Valerie. It also doesn't claim to provide premium handmade cakes – although most of its coffee is roasted in central London.

Summarizing the differences: Costa is significantly larger and part of a group, so you might expect it has significantly greater purchasing power than Patisserie Valerie. Costa doesn't make premium handmade luxury cakes. Shouldn't the operating margins of Costa be higher than Patisserie Valerie's?

To be fair, Starbucks generates operating margins of around 18%, but it has global purchasing power and has never been accused of selling artisan cakes made in London.

A simple question that should have been asked: why is our operating margin better than our global competitors?

Asking obvious questions about the numbers is in the job description of every entrepreneur, director and adviser.

APPENDIX - REGULATORY DEFINITIONS AND RECOGNITION CRITERIA

U.S. Financial Accounting Standards Board

Extracts from Statements of Accounting Concepts: CON5 Recognition & Measurement, and CON6 Elements of Financial Statements

DEFINITIONS

Assets are probable future economic benefits obtained or controlled by a particular entity as a result of past transactions or events.

Liabilities are probable future sacrifices of economic benefits arising from present obligations of a particular entity to transfer assets or provide services to other entities in the future as a result of past transactions or events.

Equity or net assets is the residual interest in the assets of an entity; the ownership interest.

Comprehensive income is the change in equity of a business enterprise during a period from nonowner sources.

Revenues are inflows or other enhancements of assets of an entity or settlements of its liabilities from its ongoing central operations.

Expenses are outflows or other using up of assets or incurrences resulting from the entity's central operations.

Gains are increases in equity from peripheral transactions.

Losses are decreases in equity from peripheral transactions.

RECOGNITION

Financial elements should be recognized when they meet the definitions above (including control and past-event derived), are measurable, relevant and reliable. Revenue activities should be "substantially accomplished" and gains "realized".

International Accounting Standards Board

Extracts from Conceptual Framework for Financial Reporting 2018

DEFINITIONS

Assets are rights (economic resources) controlled by the entity as a result of past events.

Liabilities are an obligation to transfer an asset, resulting from a past event.

Equity is the residual interest in the assets of the entity after deducting liabilities.

Income is increases in assets, or decreases in liabilities, that result in increases in equity, other than those relating to contributions from holders of equity claims.

Expenses are decreases in assets, or increases in liabilities, that result in decreases in equity, other than those relating to distributions to holders of equity claims.

RECOGNITION

Only items satisfying the definitions of assets, liabilities, equity, income or expense are recognized. Recognition must result in useful and relevant information. The recognition must be faithful, which quality includes measurability. Income and expense recognition is related to asset and liability recognition.

INDEX

X

Y

Z

BOOST YOUR BUSINESS

Do meetings with your accountant give you a sinking feeling?
Do you know what questions to ask finance experts?

Discover the levers to boost profitability, cash flow and growth.
Enquire today about a tailored business finance workshop.
Contact: joy@wealthvox.com

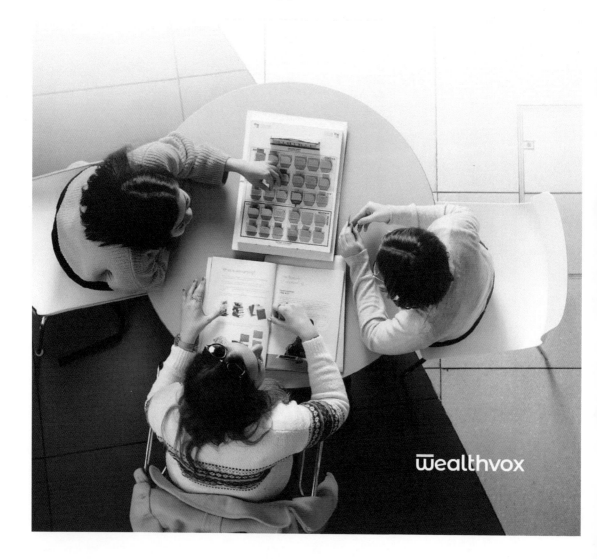

Printed in Great Britain
by Amazon

28458419R00169